THE ART OF MAKING
FERMENTED SAUSAGES

STANLEY MARIANSKI,   ADAM MARIANSKI

Bookmagic, LLC.
Seminole, Florida.

The Art of Making Fermented Sausages
Stanley Marianski, Adam Marianski

ISBN: 978-0-9824267-1-5
Library of Congress Control Number: 2009905128
First edition 2008. Second edition 2012. Third edition 2015.

Bookmagic, LLC.
http://www.bookmagic.com

Printed in the United States of America.

Table of Contents

Disclaimer

This is not a book for someone who has never made a sausage and wants to learn the skill. Basic sausage making steps must be performed at low temperatures quickly, otherwise bacteria growth will escalate. Some hobbyists may perform these operations at higher kitchen temperatures and at such conditions this is not the right place to learn the trade.

This does not mean that fermented sausages cannot be made at home. We have been making them at home for thousands of years and the slow-fermented products made the traditional way still taste better than anything made with expensive microprocessor controlled equipment.

To make great fermented sausages at home you need to:

Learn the underlaying technology behind fermentation in order to understand the process. Get familiar with basic microbiology concepts and learn how to control bacteria. Read the chapter on safety hurdles and follow these rules to the letter.

The main factor that has convinced us to write this book has been the availability of starter cultures from online distributors of sausage making equipment and supplies. *Use of starter cultures combined with good manufacturing practices* will make production of fermented sausages at home both safe and enjoyable. The information and recommendations contained in the book are presented in good faith and believed to be accurate.

Great Sausage Making

Introduction

Why write a book on making fermented sausages at home? For a very good reason – there are none. Most books about home made sausages are written by restaurant chefs or sausage making lovers who have already gained some experience in this field. The majority of those books provide very rudimentary knowledge on making sausages in general, and are loaded with hundreds of recipes which today are available for free on the Internet. These books do not tackle the subject of fermented sausages at all, and limit the discussion to saying that this is an advanced field of sausage making which is not recommended for an amateur sausage maker. Well, we think that any hobbyist could make a wonderful salami at home if only he knew how. This book aims to convince the reader that he can make any kind of a fermented sausage and the finished product will be both safe and tasteful.

For thousands of years we have been making dry fermented meats without any understanding of the process involved. Only in the last 60 years sufficient advances in the field of meat science were made, namely in microbiology, that discovered underlying reactions that accompany the fermentation and drying of meats. Until then, it was a combination of art and magic and an average hobbyist had nowhere to go.

There were some technical papers that were published in Meat Science and Food Technology journals, which were written by highly respected authorities in this field. People seldom realize that the job of the professor at a known university is not really to teach undergraduates rudimentary knowledge. This job is reserved for teaching assistants who are advanced undergraduates or graduate students pursuing a master degree. Although famous professors do teach master's and doctoral candidates, their main objective is to publish original material to bring fame to their colleges. Unfortunately these highly technical papers are written in such difficult technical terms that most of them are beyond the comprehension of an average person. They might be of interest and probably are even required to be read by college students enrolled in agriculture or meat science courses, but they are of little use to a hobbyist making meat products at home.

Thus, was born the idea of bridging the technology gap that existed between highly technical Meat Science and the requirements of the typical hobbyist making products at home. In order to simplify this knowledge to the absolute minimum, many technical terms were substituted with their equivalent but simpler terms and a number of graphs and tables were provided to make studying easier. To get the reader started, sixty-two sausage recipes supported by detailed instructions are also included.

How Our Book Differs from Others?

We have strived as well as we could to simplify the complexity of meat science and to make it understandable and friendly to a reader without going into technicalities. We could dedicate an entire chapter to a topic of meat color, but instead we explain it in a few practical sentences. The same applies to the science of meat fermentation and to all those wonderful chemical reactions that take place inside.

We aim to stay away from technical jargon and try to use simple colloquial terms instead. It is a kind of a bridge that we hope will connect advanced meat science with a hobbyist, and will bring this heavenly knowledge down to a common ground. Our aim is to help a reader understand different processes such as curing, fermentation or drying, so that he will be able to perform those tasks like a professional but will adapt them to his home conditions.

Until now this field of knowledge has been limited to just a few lucky ones but with today's meat science and starter cultures available to everybody, there is little reason to abstain from making quality salamis at home. By reading this material one can get a full understanding of the process. The purpose of this book is to explain to the reader how he can make those products at home, regardless of the climate and the outside conditions.

Stanley Marianski

Chapter 1

New Concepts of Vital Importance

Bacteria hate acidity and this fact plays an important role in the production and stabilization of fermented sausages.

The term "pH" is a measure of acidity; the lower its value, the more acidic the food. Acidity may be natural, as in most fruits, for example lemon, or added, as in pickled food. The acidity level in foods can be increased by adding lemon juice, citric acid, or vinegar, or lowered by adding baking soda, milk or water.

Bacteria will not grow when the pH is below the minimum or above the maximum limit for a particular bacteria strain. All bacteria have their own preferred acidity level for growth, generally around neutral pH (7.0). As the pH of foods can be adjusted, this procedure becomes a potent weapon for the control of bacteria.

The thermal resistance of microorganisms decreases as the pH of their medium is lowered. Most bacteria, particularly *Clostridium botulinum*, will not grow below pH 4.6. Therefore acidic foods having pH below 4.6 do not require as severe heat treatment as those with pH above 4.6 (low acid) to achieve microbiological safety.

The pH value of 4.6 is the division between high acid foods and low acid foods. Low acid foods have pH values higher than 4.6. They include red meats, seafood, poultry, milk, and all fresh vegetables except for most tomatoes. Although tomatoes generally fall on the pH dividing line at 4.6, there are varieties that have a lower pH level and there are varieties which also have a higher pH level. Tomatoes are usually considered an acidic food.

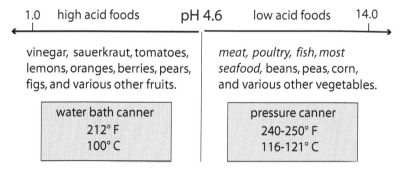

Fig. 1.1 Whether food should be processed in a pressure canner or boiling water canner depends on the acidity of the food.

Adjusting pH

The safety regulations require that low acid foods such as vegetables must be processed at 240° F (116° C) which requires a pressure canner. Acidic food such as fruits can be processed at 212° F (100° C) and that can be accomplished in an open canner. Processing soft vegetables like cucumbers at 240° F (116° C) will damage their structure and the final product will resemble a soup. The solution is to lower the pH of cucumbers so that they can be treated as fruit and processed at 212° F (100° C) or even lower. The final product, known as pickles, will have a good texture, will look like cucumbers, but will develop an acidic taste due to vinegar that was added to increase the acidity of cucumbers.

Therefore, if vegetables are to be canned as acidic foods, they must be acidified to a pH of 4.6 or lower with lemon juice, citric acid or vinegar.

This, however, comes at the expense of flavor. Acidified foods are sourly, take for example sauerkraut, pickled cucumbers or fast fermented sausage. Manufacturers do not increase acidity for flavor, they do it to save time and to extend shelf life of the product. Naturally fermented cabbage, beets or cucumbers taste much better than acidified canned products, however, they must be kept under refrigeration.

pH and Sausages

Bacteria prefer meats with a pH of 6.0 -7.0 which falls in the neutral range of the pH scale. It is in our interest to increase the meat acidity (lower pH) as this inhibits the growth of bacteria. As a result the sausage is stable and safe to consume, although it has not been submitted to heat treatment, which in many cases follows anyhow. A pH drop is accomplished by lactic acid bacteria, which consume sugar and produce lactic acid. This increases the acidity of the meat. The acidity can also be increased by directly adding additives to the meat such as Gdl (glucono-delta-lactone) and/or citric acid.

Such ingredients have to be carefully selected as they will alter the flavor of the sausage. Combining different meats and fats will produce a sausage mass of a certain pH, and the pH meat meter will provide the initial value of the pH of the mix. Foods with a low pH value (high acidity), develop resistance against microbiological spoilage. Pickles, sauerkraut, eggs, pig feet, anything submerged in vinegar will have a long shelf life. Even ordinary meat jelly (head cheese) will last longer if some vinegar is added, and this type of head cheese is known as "souse." Next time when buying meat marinade look at the list of ingredients. The list invariably includes items like vinegar, dry wine, soy sauce, lemon juice, and ingredients which are acidic or salty by nature. Although those ingredients are added mainly to tenderize meat by unwinding the protein structure, they also contribute to inhibiting the growth of bacteria. A sausage can be made safe by acidity alone if its pH is 5.3 or lower, but its flavor will be sour. To avoid this, most sausages are additionally submitted to drying or cooking as these steps add safety and less acidity (higher pH) is required.

Pure water is said to be neutral, with a pH close to 7.0. Solutions with a pH less than 7 are said to be *acidic* and solutions with a pH greater than 7 are basic or *alkaline*.

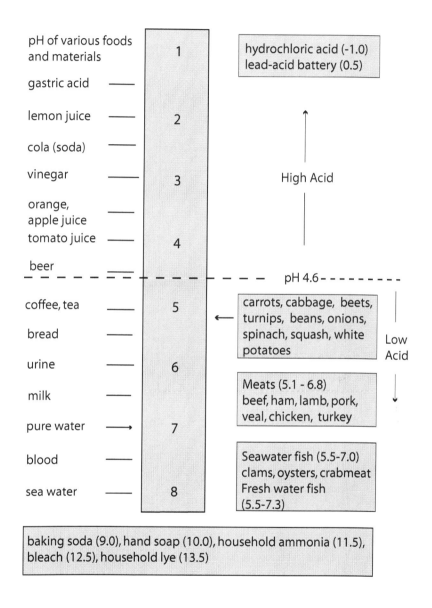

Fig. 1.2 pH of some foods.

The table on the right shows a pH value below which the listed bacteria will not grow. *Almost all fermented sausages produced in the USA today are manufactured by lowering the pH of the meat.* It is a profitable and risk free method for commercial producers, although the taste and flavor of the product leaves much to be desired. Generally a pH of less than 5.0 will severely restrict or completely stop the growth of harmful bacteria.

Name	Min pH
Salmonella	3.8
Cl.botulinum	5.0
Staph.aureus	4.2
Campylobacter	4.9
Listeria	4.4
E.coli	4.4
Shigella	4.0
Bacillus	4.3

Hanna Instruments Meat pH meter

The Hanna Instruments HI 99163 Meat pH Meter is of great value for the pH analysis of meat products. This pH meter is simple to use with only two buttons. The replaceable penetration blade allows the user to measure not only the surface, but also the internal pH of the meat. The unit is very accurate and the reading is obtained within seconds.

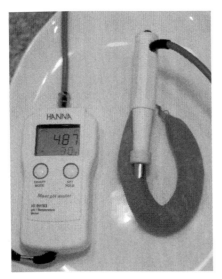
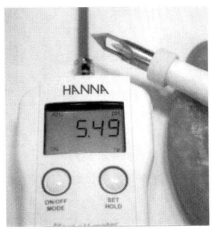

Photo 1.1 and **Photo 1.2** HI 99163 Portable Meat pH Meter.

Photo and information courtesy Hanna Instruments

http://www.hannainst.com

The probe has a built-in temperature sensor that provides automatic temperature compensation and its external body material is non-toxic and food compatible. The replaceable penetration blade allows the user to measure not only the surface, but also the internal pH of the meat.

14

Specifications:
Range pH -2.00 to 16.00 pH
Range Temperature -5.0 to 105.0°C / 23.0 to 221.0°F
Resolution pH 0.01 pH
Resolution Temperature 0.1°C / 0.1°F
Accuracy pH ±0.02 pH
Environment: 0 to 50°C (32 to 122°F); RH max 100%
Dimensions: 150 x 80 x 36 mm (5.9 x 3.1 x 1.4")
Weight: 210 g (7.4 oz.)
Battery Type / Life   3 x 1.5V AA / approx. 1500 hours of continuous use: auto-off after 8 minutes of non-use

There are many companies making pH measuring equipment. Large bench models are expensive and will be used by the professionals who establish thermal processes for canned foods.

pH Test Strips

There is another simpler method for measuring pH that uses disposable testing strips made by: *Micro Essential Laboratory, Inc., www.microessentiallab.com* and available from *the Sausage Maker Inc., www.sausagemaker.com*

Photo 1.3 pH testing strips
pH range: 3.9 - 5.7.

Photo 1.4 pH testing strips
pH range: 4.9 - 6.9.

These two strips will cover the entire range of pH values of fresh materials (meats and fats) and finished sausages. To use, mix 1 part finely chopped meat and 2 parts distilled water, tear off a strip of pH paper, dip into test solution, and match immediately to color chart. No technical training is necessary. The results may be less accurate than those obtained with a pH meter, but the strips are very inexpensive. They can also be obtained at any pet store that sells fish.

Aw - Water Activity

All microorganisms need water to live, when enough of the water is removed they will stop growing and die. This statement explains the science of drying foods.

All microorganisms need water and the amount of water available to them is defined as water activity. Water activity (Aw) is an indication of how tightly water is "bound" inside of a product. It does not say how much water is there, but how much water is *available* to support the growth of bacteria, yeasts or molds. Adding salt or sugar "binds" some of this free water inside of the product and lowers the amount of available water to bacteria which inhibits their growth.

Below certain Aw levels, microbes cannot grow. United Stated Department of Agriculture guidelines state that:

"A potentially hazardous food does not include . . . a food with a water activity value of 0.85 or less."

A simple scale is used to classify foods by their water activity and it starts at 0 (bone dry) and ends on 1 (pure water).

Freshly minced meat possesses a very high water activity level around 0.99, which is a breeding ground for bacteria. Adding salt to meat drops this value immediately to 0.96-0.98 (depending on the amount of salt), and this already creates a safety hurdle against the growth of bacteria. It was also discovered that the addition of sugar would preserve foods such as candies and jellies. Both factors contribute to lowering the water activity of the meat. This may be hard to comprehend as we don't see water evaporating suddenly when salt is added to meat.

Water activity (Aw) of some foods	
Pure water	1.00
Fresh meat & fish	0.99
Bread	0.99
Salami	0.87
Aged cheese	0.85
Jams & jellies	0.80
Plum pudding	0.80
Dried fruits	0.60
Biscuits	0.30
Milk powder	0.20
Instant coffee	0.20
Bone dry	0.00

Well, this is where the concept of water activity becomes useful. Although the addition of salt to meat does not force water to evaporate, it does something similar: it immobilizes free water and prevents it from reacting with anything else, including bacteria. The same happens when we freeze meat though we never think of it. Frozen water takes the shape of solid ice crystals and is not free anymore. It is like stealing food from bacteria, the salt locks up the water creating less favorable conditions for bacteria to grow and prosper. As we add more salt, more free water is immobilized, however, a compromise must be reached as adding too much salt will make the product unpalatable.

Too much salt may impede the growth of friendly bacteria, the ones which work with us to ferment the sausage. The manipulation of water content in processed meat is very important to the successful production of the traditionally made slow-fermented sausages. Water exists in meat as:

- **Bound** (restricted or immobilized water) - structurally associated with meat proteins, membranes and connective tissues. This water (3-5% of total water) can only be removed by high heat and is not available for microbial activities.

- **Free** or bulk water - held only by weak forces such as capillary action. This free water is available for microorganisms for growth.

It can be seen in the table that except *Staphylococcus aureus*, the growth of other microorganisms is severely restricted below Aw 0.92. This is why drying is such an effective method of preventing bacteria growth and preserving foods in general.

Minimum Aw requirements for microorganism growth	
Molds	0.75
Staphylococcus aureus	0.85
Yeasts	0.88
Listeria	0.92
Salmonella	0.93
Cl.botulinum	0.93
E.coli	0.95
Campylobacter	0.98

Water Activity Meter

Photo 1.5 Originally designed for government inspectors, the 4-inch Pawkit is a reliable water activity instrument for use on-the-go. A push of a button brings an accurate reading within five minutes.

Range: 0 to 1.0 Aw
Resolution: plus, minus 0.01 Aw
Accuracy: plus, minus 0.02 Aw
Case dimensions: 3.5 x 4"
Weight: 115 g (4 oz).

Photo courtesy:

Decagon Devices Inc,
Pullman, WA,USA.
www.decagon.com

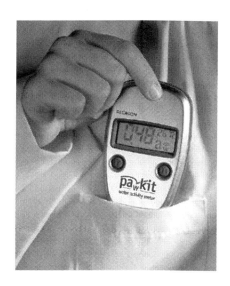

Pawkit uses a dielectric humidity sensor to measure the Aw of a sample. In an instrument that uses this technique, a special polymer is placed between two porous electrodes in the headspace of a sealed chamber. The electrical properties of the polymer change depending on the relative humidity of the chamber. The electrodes give a signal based upon the relative humidity in the closed chamber. This signal is then translated by the software and displayed as water activity on the instrument's screen. At equilibrium, the relative humidity of the air in the chamber is the same as the water activity of the sample. The Pawkit is accurate to ±0.02 aw. For many applications, this accuracy is more than adequate. If you require higher accuracy in your measurements, we recommend you use Decagon's AquaLab water activity meter, which is a lab-grade, bench-top instrument that has an accuracy of ±0.003 aw.

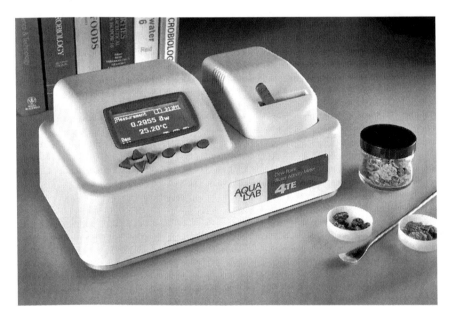

Photo 1.6 AquaLab 4TE benchtop water activity meter is a lab-grade, bench-top instrument that has an accuracy of ±0.003 aw.

Photo courtesy Decagon Devices Inc., www.decagon.com

Drying Food

When water is eliminated, bacteria cannot eat, so they will not grow and will eventually die. This is the basic concept of drying foods.

How do Bacteria Eat?

In order to remain alive the microorganisms need nutrients and moisture. They do not have mouths so they have to absorb food differently. They have to dissolve food in water first and then the food can be absorbed. Bacteria are like a sponge, they absorb food through the wall, but the food must be in a form of a solution. Imagine some sugar, flour or bread crumbs spilled on the table. Place a dry sponge on top of the sugar and you will see that the sponge will not pick up any of the ingredients. Pour some water over the ingredients and repeat the sponge procedure. The sponge will absorb the solution without any difficulty.

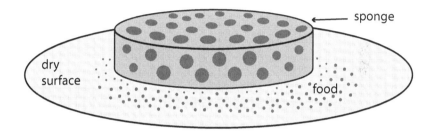

Fig. 1.3 Sponge will not pick up food particles from a dry surface.

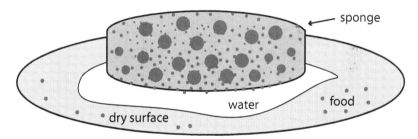

Fig. 1.4 Sponge easily picks up food particles that dissolved in water.

Air Speed

Air speed is a factor that helps remove moisture and stale air, and of course it influences drying. Sausages will dry faster at higher temperatures, but in order to prevent the hardening of the sausage surface, the long term drying must be between 12-15° C (53-59° F). The speed of drying does not remain constant, but changes throughout the process: it is fastest during the beginning of fermentation, then it slows down to a trickle. At the beginning of fermentation humidity is very high due to the high moisture content of the sausage.

When starter cultures are used, the temperature is at the highest during fermentation as some cultures are designed to ferment at 35-45° C, 95-113° F. *Such temperatures enormously* speed up moisture removal from the sausage. The surface of the sausage contains a lot of moisture which must be continuously removed otherwise slime and mold might appear. If the sausages are soaking wet during fermentation, the humidity should be lowered. At the beginning of fermentation the fastest air speed is applied, about 0.8 - 1.0 m/sec. *The speed of 3.6 km/h (2.2 mile/hour) corresponds to the speed of 1 meter/second.* Ideally, the amount of removed moisture should equal the amount of moisture moving to the surface.

Fermentation is performed at high humidity (92-95%) to prevent case harden-ing. If the humidity were low and the air speed fast, the moisture would evaporate from the surface so fast, that the moisture from the inside of the sausage would not make it to the surface in time. The surface of the casing will harden, creating a barrier to the subsequent drying process. *In slow-fermented sausages* this will cre-ate a big problem as the inside of the sausage may never dry out and the product will spoil. As the sausage enters the drying stage, less moisture remains inside and the humidity and air speed are lowered. After about a week the air speed is only about 0.5 m/sec and after another week it drops to *0.1 m/sec (4 inches/sec).* It will stay below this value for the duration of the drying.

Fast moisture removal is not beneficial in *fast-fermented sausages* either. Lactic acid bacteria need water to grow and if we suddenly remove this moisture, they would produce lactic acid at a slower rate. The technology of making fast-fermented sausages relies on a rapid pH drop and not on drying so the air speed control is less critical.

It should be noted that in slow-fermented sausages yeasts and molds often appear during the drying process. This induces a "reversed" fermentation as these microorganisms consume some of the lactic acid that was produced during fer-mentation and leave behind a small amount of ammonia which is alkaline. This alkalinity will lower the overall acidity of the sausage and is the main factor con-tributing to a milder flavor in slow-fermented sausages.

There are processors of dry products that limit the entire process to one long drying step. The stuffed sausage is introduced into the drying chamber at 6-15° C (42-58° F), where it remains for the rest of the process.

Color and flavor forming bacteria (*Staphylococcus, Kocuria*) are aerobic (need oxygen to survive) and are concentrated close to the surface of the sausage where they easily find oxygen. They are sensitive to changing water activity levels and very fast drying at low humidity levels will prematurely dry out the surface of the sausage. A gray surface ring is a typical example. Like other bacteria, they need moisture to grow and the dry surface area will affect their growth. This will affect the development of proper color and flavor.

Drying basically starts already in the fermentation stage with the humidity kept at a high level of about 90-95%. Air flow is quite fast (0.8 m/sec) to permit fast moisture removal but the high humidity level moisturizes the surface of the casing preventing it from hardening.

Drying continues after the fermentation stage and more moisture is removed from the sausage. This becomes easier in time as the acidity weakens the forces that bind water. As the Aw (water activity) keeps dropping lower, the humidity level is decreased to about 0.85-90%. Because the sausage contains less moisture, less moisture appears on the surface and maintaining previous fast air flow may harden the surface of the casing so the air speed is decreased to about 0.5 m/sec (1.8 miles/per hour) which corresponds to a slow walk. The process continues until the desired amount of dryness (weight loss) is obtained. At home conditions this can be calculated by weighing test sausages.

Drying is usually performed at 12-18° C (54-66° F) and decreasing humidity, from about 85% to 65-70%. Higher temperatures and humidity over 75% will promote the development of mold on the surface of the sausage.

When making slow fermented sausages without starter cultures, drying temperatures should fall in 12-15° C (54-59° F) range. *Staph. aureus* starts growing faster at 15.6° C (60° F) and obviously it is best to avoid this and higher temperatures.

After 3 months of drying, the sausage will last almost indefinitely as long as it is kept in a cool (12° C, 44° F) and dark place, at about 60% humidity. If during storage humidity is much higher (>75%) the mold will grow on its surface. If the humidity is very low, the sausage will lose too much moisture which will make sausage production less profitable.

One may say why not to dry a sausage very quickly and be done with all this pH stuff and bacteria. Well, there are basically two reasons:

1. The outside layer of the sausage must not be hardened as it may prevent the removal of the remaining moisture. It may affect the curing of the outside layer which will develop a gray ring that will be visible when slicing the sausage.

2. Bacteria naturally found in meat and/or introduced starter cultures need moisture to grow. They have to go through the so called "lag phase" first. Only then, can they metabolize sugar and produce lactic acid. Once, when a sufficient pH drop is obtained, lactic acid bacteria slow down growing and more moisture can be removed.

Drying Sausages

Removing water content by drying a sausage is a slow process. We could dry sausages at higher temperatures by applying fast air speed, but that would only harden their surfaces, trapping the moisture inside causing the sausages to spoil. Slow, controlled drying is the method applied to traditionally made slow-fermented sausages which require three months or more to produce. As the process proceeds, water starts to evaporate (water activity decreases), making meat stronger against spoilage and pathogenic bacteria. There eventually comes a point, when there are no bacteria present and the meat is microbiologically stable. It will not spoil, as long as it is kept at low temperatures and at low humidity levels. If the temperature and humidity go up, new bacteria will establish a colony on the surface and will start moving towards the inside of the sausage. The mold immediately appears on the surface.

Sausages dry *from inside out*. For a correct drying process, there must be a balance between moisture diffusion towards the surface and moisture evaporation from the surface. If diffusion is faster than evaporation, moisture will accumulate on the surface of the sausage, causing it to be slimy. Yeasts and molds will soon follow. If evaporation is faster than diffusion, the outside surface area of the sausage will dry out and harden, and will act as a barrier to subsequent moisture removal. As a result moisture will be trapped inside of the sausage, creating favorable conditions for the growth of spoilage and pathogenic bacteria.

Drying is affected by:

- humidity - higher humidity, slower drying.
- temperature - higher temperature, faster drying.
- air flow - faster air flow, faster drying.

The moisture removed from the surface is replaced by the moisture coming from the inside of the sausage.

This is equilibrium state:

diffusion rate = evaporation rate

Fig. 1.5 Balanced moisture removal.

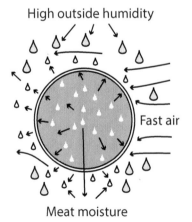

High outside humidity

Fast air

Meat moisture

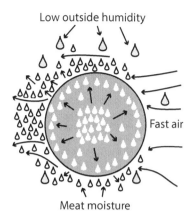

Low outside humidity

Fast air

Meat moisture

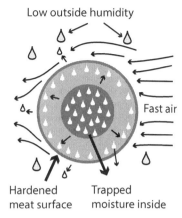

Low outside humidity

Fast air

Hardened meat surface

Trapped moisture inside

Fig. 1.6 Fast moisture removal. Inside moisture travelling towards the surface cannot keep up with the moisture removed from the surface. The sausage becomes dry on the outside and moist inside.

Fig. 1.7 Trapped moisture. The pronounced effect of fast drying. The surface is dry and there is a visible grayish ring on a sliced sausage. If the surface hardening occurs in the first stages of drying, the inside moisture may be permanently trapped and bacteria may spoil the sausage.

Fig. 1.8 Finely minced sausage. In a fine grind the particles are very small and moisture has to overcome more surface area on its way to the surface. *Its path is longer.* The air speed can be slower. This problem is magnified in a large diameter sausages, which should be dried at a slower pace.

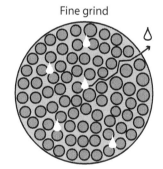

Fine grind

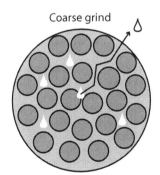

Coarse grind

Fig. 1.9 Coarse minced sausage. In coarse ground meat the moisture has more free room and a *shorter distance to the surface.*

A medium diameter sausage might experience 1.0-1.5% weight loss per day when in a fermenting room. The same sausage should lose about 0.5-0.7% of its weight per day when in a drying chamber.

For the perfect drying the humidity of the drying room should be 5% lower than the water activity (Aw) within the sausage. This requires water activity measurements and computer operated drying chambers where parameters such as temperature, humidity and air speed are continuously monitored and readjusted. This relationship remains constant and every time the water level drops, the humidity is lowered accordingly. Water activity (Aw) can be lowered faster in a sausage which contains more fat than a leaner sausage. Meat contains about 75% of water but the water content of fat is only about 10-15%. A fatter sausage containing less meat also contains less water and will dry out faster.

Increasing the acidity of the meat facilitates drying and the movement of moisture towards the surface is much smoother. As the pH drops, it approaches the isoelectric point of the myofibrillar proteins (actin and myosin) where their ability to bind water reaches a minimum. This happens around pH of 4.8-5.3. In simple words, *lowering pH aids in the removal of moisture*. Depending on the method of manufacture, diameter of a casing and the content of fat in a sausage mass, fermented sausages lose from 5-40% of their original weight.

Notes:

- The length of the sausage has no influence on drying time.
- Sausages should be dried at a rate not higher than the moisture losing ability of the sausage.
- Traditionally made sausages have pH of about 5.3 and Aw about 0.88 at the end of the drying process.
- Overloading the drying chamber can impede the air movement.
- Air speed - higher air speed, faster drying. The average air speed varies between 0.5 and 0.1 m/sec
- Casing type (pore size) - bigger pores, faster drying.
- Amount of fat - more fat in sausage, faster drying.
- Particle size - bigger size, faster drying.
- Sausage diameter - bigger diameter, slower drying.
- In general, when pH drops rapidly the sausage dries faster.
- Molds will develop more quickly if there is no air draft at all.
- If the outside of the sausage becomes greasy, it should be wiped off with a warm cloth otherwise it may inhibit drying.
- The speed of 3.6 km/h (2.2 mile/hour) corresponds to the speed of 1 meter/second which is basically a walking speed.
- The air speed of 0.5 m/sec (1.8 miles/per hour) corresponds to a slow walk.
- Often air speed is given in air changes per minute. Typical values for *fermentation* rooms are 4-6 air changes per minute, and less than 2 air changes per minute for *drying* chambers.

Humidity Control

Humidity, or better said the "relative humidity" defines how much water is present in the air at a particular temperature. The air always contains some water vapor and although we don't see it, it is there and it has a certain mass. *The higher the temperature the more water can be held by air and vice versa.* Humidity changes throughout the day and is dependent upon temperature. *When the temperature goes up, the humidity goes down and vice versa.* This means that there is higher humidity in the air at night when temperatures are lower. When the clouds come in and it starts to drizzle, the humidity goes up immediately. There is more humidity in areas containing many lakes, rivers or being close to the sea shore. Arid areas such as deserts or mountains have less water and subsequently less humidity.

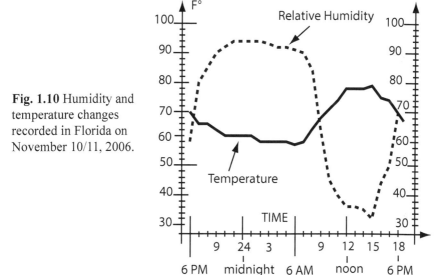

Fig. 1.10 Humidity and temperature changes recorded in Florida on November 10/11, 2006.

As documented on the graph, there was a steep rise in humidity levels (from 60 to 90%) when the temperature dropped from 70° F (6 PM) to 62° F (11 PM). These high humidity levels continued until 7 AM. There was a big drop in humidity levels from 90 to 36%, when the temperature increased from 60° (7 AM) to 77° F (12 AM-noon). At 7 AM there was so much humidity that there was a fog all over the area which completely disappeared one hour later.

25

Photo 1.7 - 7 AM, fog, 90% humidity.

Photo 1.8 - 8 AM. clear, 84% humidity.

This humidity behavior can be used to our advantage when a large drying chamber or smokehouse is located outside. The amount of moisture in the air is fixed for at least some time but raising the temperature lowers the relative humidity. As you cannot change the physical location of the drying chamber, you have to learn how to go around it.

- There are portable devices (humidifiers and dehumidifiers) which can be placed inside of the drying chamber. They are inexpensive and have a thermostat which allows automatic humidity control.

- In smaller chambers such as an old refrigerator box, the simplest humidifier is a bowl filled with water that is placed inside. The larger surface area of the dish, the more evaporation will take place.

- To increase humidity, sausages can be periodically sprayed or immersed briefly in water.

- Humidity testers are inexpensive and there is no excuse for not having one.

- In home freezer or refrigerator humidity varies between 40-50%.

For controlled drying humidity should lag the sausage Aw from 0.2 to 0.5, 0.3 being the average.

Example: sausage Aw 0.95, humidity 92%, Sausage Aw 0.92, humidity 89%. sausage Aw 0.89, humidity 0.86 etc.

Chapter 2

The Magic Behind Fermented Sausages - *It's All About Bacteria*

Understanding Bacteria

Learn how to work with and how to control bacteria. After all, they and not you, make the sausage, you are just the driver. Making fermented sausages is a combination of the art of the sausage maker and unseen magic performed by bacteria. The friendly bacteria are working together with a sausage maker, but the dangerous ones are trying to wreak havoc. Using his knowledge the sausage maker monitors temperature and humidity which allows him to control reactions that take place inside the sausage. This game is played for quite a while and at the end a high quality product is created.

This is basically how they have been made for centuries, but recently we have come to understand the inner Whys and Hows of the fermentation process. Food safety is nothing else but the control of bacteria, but first we have to learn how bacteria behave. Once one knows what bacteria like or dislike, it will be very simple to produce safe products with a long shelf life. Let's make something clear: it is impossible to eliminate bacteria altogether, life on the planet will come to a halt. They are everywhere: on the floor, on walls, in the air, on our hands and all they need to grow is moisture, nutrients and warm temperature. Let us quote an old military motto: *"You have to know your enemy if you want to win the battle"* holds true for making fermenting sausages and only by understanding bacteria behavior we can fight or control them. We have to create conditions that will:

- Inhibit spoilage and dangerous bacteria.
- Take a good care of friendly bacteria so they can prosper and work for us.

Microorganisms

All microorganisms can be divided into the following groups:

- Bacteria
- Yeasts
- Molds

They all share one thing in common: they want to live and given the proper conditions they will start multiplying. They don't grow bigger, they just divide and divide until there is nothing for them to eat, or until conditions become so unfavorable that they stop multiplying and die.

Fig. 2.1 Bacterial growth. A bacterial cell enlarges in size, then a wall separates the cell into two new cells exactly alike.

All bacteria need moisture, nutrients, and warm temperatures to grow. *Keeping them at low temperatures does not kill them, but only stops them from multiplying.* Once when the conditions are favorable again, they will awaken and start growing again. Some bacteria tolerate the presence of salt better than others and we take advantage of this when curing meats. Most bacteria need oxygen (aerobic), others thrive without it (anaerobic).

Meat contains about 75% of water and this moisture is the main reason that meat spoils. It is a community pool and if the weather is warm, all bacteria types go swimming. They are having a lot of fun but what's worse, given favorable conditions they can double up in numbers every 20 minutes. In a refrigerator their number will also grow, albeit at a reduced pace, but they can double up in 12 hours. Only deep freezing stops bacteria from contaminating meat, however, even then they don't die, but only go to sleep. With the raise of temperature the conditions for bacteria growth become favorable again and they will wake up and grow again. At room temperatures bacteria will grow anywhere they have access to nutrients and water.

Restricting Bacteria Growth

Bacteria are walking their way into the meat from the outside. Most of them need oxygen to survive and there is a lot of air between particles of minced meat. Meat which is finely comminuted is at higher risk due to its large surface area, and this is why ground meat has the shortest life. We all know that meat left at room temperature will spoil in time and that is why it is kept in a refrigerator/freezer. Yet fermented dry or air dried sausages are made of raw meat and are neither cooked nor refrigerated. What makes them safe? Well, it is our job to provide safety by restricting growth of undesirable bacteria. Bacteria growth can be restricted by:

- Exposure time
- Temperature
- Acidity
- Moisture
- Salt

Number of bacteria	Elapsed time
10	0
20	20 minutes
40	40 minutes
80	1 hour
160	1 hour 20 min
320	1 hour 40 min
640	2 hours
1280	2 hours 20 min
2560	2 hours 40 min
5120	3 hours
10,240	3 hours 20 min
20,480	3 hours 40 min
40,960	4 hours
81,920	4 hours 20 min
163,840	4 hours 40 min
327,680	5 hours
655,360	5 hours 20 min
1,310,720	5 hours 40 min
2,621,440	6 hours

Bacteria Growth in Time

Under the correct conditions, bacteria reproduce rapidly and the populations can grow very large. *Temperature and exposure time are the factors that affect bacterial growth the most.* Looking at the table it becomes very clear what happens to a piece of meat left on the kitchen table on a beautiful and hot summer day.

Bacteria Growth With Temperature

Most of them love temperatures that revolve around the temperature of our body 98.6° F (36.6°C). Holding products at temperatures higher than 130° F (54° C) restricts their growth. Increasing temperature over 140° F (60° C) will start killing them.

All bacteria hate cold, and around 32° F, (0° C) they become lethargic and will become dormant when the temperature drops lower.

It can be seen on the right that at 32° F (0° C) bacteria needs as much as 38 hours to divide in two. That also means that if our piece of meat had a certain amount of bacteria on its surface, after 38 hours of lying in a refrigerator the amount of bacteria will double. If we move this meat from the refrigerator to a room having a temperature of 80° F (26.5° C), the bacteria will divide every hour (12 times faster). At 90° F (32 C)° they will be dividing every 30 minutes.

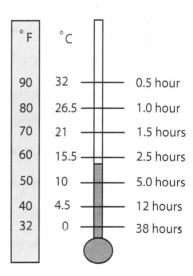

Fig. 2.2 Bacteria growth with temperature.

The above drawing (Fig. 2.2) has been compiled from the data we found at the College of Agriculture, Auburn University, Alabama. It shows the time that is required for one bacteria cell to become two at different storage temperatures. Looking at the above drawing we can see that once the temperature reaches 50° F (10° C), bacteria will double up twice as fast every time we raise the temperature by about 10° F. From the above examples we can draw a logical conclusion, that if we want to process meats *we should perform these tasks at temperatures not higher than 50° F (10° C)*. And those are the temperatures present in meat processing plants. You might say that lowering the temperature of the room will be better still. Of course it will be better, but people working in such conditions for 8 hours a day will find it very uncomfortable. Keep in mind that meat is processed at 50° F (10° C) just for a short while and then it goes back into a cooler. Bacteria growth data in the above tables hold true for optimal conditions: no salt or nitrite and ample supply of moisture. Once we introduce conditions that are unfavorable to bacteria (salt, nitrite, acidity), their growth will be inhibited.

Below 45° F (7° C) bacteria grow slowly and at temperatures above 140° F (60° C) they start to die. In the so called "danger zone" between 40-140° F (4-60 ° C) bacteria are growing very well. For instance, the infamous *E.coli* grows best at 98° F (37° C) and *Staph. aureus* at 86-98° F (30-37° C). Certain types for example *Clostridium botulinum* are able to survive high temperatures because they form spores. Spores are special cells that envelop themselves in a protective shell (cocoon) and become resistant to harsh environmental conditions. Once conditions become favorable, the cells return to the actively growing state.

Restricting bacterial growth by acidity, moisture and salt is explained in detail in Chapter 6 Safety Hurdles.

Bacteria Types

Bacteria which are of concern to us can be classified as:
- Food spoilage bacteria.
- Dangerous (pathogenic) bacteria.
- Beneficial bacteria.

Food Spoilage Bacteria - How Do Bacteria Spoil Food?

Microorganisms, like all living creatures must eat. Spoilage bacteria break down meat proteins and fats causing food to deteriorate and develop unpleasant odors, tastes, and textures. Fruits and vegetables get mushy or slimy and meat develops a bad odor. They don't use the toilet, but they excrete the waste which we end up eating. This is the unpleasant tasting "spoilage." Most people would not eat spoiled food. If they did, however, they probably would not get seriously sick. Bacteria such as *Pseudomonas spp.* or *Brochotrix thermosphacta* cause slime, discoloration and odors but do not produce toxins. There are different spoilage bacteria and each reproduces at specific temperatures. Some can grow at low temperatures in the refrigerator or freezer. Others grow well at room temperature and in the "Danger Zone" (40-140° F, 4-60° C). Most spoilage bacteria are easily killed by the temperature of boiling water, 212° F, 100° C. Under the correct conditions, spoilage bacteria reproduce rapidly and their populations can grow very large. Spoilage bacteria love moisture and stop growing at Aw < 0.97.

Pathogenic Bacteria

It is commonly believed that the presence of bacteria creates immense danger to us but this belief is far from the truth. The fact is that a very small percentage of bacteria can place us in any danger, and most of us with a healthy immune system are able to fight them off. *Pathogenic bacteria cause illness.* They grow rapidly in the "Danger Zone" and *do not generally affect the taste, smell, or appearance of food.* Food that is left too long at warm temperatures could be dangerous to eat, but smell and look just fine. *Clostridium botulinum, Bacillus cereus* or *Staphylococcus aureus* infect food with toxin which will bring harm to us in just a few hours. Still others like *Salmonella* or *Escherichia coli* will find the way with infected meat into our intestines and if present in sufficient numbers will pose a serious danger. The table below shows the ability of common pathogenic bacteria to survive at low pH and Aw levels.

Name	Temperature in ° C			Min pH	Min Aw	O_2 needs
	Minimum	Optimum	Maximum			
Salmonella	7	35 - 37	45	3.8	0.94	FA
Cl.botulinum	3	18 - 25	45	5.0	0.97	QA
Cl.perfringens	12	43 - 47	50	5.5	0.93	QA
Staph.aureus	6	37	48	4.2	0.85	FA
Campylobacter	30	42	45	4.9	0.98	MA
Listeria	-1.5	37	45	4.4	0.92	FA
E.coli	7	37	46	4.4	0.95	FA
Shigella	7	35-37	47	4.0	0.91	FA
Bacillus	4	30 - 37	55	4.3	0.91	FA

A: Facultative anaerobic feels comfortable in oxygen but can live without it.
OA: Obligate anaerobic cannot grow in presence of oxygen.
MA: Microaerophile bacteria like very little oxygen (5%) and low levels of CO_2 (carbon dioxide-10%).
The min pH and Aw are the lowest values at which the above bacteria can survive.

Most pathogenic bacteria, including *Salmonella, E.coli 0157:H7, Listeria monocytogenes*, and *Campylobacter,* can be fairly easily destroyed using a mild cooking process. Maintaining a minimum temperature within the range of 130-165° F (54-74° C) for a specific amount of time will kill them. However, cooking will not destroy several of these toxins once they have formed in food. Pathogenic bacteria hate cold conditions and lie dormant at low temperatures waiting for an opportunity to jump into action when the conditions get warmer again. They all die when submitted to the cooking temperature of 160° F (72° C). However, most fermented sausages are never cooked, so different strategies must be implemented to keep them at bay. Fighting bacteria is a never ending battle, but at least we can do our best to turn the odds in our favor, and make life miserable for our enemy. A fully cooked piece of meat if left at warm temperature will spoil again, as new bacteria will jump on its surface and will start moving inside.

Control of Microbiological Hazards Associated with Fermented Sausages

Staphylococcus aureus *This bacteria, often called "staph", is present in the nose, throat, skin and hair of many healthy individuals*	Contamination is most often caused by human contact with hands (raw and cooked foods) and can be controlled by hand sanitation and the use of disposable gloves. *Staphylococcus aureus* is very resistive to drying and in the presence of oxygen can survive at water levels down to 0.86. Without oxygen it will not grow below Aw 0.90. At 60° F (15.6° C) it starts to grow rapidly. It can withstand up to 15% salt. Temperature control is the best way to minimize the growth of *S. aureus* and development of its toxin as it can be killed by mild heat. A rapid drop to pH <5.3 slows *S. aureus* growth.
E. coli 0157:H7 *The bacteria resides in the intestinal tracts of animals, especially cattle, and can be shed in feces. During the slaughter, the bacteria can contaminate the carcass.*	*E.coli 0157:H7* is a hardy pathogen that can survive both refrigerator and freezer storage. It survives the acidic environment well all the way down to pH 4.0. The procedures used for the destruction of *E.coli 0157:H7* include a combination of controls for pH, Aw, and temperature. It multiplies very slowly at refrigerator temperatures. A thorough cooking is the most reliable method to destroy this pathogen.
Listeria monocytogenes *Present in soil, vegetation, water and can be carried by humans and animals. It can be found at at every level of the meat processing chain and in a variety of meat products.*	*Listeria monocytogenes* can grow with or without oxygen, it can survive dry conditions and is a very salt tolerant organism. Listeria has a wide temperature growth range from 36-112° F (2-44° C). At 39° F (4° C) it can double in numbers every 1.5 days. In fermented sausages *L. monocytogenes* is controlled through a combination of low pH, high levels of salt, drying process, protective cultures like Bactoferm ™ F-LC and varying degrees of heat processing.

Salmonella	Salmonella grows very slow below 50° F (10° C). It can grow with or without oxygen and in a range of temperatures from 40-117° F (5-47° C). It does not grow above 130° F (54° C) and at low pH levels. *Salmonella* is heat-sensitive and cooking meat (150-165° F, 65-74° C) will rapidly destroy it.
Salmonella is carried in the intestinal tracts of sheep, cattle, swine and poultry.	
Campylobacter *Fecal contamination of raw poultry meat*	Cross contamination from raw meat or poultry drippings or consumption of under cooked food. *Campylobacter* is sensitive to heat and drying and it does not grow in acidic food. It survives, but it does not grow during refrigeration. Prefers reduced oxygen environment and grows best at human body temperature.
Clostridium botulinum *Soil and the intestinal tract of animals*	Grows best without oxygen and it can grow in most low-acid foods. Bacteria can protect itself by forming spores (shells) which are extremely heat resistant and can resist boiling water temperature for 5 hours. pH 4.6 prevents bacteria growth and toxin production. Addition of sodium nitrite is the most effective hurdle.

Toxins

Toxins of most concern are produced by *Clostridium botulinum, Clostridium perfringens, Bacillus cereus*, and *Staphylococcus aureus*. All are the result of the growth of bacteria in foods that have been mishandled. Proper cooking, fermentation, cooling, and storage of food can prevent the growth of these bacteria and more importantly, the production of their toxins. Thermal processing (canning) at a minimum retort temperatures of greater than 240° F (116° C) for a specific amount of time is necessary to destroy most spores and toxins.

Note: botulism is covered in detail in Appendix.

Beneficial Bacteria

Without beneficial bacteria it will not be possible to make fermented sausages. They are naturally occurring in the meat, but are commonly added into the meat in the form of starter cultures. There are two classes of beneficial (friendly) bacteria:

- Lactic acid producing bacteria - *Lactobacillus, Pediococcus.*
- Color and flavor forming bacteria - *Staphylococcus, Kocuria* (previously known as *Micrococcus*).

In the past, without much knowing, we have been growing beneficial bacteria during the curing process.

Lactic Acid Bacteria

The lactic acid bacteria are the engine that powers making fermented foods. They are responsible for the fermentation of yogurt, cheese, sauerkraut, pickles, beer, wine, cider, kimchi, cocoa, sourdough bread and other fermented foods. All lactic acid bacteria are micro-aerophilic, that is they require very small amounts of oxygen to function. Their diet is a simple one; all they eat is sugar. The lactic acid bacteria belong to two main groups:

- Homofermenters - produce mainly lactic acid.
- Heterofermenters - produce lactic acid, ethyl alcohol, acetate and carbon dioxide. By producing more components, they contribute more towards the flavor of the product.

The lactic acid producing bacteria family consists of many different strains and each of them displays different optimal temperature for growth, the fact which helps us to select fermentation temperature.

Name	Optimum temperature		Salt limit (% salt-in-water)
	°C	°F	
Lactobacillus sakei	30	86	9
Lactobacillus farciminis	37	99	10
Lactobacillus plantarum	30	86	13
Lactobacillus curvatus	24	75	10
Lactobacillus pentosus	35	95	9
Pediococcus acidilactici	40	104	10
Pediococcus pentosaceus	35	95	7

These are highly competitive microorganisms and can grow with or without air. Typically, the initial counts of lactic acid bacteria in raw meat mixes are around 1,000 - 10,000 cells/g. During fermentation, those numbers increase to 10,000,00 - 100,000,000 cells/g. These bacteria are directly responsible for fermentation and they accomplish this by consuming sugar and producing lactic acid. This makes sausages safe, but imparts a tangy-sourly flavor to the product which becomes more pronounced as more sugar is added. Lactic acid bacteria contribute little towards the development of flavor although *Pediococcus* spp. possess some proteolytic ability (breaking down meat proteins).

By producing lactic acid, bacteria indirectly influence the taste of the sausage. In most cases this sourly flavor is off set by the introduction of spices, different sugars and flavoring syrups. The most useful lactic acid bacteria families are:

- ***Lactobacillus***: *(Lb.sakei, Lb.plantarum, Lb.farcimis, Lb.curvatus).*
- ***Pediococcus***: (*Pediococcus pentosaceus, Pediococcus acidilactici).*

34

They exhibit different optimal growth temperatures and can be chosen for making fast or slow-fermented sausages. With a fast-fermented cultures a sausage can be made in 7 days what amounts to higher profits. *Pediococcus acidilactici* allows fermentation at temperatures as high as 45° C (113° F). Lactic bacteria cause rapid acidification of meat by metabolizing sugar. They produce not only lactic acid but also acetic acid, ethanol, different aromas, bacteriocins and other enzymes. Lactic bacteria are quite resistant to small changes in water activity but their action slows down when Aw of 0.95 is reached. This means that fast fermented sausages *must not lose moisture too fast,* otherwise the fermentation process will suffer. Lactic acid bacteria exhibit a *higher salt tolerance* than spoilage or pathogenic bacteria but not as high as color and flavor forming *Staphylococcus spp.* Being an acid producer, lactic acid bacteria can *tolerate high acidity* levels (pH as low as 3.0). Not all lactic acid bacteria that reside in meat are desirable. For example, *L. viridescens* can cause the greening of meat due to the production of hydrogen peroxide, *L. brevis* and *L. mesenteroids* can cause gas production and unacceptable souring. *Brochrothrix* can cause souring, off flavors and odors. This is why starter cultures are so popular as they allow us to introduce bacteria with preselected characteristics into meat.

Color and Flavor Forming Bacteria

These bacteria are responsible for *the color, taste and the flavor of the sausage. They are not directly involved in the fermentation process.* Bacteria strains such as *Staphylococcus* and *Kocuria* (formely *Micrococcus)* belong to the *Micrococcaceae* family and are known to be the main mechanisms of producing nitrite from nitrate during the curing process.

Without these bacteria it will not be possible to produce traditional salami. Dry fermented sausage containing an insufficient number of these bacteria will not cure properly, and ultimately the color and the flavor of the meat will suffer. In addition, the microbiological safety of a dry sausage will be at risk as these bacteria force nitrate into releasing nitrite.

Staphylococcus and *Kocuria* do not perform well at high acidity levels (pH < 5.4) and their performance in fast-fermented sausages (fast pH drop) is severely restricted. They grow very slowly and are best used in slow-fermented sausages which are made with nitrate or nitrite/nitrate. Even so, by the time the sausage enters the ripening stage, the number of *Staphylococcus* might be quite small. To ensure the desired activities (and flavor production) of these bacteria in the late ripening/drying stage, a sufficient number of bacteria (10^6 - 10^7 /g of meat) in a form of starter cultures should be added. They might not grow much in the late ripening stage but they will still react with the meat.

Name	Optimum temperature		Salt limit (% salt-in-water)
	°C	°F	
Staphylococcus carnosus	30	86	16
Staphylococcus xylosus	30	86	15
Micrococcaceae spp.	30	86	16

Today most meat products contain sodium nitrite which does not depend on the bacterial action of curing bacteria to produce nitrite. The direct introduction of nitrite (cure #1) to sausage mince guarantees the characteristic pink color, providing that meat with enough myoglobin was selected. In a case of slow fermented sausages which often use nitrite and nitrate together, *Staphylococcus* and/or *Kocuria* bacteria are needed to force nitrate into releasing nitrite which in turn will start curing meat. Although nitrite will start reacting with myoglobin immediately, it dissipates in meat rapidly, however, nitrate lasts much longer. If nitrite were used alone, the color development would suffer, at least in slow fermented products. For this reason nitrite and nitrate are added together (cure #2).

As a rule *Staphylococcus* spp. are preferred to *Micrococcus* spp. as they exhibit higher salt tolerance and they require less oxygen. This allows *Staphylococcus* spp. to be active deep inside of the sausage whereas *Micrococcus* spp. being aerobic (need oxygen) are more active in the surface area. In addition to possessing nitrate reductase (releasing nitrite from nitrate), they produce the enzyme catalase which protects the sausage against oxygen activity and delays the rancidity of fats. *Staphylococcus* can tolerate lower water levels quite well and will react with meat for a very long time, *being the main factor* which creates flavor and aroma in traditionally made slow-fermented sausages. Most color and flavor forming bacteria can grow in the presence of 5% salt. In addition to their nitrate to nitrite reducing capabilities, these bacteria are known to contribute to flavor development by:

- Proteolysis-break down of proteins into free amino acids.
- Lipolysis-break down of fats into free fatty acids.
- Catalase activity-ability to bind oxygen and to convert undesired hydrogen peroxide (H_2O_2) to water and molecular oxygen.

Once free amino acids and free fatty acids are produced, many involved reactions will take place during fermentation and the drying stages of traditionally made sausages. In slow-fermented sausages, the final pH (5.3-5.5) is achieved very slowly, and is not low enough to inhibit the action of curing and flavor developing bacteria. When making fast-fermented sausages the pH drop below 5.0 can be obtained within 12-24 hours and that will prevent acid sensitive color and flavor forming bacteria from reacting with meat. As a result no proteolysis and lipolysis will take place, and the sausage will not develop a traditional salami flavor.

The flavor of the fast-fermented sausage is tangy and sourly which is the result of lactic acid produced by lactic acid bacteria. Such sausages (fast-fermented or semi-dry) are perfectly acceptable in the USA and Northern Europe, although people in countries such as Italy or Spain may have a different opinion.

In the past most regular sausages were made with nitrate and it was well known though not understood, that sausages that were cured at higher temperatures 46° F (8° C) exhibited stronger color and better quality. Years later we discovered, that at higher temperatures curing bacteria grew and reacted with meat faster which led to stronger color and better flavor. The serious drawback to this method is that spoilage and pathogenic bacteria will also grow faster at higher temperatures.

Yeasts

Yeast and molds grow much slower than bacteria and they develop later in a drying process. This means they are normally a part of the traditionally made sausage process. They metabolize some of the lactic acid that was created during the fermentation stage thus increasing pH (lowering acidity) what as a result improves flavor in a slow-fermented product. They don't seem to be affected by a pH drop in the fermentation stage and will grow in a vast range of temperatures (8-25° C, 46-78° F), as long as there is high humidity in a chamber. They are less sensitive to increased salt levels than lactic acid bacteria. Yeasts need little oxygen to survive, and live on the surface or near the surface inside of the sausage, but molds will grow only on the surface. Popular yeasts: *Debaromyces hansenii, Candida formata.* Those are the preferred species as they exhibit a high salt tolerance. *D. hansenii* decomposes peroxides and consumes both lactic and acetic acids which are present in fermented sausages. As a result pH increases and the meat is less acidic which contributes to the milder flavor. In addition *D. hansenii* produces ammonia, which has a pH of about 11.5 and this creates a new and higher pH of the meat (less acidic). *D. hansenii*, similarly to *Staphylococcus* spp., can break down meat proteins (proteolysis) and fats (lipolysis), contributing to flavor development.

Molds

Molds are aerobic (need oxygen) and will grow on the surface of the sausage only. Vacuum packed products do not develop molds. On fermented European sausages, the development of mold is often seen as a desired feature as it contributes to the flavor of the sausage. The positive characteristics of molds are numerous:

- They help to moderate drying and prevent oxygen from reaching the inside of the sausage, which prevents loss of color and delays rancidity of fats.
- They can metabolize lactic acid which causes an increase in pH (lower acidity) and contributes to a mellower flavor.

- By consuming oxygen and producing catalase, they reduce chemical lipid oxidation and rancidity of fats.
- *P. nalgiovense* mold affects flavor formation by promoting lipolytic and proteolytic activities.

Popular mold cultures: *Penicillium nalgiovense, Penicillium chrysogenum, Penicillium roqueforti (used in cheese), Penicillium camemberti (used in cheese).*

Photo. 2.1 Molded and unmolded salami.

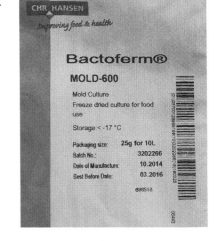

Photo. 2.2 Chr-Hansen Mold 600 starter culture.

Chapter 3

Fermentation Step By Step

In simple terms *meat fermentation is spoilage of meat by bacteria*. Leaving meat at room temperature to itself will result in a spoilage, but if the process is properly controlled, the result is a quality fermented product. Meat fermentation is accomplished by lactic bacteria, either naturally present in meat or added as starter cultures. These bacteria feed on sugars and produce lactic acid and small amounts of other components. Increased amount of lactic acid results in higher acidity (lower pH) what not only creates a highly desirable product, but also prevents the growth of spoilage and pathogenic bacteria. When a sausage is introduced into a fermentation chamber, the bacteria hold all cards in their favor:

- Warm temperature - right inside of the danger zone.
- Moisture - meat contains 75% water.
- Food - little sugar is present in the meat itself (glycogen) but extra amounts are usually added.
- Oxygen - present in air. Food spoilage bacteria require oxygen to grow.

When a sausage is stuffed *the only barrier that protects the meat from spoiling is salt and nitrite.* Fresh meat always contains some bacteria and they will grow in time. Initially, there is fierce competition among different groups of bacteria for food, but beneficial bacteria slowly but steadily gain the upper hand in this fight by eliminating spoilage and pathogenic types. "Survival of the fittest" at its best. The reason that beneficial bacteria get the upper hand in this war is that they are:

- Stronger competitors. This becomes much more pronounced when starter culture is added which brings millions of beneficial bacteria into the mix.
- Better tolerate exposure to salt, nitrite and decreased water levels than undesirable bacteria types.

The addition of salt, nitrite and starter cultures creates favorable fermentation conditions, however, spoilage and dangerous bacteria such as *Listeria monocytogenes, Salmonella, Staphylococcus aureus* and *E. coli 0:157:H7* are still able to grow, although at a much slower pace. When a sausage is placed in a warm fermentation chamber, *all bacteria* types spring into action and start to multiply, but they react to the new environment differently:

- **Food spoilage bacteria** (*Pseudomonas*) need oxygen and start to choke as there is little air inside of the sausage. The salt and lowered moisture further inhibits their growth. Once lactic acid bacteria start to produce lactic acid, the increased acidity inhibits spoilage bacteria even more.

- **Lactic acid bacteria** (*Lactobacillus* and *Pediococcus*) are quite resistant to salt and function well at slightly reduced water levels. They start to metabolize sugar and produce lactic acid which increases acidity and creates a barrier against undesirable types. As they grow in numbers, they eat more sugar and produce more lactic acid.

- **Color and flavor forming bacteria** (*Staphylococcus* and *Kocuria*) tolerate increased salt levels very well, but they grow slowly. They can grow in the presence of oxygen or without it. They are sensitive to acidity and at pH below 5.5 they become less effective. They need not days, but months of time to break meat proteins and fats in order to produce all those aroma releasing enzymes. In fast-fermented sausages a drop of pH 5.0 can be achieved in just 12 hours giving them no chance to perform.

- **Pathogenic bacteria** (dangerous) are kept in check primarily by salt and nitrite. Once lactic acid bacteria start making lactic acid, this increasing acidity starts to inhibit pathogenic bacteria, especially *Staphylococcus aureus,* which is very sensitive to acidity though it functions very well at low moisture levels (down to Aw 0.86). In addition, some lactic acid bacteria strains (*Pediococcus acidilactici, Lactobacillus curvatus*) can produce bacteriocins that are very hostile towards wild and unwanted lactic bacteria strains and pathogenic *Listeria monocytogenes.*

The main product of fermentation is lactic acid and the main cause is an increased acidity of meat. The more sugar that is metabolized by the lactic acid bacteria, the more lactic acid is produced and the higher acidity of meat is obtained. *The speed of fermentation is directly proportional to the temperature* so the fermentation proceeds faster at higher temperatures. If the fermentation temperature drops to <53° F (12° C), the lactic acid bacteria may stop metabolizing sugar. *How acidic the sausage becomes depends on the amount and type of sugar introduced.* If more sugar is added, a higher acidity (lower pH) is obtained and the sausage gains a more sourly flavor.

In traditionally made slow-fermented dry sausages, the proper fermentation can take place only if there is a sufficient number of lactic bacteria in the meat to begin with. To increase their number a long curing step was performed which allowed lactic acid bacteria to grow. Unfortunately, spoilage and pathogenic bacteria were growing as well, although at a much slower rate due to the effects of salt and nitrate. In the latest production methods, huge numbers of lactic acid bacteria in the form of *starter cultures* are introduced into the meat right at the beginning of the process and that guarantees healthy and strong fermentation. These armies of beneficial bacteria start competing for food with other undesirable bacteria types, decreasing their chances for growth and survival. Fermentation stops when no more lactic acid is produced by bacteria. This happens when:

- No more sugar is available to lactic acid bacteria.
- There is not enough free water (Aw < 0.95) available. This can happen when a sausage dries rapidly in low humidity or air speed is too fast.
- Temperature is lowered below 53° F (12° C), or product is heated above 120° F (50° C) which may kill bacteria.

Fermentation is performed by *Lactobacillus* or *Pediococcus* lactic acid bacteria. *Lactobacillus* and *Pediococcus* require different temperatures for growth and this is what basically separates them. Depending on the type of a sausage desired different amounts and types of sugars will be chosen and in each case fermentation will run differently. In the past, all was very simple as traditional sausages were manufactured with very little or none at all sugar. Potassium nitrate was added as sodium nitrite was not yet discovered.

Today the commonly available starter cultures help us to produce fermented sausages of many types such as slow or fast-fermented, dry or semi-dry, sliceable or spreadable, with mold or without.

Choosing a type of sausage to make decides the choice of starter culture and establishes parameters of the fermentation process as different cultures prefer different fermentation temperature. Based on that choice, the proper type and amount of sugars will be added into the mix.

The process of meat fermentation in slow or fast-fermented products varies slightly. The processing steps prior to the fermentation stage such as meat selection, curing, grinding, mixing and stuffing remain similar in both cases. Nowadays, starter cultures are added regardless of what sausage type is produced.

The fermentation process is influenced by:

- Temperature (the most important factor).
- Type of sausage desired and starter culture chosen, the time can be from 12 hours to many days.
- The method of production (chance, back slopping or starter cultures).
- Sugar type.
- pH lowering additives (Gdl, citric acid).
- Meat used, pork ferments faster than beef as it has a lower starting pH.

When a stuffed sausage is placed in a warm fermentation chamber lactic acid bacteria suddenly wake up and enter the "waiting" stage which is known as *lag phase*. They sit, they look around, they start consuming sugars, they are getting comfortable and ready for the war. If anybody made his own wine, he will recognize the similarity. At this period the sausage is at the highest risk as other bacteria types will try to grow as well. The only protection is nitrite and salt that were added into the mix. Then, all types of bacteria go on a rampage and start to multiply.

The speed in which they will keep on growing (not in size but in number), depends on the temperature. The amount of acid they will produce depends on the type and the total amount of sugar added.

In general, *faster fermentation results in a lower pH even if the same amount of sugar is added.* According to Chr. Hansen a 5° C increase in temperature, if close to the optimum growth temperature for the specific lactic acid bacteria, doubles the rate of lactic acid formation.

The temperature of the sausage should increase to the recommended fermentation temperature of a particular culture as fast as possible to create the best starting conditions for the growth of starter culture bacteria. If the temperature is increasing slowly, the bacteria that are naturally present in meat will have favorable conditions to grow before culture bacteria start competing with them.

Fermentation starts at a high humidity (> 90%) to slow down the moisture removal from the sausage. Adding 3% salt will drop Aw water activity to 0.96-0.97 and if at humidity were below 90% the drying may proceed too quickly. As a result Aw may drop below Aw 0.95 which will have a detrimental effect on the growth of lactic acid bacteria and fermentation may be inhibited. All bacteria types need free water to survive and lactic acid bacteria are not an exception.

If humidity is high but air speed is restricted, too little drying will take place which is indicated by slime that forms on the sausage. Once the fermentation has taken place the drying can be more aggressive.

The End of Fermentation

Without performing pH acidity tests it is impossible to predict exactly when the fermentation ends and the drying begins, as both processes are closely related.

The sausage pH, not the time, is the factor that determines when the fermentation is completed.

When the lowest pH reading is obtained we may assume that the fermentation stage has ended. The question is even harder to answer in the case of slow-fermented products which are made with little sugar as this results in a slow and small pH drop. Once the fermentation starts, it will continue until the sugar supply is exhausted providing that there is sufficient moisture inside the sausage (Aw > 0.95).Then the sausage enters the drying stage at a lower temperature although in reality *it starts drying already in the fermentation stage.*

42

Traditional Slow Fermenting Process

The production of traditionally fermented sausages is possible because of:

- Naturally present bacteria inside of the meat.
- Bacteria residing on the premises and equipment, including our body.

In traditionally made sausages the total drop of pH and resulting acidity will be small, around pH 5.3 or higher, due to a very little sugar (around 0.3%) and in some cases none at all. Even if no sugar is introduced, some fermentation will still take place as meat contains a little amount of sugar (glycogen). For safety reasons slow-fermented sausages are made with 3% or more salt. This amount of salt combined with nitrite and low temperatures prevent undesirable bacteria from growing.

Lactic acid, color and flavor forming bacteria grow quite well at slightly elevated salt levels, but spoilage and pathogenic bacteria find a salty environment increasingly hostile. If you look at the Fig. 3.1 drawing on the next page you will see that as lactic, curing and flavor bacteria start growing, the number of spoilage and pathogenic bacteria starts to decrease. As lactic acid bacteria consume sugar they produce acidity which makes meat more resilient to undesirable bacteria. It seems logical that it shall be in our interests to create plenty of acidity as soon as possible to guard meat against spoilage. Well, this is often done, however, it introduces a sourly flavor which not everybody likes.

Color and flavor producing bacteria are somewhat salt tolerant, however, they do not tolerate acidity well. *Color and flavor forming bacteria (Micrococcus and Staphylococcus) are responsible for the development of flavor* which they accomplish by breaking down meat proteins and fats. This proceeds very slowly and needs not days, but months of time and is typically associated with traditionally fermented sausages. As curing bacteria multiply in numbers, they force nitrate, which is usually added to slow fermented products, into releasing nitrite which contributes to a strong curing color. Once acidity reaches pH 5.4, the curing and flavor bacteria become less effective and will stop working when acidity increases to pH 5.0. This can be seen on the graph where pH and flavor bacteria curves cross together. It is in our interest to delay increase in acidity for as long as possible so that flavor producing bacteria will keep on working.

As the growth of any bacteria is directly related to the increase in temperature, lactic acid bacteria will grow faster and will produce more lactic acid at higher temperatures. High temperature can increase the production of lactic acid so fast that curing and flavor bacteria will prematurely stop working. The sausage will be stable, but no more flavor development will take place. Traditionally made sausages are usually fermented at moderate temperatures around 68° F (20° C). At these temperatures lactic acid bacteria metabolize sugar slowly which results in a slow increase in the acidity of the meat. The pH drop is accompanied by *slow drying* at high humidity levels so there is a slow removal of moisture which does not inhibit the action of lactic acid or color and flavor forming bacteria.

Because acidity accumulation (pH drop) is directly proportionate to the amount of introduced sugar, the amount of added sugar should not be higher than 0.5%. If less than 0.3% sugar is added the acidity will not reach pH 5.0 and curing and flavor bacteria will work at their fullest. As the pH of the sausage drops below pH 5.3 moisture removal becomes easier. At around pH 4.8 a point is reached, called isoelectric point, when water holding forces become weaker and the sausage starts drying fast. Slow-fermented sausages usually do not develop so much acidity.

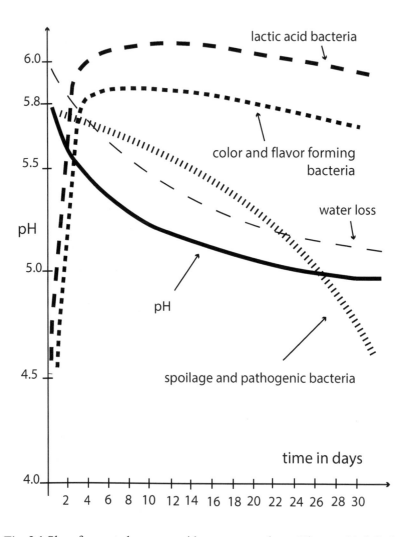

Fig. 3.1 Slow-fermented sausage without starter culture. Nitrate added, little sugar. Fermented at 64-70° F (18-20° C).

Data of Nurmi (1966)

There is less and less free water available to bacteria and this creates an additional hurdle against their growth. The sausage becomes much firmer. Once the supply of sugar is exhausted, the lactic acid bacteria go dormant but curing and flavor producing bacteria (*Micrococcus* and *Staphylococcus*) continue working as long as acidity is not higher than pH 5.0. When the sugar supply is fully exhausted, lactic acid producing bacteria (*Lactobacillus* or *Pediococcus*) die.

Influence of Sugar on Fermentation Process

For the sausage to be considered microbiologically safe a pH drop below 5.30 must be attained within the prescribed time. (see USA standards in Chapter 8). The data below shows that for slow-fermented T-SPX culture being fermented at 75° F (24° C), this will occur within 48 hours (curves 1, 2 and 3).

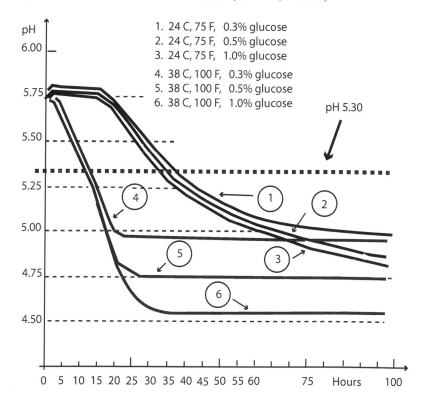

Fig. 3.2 Influence of amount of glucose on the pH-decrease induced by the traditional fermenting culture T-SPX, containing a *P. pentosaceus* bacteria strain, at two temperatures: 24° C (75° F), 38° C (100° F).

Data of Chr. Hansen

The 1,2,3 curves remain almost the same during the first 48 hours, regardless of the amount of sugar added. At 38° C (100° F) the pH drop is faster (curves 4, 5 and

45

6) and the sausage is stable within 24 hours of fermenting. When making a traditional fermented sausage, the pH values should not fall below 4.8-5.0 as this will inhibit the action of color and flavor forming bacteria which are sensitive to acidity. To meet this requirement when applying T-SPX culture shown in the graph above, fermentation temperatures must be kept in the 68-75° F (20-24° C) range and only a small amount of glucose should be added (0.2-0.3%).

Influence of Temperature on Fermentation Process

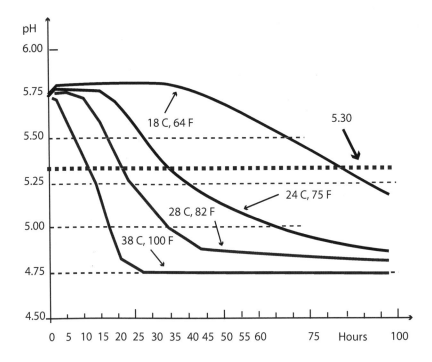

Fig. 3.3 Influence of fermentation temperature on the pH-decrease induced by the traditional fermenting culture T-SPX, containing a *P. pentosaceus* bacteria strain. Sausage mince contains 0.5% glucose.

Data of Chr. Hansen

Above figure shows the culture profile for the pH decrease of the T-SPX Chr. Hansen culture, containing traditional and fast fermenting *P. pentosaceus strain* which has an optimum growth temperature around 95° F (35° C). The culture, however, can also be applied at lower temperatures where it will ferment slower. The pH drop will be determined by the amount of added sugar. The data displayed in the graph prove how important the role of temperature is in the fermentation process. Cultures containing different bacteria strains have a different optimum growth temperature, but the general profile will look like the graphs shown above.

46

Fast Fermenting Process

Fast-fermented products are economically produced sausages that end up in local supermarkets or as pizza toppings. They are characterized by a fast drop in pH that increases the acidity to such a level that a sausage can be made within 7 days and be microbiologically stable. Its tangy flavor is already set and will not be improved with additional drying, as flavor forming bacteria cannot tolerate such high acidity levels. A few days of drying will add to the overall safety of the sausage, but there is no need for long term drying as it will only decrease the weight of the sausage.

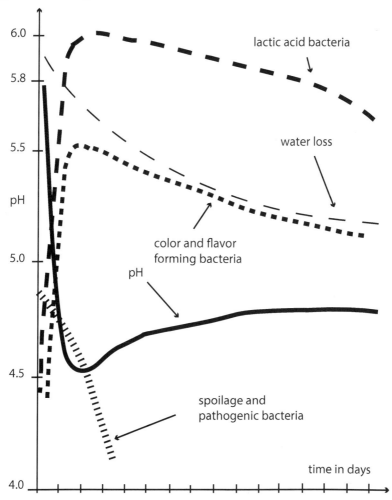

Fig 3.4 Fast-fermented sausage without starter cultures. Nitrite added plus a large amount of sugar. Fermented at 75° F (24° C).

Data of Reuter at al. (1968)

47

Influence of Sugar on Fermentation Process

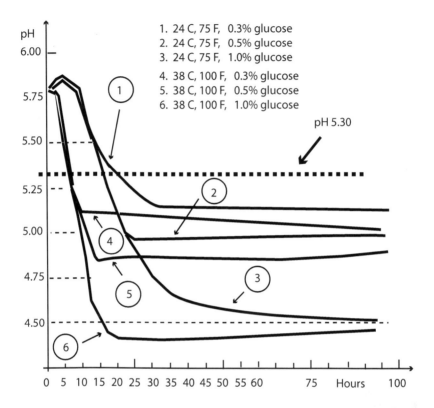

Fig. 3.5 Influence of amount of glucose on the pH-decrease induced by the fast fermenting culture F-1, containing a *P. pentosaceus* bacteria strain, at two temperatures: 75° F (24° C) and 100° F (38° C).

Data of Chr. Hansen

From the above graph it can be easily deduced that F-1 fast-fermenting culture at 100° F (38° C) fermentation temperature will make sausages microbiologically safe (pH<5.3) within 12 hours (curves 4, 5 and 6). At 75° F (24° C) they will be safe within 24 hours (curves 1, 2 and 3). As these sausages are generally smoked and either partially or fully cooked, the smoke can now be applied.

A fast-fermented sausage can be made in a short time due to the following factors:

- Addition of a large amount (0.7-1%) of fast fermenting sugar (dextrose).

- Addition of fast fermenting starter cultures which allow to undertake the fermentation process at temperatures as high as 104° F (40° C).

48

- Additions of additives such as Gdl (glucono-delta-lactone) and citric acid which can drop acidity even faster and without involving bacteria.
- Addition of sodium nitrite which does not need curing bacteria for the development of color.

Influence of Temperature on Fermentation Process

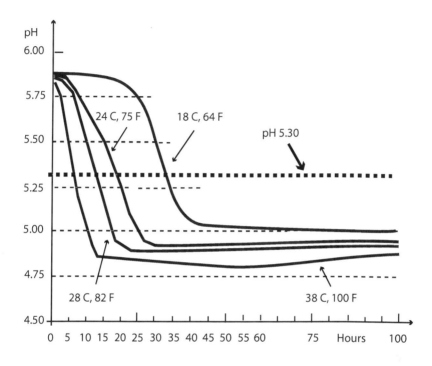

Fig. 3.6 Influence of fermentation temperature on the pH-decrease induced by the fast fermenting culture F-1, containing a *P. pentosaceus* bacteria strain. Sausage mince contains 0.5% glucose.

Data of Chr. Hansen

The curing step may be omitted as color and flavor forming bacteria will not have enough time to react with the meat and develop salami type flavor. This is compensated by adding more spices and combinations of slow and fast acting sugars and fruit syrups. Besides, a rapid pH drop during the fermentation stage will inhibit their action anyway as they are *are sensitive to acidity*.

It is questionable whether enough lactic acid bacteria can grow during the curing step to perform a fast pH drop without using starter cultures or adding Gdl. Adding starter cultures assures the introduction of a large number of lactic acid

49

bacteria which at these high temperatures will metabolize sugar very fast. This leads to a rapid increase in the acidity of the meat. The whole strategy behind making fast-fermented sausages relies on a *rapid increase in acidity* and this can be accomplished in two ways:

- Addition of a fast-fermenting *starter culture* plus a sufficient amount of sugar. The introduction of more sugar leads to lower pH and stronger acidification.
- Addition of Gdl and citric acid (or both) plus a sufficient amount of sugar.

Adding Gdl must be carefully monitored as too much may be added. This will increase the acidity so rapidly that the growth of all bacteria will be adversely affected. The sausage will be safe to consume but its flavor will suffer. If you keep stuffed sausage in vinegar for a sufficient time it will acquire enough acidity to be safe, but it will taste sourly. The best example is Czechoslovakian *Utopence* sausage which is preserved in vinegar, however, it is not a fermented product. Note that *lowering temperature will not stop* chemicals from reacting with meat. They will react until all of them are used up.

To speed up the development of curing color, ascorbic acid (vitamin C) is often added to the sausage mince. Fast-fermented sausages are fermented at relatively high temperatures around 78-86°F (30-35°C), sometimes even at 113° F (45° C).

Stopping Fermentation

When the desired pH has been reached but there is a suspicion that it may still drop lower, the best action is to lower the temperature to 53° F (12° C). The remaining unfermented sugar will offset the acidic taste of the fast-fermented sausage and will contribute to stronger color and flavor in slow-fermented types. Lowering temperature when too much Gdl was added will only slow down fermentation, which will continue until all Gdl was converted into gluconic acid. It is relatively easy to stop fermentation of fast-fermented sausages at any desired pH level (if no chemical acidulants were added) by submitting sausages to a thermal process what will kill the fermenting bacteria.

Summary of Critical Points

- The speed of fermentation depends mainly on the temperature. It does not depend on the amount sugar, but it may be influenced by the type of sugar.
- The pH drop and the resulting acidity depends on the amount of introduced sugar.
- Starter cultures allow precise control of fermentation.
- The sausages with the final pH of 5.0 or higher develop a mild taste.

Chapter 4

Starter Cultures

The preservation of meats by fermentation has been practiced for centuries. Traditional practices relied on indigenous bacteria present in meat and in the environment. These techniques are being replaced by the application of commercially grown starter cultures. Fermentation technology has become a huge part of food science and to be able to choose the right culture for a particular product, requires a basic understanding of microorganisms and their behavior. Americans were the first ones to experiment with bacteria in order to produce sausages faster and cheaper. In 1940 the first US patent # 2,225,783 was granted to Jensen & Paddock for their research on *Lactobacilli* bacteria in making fermented sausages. Although the theory was solid, it was difficult to produce *Lactobacilli* starter culture on a commercial scale, as there were problems with freezing bacteria and reactivating them later. More research was done and *Pediococcus*

cerevisiae was discovered which would survive freezing and drying techniques. Thus, the practice of adding starter cultures to sausages was first born in the USA. *Pediococcus* cultures performed best at high temperatures and the manufacturers embraced this technology. As a result, sausages were made faster and at reduced costs.

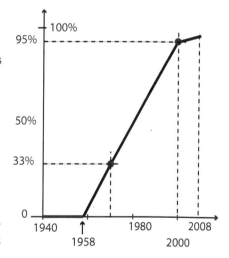

Fig. 4.1 Starter culture development.

In Europe where the tradition of making fermented sausages dates back thousands of years, sausages were always fermented at much lower temperatures which lead to a much milder flavor. For that reason American fast acting starter cultures were not really embraced. These cultures produced lactic acid so fast, that this sudden increase of acidity prevented color and flavor forming bacteria from reacting with meat. As a result there was no development of the expected and well liked flavor. The first

European cultures produced in the 1950's were curing cultures aimed at color and flavor development. In 1957 Niinivaara introduced a new strain of bacteria called *Micrococcus*. In the 1960's more curing bacteria strains were introduced i.e. *Staphylococcus carnosus* which is still used today.

The first lactic acid bacteria of practical and universal use was an isolated bacteria from a fermented sausage in 1966 by Nurmi. It was called *Lactobacillus plantarum* and it could be used at moderate temperatures 68-72° F (20-22° C). It is still in use today. Then in the 1970's researchers combined lactic acid bacteria and curing bacteria together to form multi-strain cultures. Those cultures in addition to fermenting meat can speed up development of color, flavor and fight off other undesirable bacteria. Today, there are cultures for all kinds of foods, including a group of microorganisms known as probiotics. Probiotics are live microorganisms that when consumed as part of the food, provide a health benefit for the host. Sauerkraut is the best known probiotic and it is the result of fermenting cabbage by *Lactobacillus plantarum* bacteria, the same type that is used for making fermented sausages.

Although lactic acid bacteria are naturally present in meat, the quantity and qualities are hard to predict. In most cases they are of a hetero-fermentative type but being of wild variety they not only produce lactic acid by metabolizing carbohydrates, but also create many different reactions which can produce unpleasant odors and affect the entire process.

Starter cultures are of a homo-fermentative type and will produce lactic acid only, although some strains will develop mold or stronger color.

One gram of culture introduces up to 10 millions of bacterial cells what assures microbial dominance over other undesirable microorganisms that might be present. Those other microorganisms might be unwelcome lactic acid bacteria that were naturally present in meat or pathogenic bacteria that must be eliminated.

The commercial starter cultures are produced by isolating the desired bacteria strains that are naturally found in meat products. Next, by purifying and then growing them under controlled laboratory conditions the desired characteristics are obtained. Then they are concentrated and preserved by freezing or drying.

4.1 Culture Types

Cultures can be classified into the following groups:

- Lactic acid producing cultures.
- Color and flavor forming cultures.
- Surface coverage cultures (yeasts and molds).
- Bio-protective cultures (producing bacteriocins). You may think of bacteriocins as some kind of antibiotics which kill unwanted bacteria.

The advantages of starter cultures are numerous:

- They are of known number and quality. This eliminates a lot of guessing as to whether there is enough bacteria inside the meat to start fermentation, or whether a strong curing color will be obtained.
- Cultures are optimized for different temperature ranges that allow production of slow, medium or fast-fermented products.
- Starter cultures speed up the manufacturing process.
- Production of fermented sausages does not depend on "secrets" and a product of constant quality can be produced year round in any climatic zone as long as proper natural conditions or fermenting/drying chambers are available.
- They provide safety by competing for food with undesirable bacteria thus inhibiting their growth.

The most important microorganisms used in starter cultures are:

Microorganism	Family	Species	Use
Lactic Acid Bacteria	Lactobacillus	L.plantarum	acid production
		L.pentosum	acid production
		L.sakei	acid production
		L.curvatus	acid production
	Pediococcus	P.acidilactici	fast-fermented
		P.pentosaceus	acid production
Curing, Color and Flavor Producing Bacteria	Kocuria (Micrococcus)	K.varians	curing
	Staphylococcus	S.xylosus	flavor and color
		S.carnosus	flavor and color
Yeasts	Debaryomeces	D.hansenii	flavor
	Candida	C.famata	flavor
Molds	Penicillium	P.nalgiovense	white mold
		P.chrysogenum	white mold

In addition to being very strong competitors for nutrients against pathogenic and spoilage bacteria, lactic acid bacteria are known to produce compounds named "bacteriocins" which can act against other microorganisms. *Pediococcus acidilactici* and *Lactobacillus curvatus* are known bacteriocins producers, especially effective against the growth of *Listeria monocytogenes.*

4.2 Chr. Hansen Starter Cultures

There are many manufacturers of starter cultures that are used in Europe and in the USA. We are going to list products made by the Danish manufacturer "Chr. Hansen" as their products demonstrate superior quality and are easily obtained from American distributors of sausage making equipment and supplies. Even more, the company offers wonderful technical support and we are deeply indebted to them for detailed specifications about their products.

4.2.1 Acidifying Cultures

Lactobacillus

All *Lactobacillus* bacteria strains used in starter cultures are homo-fermentative (producing a fermentation resulting wholly or principally in a single end product), which grow best at low oxygen levels and their main fermentation product from sugar is lactic acid. On the contrary, endogenous (naturally occurring) *Lactobacillus* bacteria found in meats are hetero-fermentative (producing fermentation resulting in a number of end products) and in addition to lactic acid will also produce volatile acids and carbon dioxide. Those byproducts react with meat and achieving a constant quality product is hindered.

Culture	L. pentosus	L. sakei	L. plantarum	L. farciminis	L. curvatus
Opt. growth temp.°C/°F	35/95	30/86	30/86	37/99	30 or 37° 86 or 99°
Fermentable sugars					*
Glucose (dextrose)	+	+	+	+	
Fructose	+	+	+	+	
Maltose	+	-	+	-	
Lactose	+	-	+	(-)	
Saccharose (sucrose)	+	-	+	+	

Acidifying species offered by Chr. Hansen. All Lactobacillus species are able to ferment simple sugars glucose and fructose.

* Strain dependent, please refer to product sheets

Pediococcus

Pediococcus species used in starter cultures are homo-fermentative (producing a fermentation resulting wholly or principally in a single end product) which grow best at low oxygen levels. These bacteria strains in general grow at higher temperatures and metabolize most sugars.

54

Culture	P. pentosaceus	P. acidilactici
Opt. growth temp.°C/°F	35/95	40/104
Fermentable sugars		
Glucose (dextrose)	+	+
Fructose	+	+
Maltose	+	+
Lactose	(+)	(+)
Saccharose (sucrose)	+	(+)

4.2.2 Color and Flavor Forming Cultures

Staphylococcus

The *Micrococcaceae* species cover different strains of *Staphylococcus* and they are encountered in fermented meats. The strains of most importance are *S. xylosus, S. saprophyticus* and *S. carnosus*.

Culture	S. carnosus	S. xylosus	Micrococcaceae spp.
Opt. growth temp.°C/°F	30/86	30/86	30/86
Fermentable sugars:			
Glucose (dextrose)	+	+	+
Fructose	+	+	+
Maltose	-	+	-
Lactose	+	+	+
Saccharose (sucrose)	-	+	-

Staphylococcus are oxygen hungry during growth and may find insufficient air inside firmly stuffed sausage what may limit their growth to the surface areas only. However, they are capable of using nitrate (in cure #2) as an electron acceptor instead of oxygen during respiration, which will promote their survival. As long as sufficient number of bacteria (10^6-10^7 cfu/g) are introduced to the sausage mince they will produce flavors even though they might not significantly grow in numbers.

4.2.3 Yeasts and Molds

Yeasts and molds consume lactic acid and acetic acid which lowers pH of the sausage and removes some of the sourness taste. Additionally, they produce ammonia (pH 11.5) which increases sausage pH.

In addition cultured molds for example Mold-600, produce an attractive white mold on the surface of the sausage which is desired by many customers.

4.3 Guidelines for Choosing Chr. Hansen Starter Cultures

4.3.1 Starter cultures for traditional fermented sausages

In the production of traditional style sausages, the fermentation profile must have a short lag phase in order to ensure the growth of the added starter culture at the expense of the unwanted bacteria. The acidification profile must be rather flat not going below pH 4.8-5.0 at any time. This will ensure that *Staphylococci* maintain their activity over a longer period of time; foremost their nitrate reductase and flavor forming activities. The cultures listed above are specifically selected for traditional fermentation profiles applying fermentation temperatures not higher than 75° F (24° C).

Culture	Bacteria included	Characteristics
T-RM-53	*Lactobacillus sakei* *Staphylococcus carnosus*	Aromatic culture with mild acidification.
T-SP	*Pediococcus pentosaceus* *Staphylococcus carnosus*	Aromatic culture with mild acidification.
T-SPX	*Pediococcus pentosaceus* *Staphylococcus xylosus*	Aromatic culture with mild acidification. The high concentration of *Pediococus pentosaceus* gives a controlled and moderate pH drop. The acidification gives a mild lactic acid taste. *Staphylococcus xylosus* gives good color formation and stability. Furthermore *Staphylococcus xylosus* gives a very round and mild flavor which is very typical for South European salami types such as Milano.
T-D-66	*Lactobacillus plantarum* *Staphylococcus carnosus*	Aromatic cultures with intermediate acidification.
T-SC-150	*Lactobacillus sakei* *Staphylococcus carnosus*	Aromatic cultures with intermediate acidification. Gives a product flavor which is very typical for German salami such as Westphalia salami type. The acidification leads to a clear lactic acid taste. The used Lactobacillus sakei has a very good growth potential and is able to suppress the growth of a lot of indigenous bacteria. *Staphylococcus carnosus gives good color stability and a mild aroma. Attention: this Lactobacillus sakei is sucrose negative.*
T-SL	*Lactobacillus pentosus* *Staphylococcus carnosus*	Aromatic cultures with intermediate acidification.
TRA-DI-302	*Lactobacillus sakei* *Staphylococcus xylosus* *Staphylococcus carnosus*	Same features as T-SC-150, but the combination of the two *Staphylococci* leads to a more intensive color formation and a slight milder aroma.

56

SM-182	*Lactobacillus sakei* *Staphylococcus carnosus* *Debaromyces hansenii*	Same features as T-SC-150, but the yeast *Debaromyces hansenii* introduces a more "Mediterranean" flavor.
BFL-T03	*Pediococcus pentosaceus* *Staphylococcus carnosus ssp.*	Same features as T-SPX, but the new developed *Staphylococcus carnosus ssp.* gives a milder and more "Mediterranean" flavor.
SM-181	*Lactobacillus sakei* *Staphylococcus xylosus*	The sucrose positive *Lactobacillus sakei* gives a moderate pH drop. This *Lactobacillus sakei* has a very good growth potential and is able to suppress the growth of a lot of indigenous bacteria. *Staphylococcus xylosus* gives good color formation and stability. The very high number of *Staphylococcus xylosus* leads to a very round and mild "Mediterranean" flavor.

4.3.2 Starter cultures for fast-fermented sausages

In the production of North European and US style sausages, the fermentation profile must have a very short lag phase in order to rapidly on-set fermentation and exhibit a fast drop in pH to below 5.3 within 30 hours as a minimum. This ensures an efficient inhibition of unwanted bacteria and an early on-set of fast drying. Total production time is typically less than 2 weeks.

In the past, fast-fermented sausages were produced by introducing a large amount of sugar and maintaining high fermentation temperatures. In the US style fast-fermented sausages, 95-113° F (35-45° C), very fast pH drop, low final pH < 4.8), *Staphylococci* are not added to the culture since they generally do not survive such fast pH lowering.

Culture	Bacteria included	Characteristics
F-RM-52	*Lactobacillus sakei* *Staphylococcus carnosus*	Fast culture targeted for fermentation temperatures 70-90° F (22-32° C).
F-RM-7	*Lactobacillus sakei* *Staphylococcus carnosus* *Staphylococcus xylosus*	Fast culture targeted for fermentation temperatures 70-90° F (22-32° C).
F-SC-111	*Lactobacillus sakei* *Staphylococcus carnosus*	Fast culture targeted for fermentation temperatures 70-90° F (22-32° C). Same features as T-SC-150, but faster in pH drop by different amount and production treatment of the applied *Lactobacillus sakei*. (Faster version of T-SC-150).
F-1	*Pediococcus pentosaceus* *Staphylococcus xylosus*	Fast culture targeted for fermentation temperatures 70-90° F (22-32° C). Same features as T-SPX, but faster in pH drop by different amount and production treatment of the applied *Pediococcus pentosaceus*. (Faster version of T-SPX).

LP	*Pediococcus pentosaceus*	Fast cultures targeted for fermentation temperatures 70-90° F (22-32° C).
LL-1	*Lactobacillus curvatus*	
CSL	*Lactobacillus curvatus* *Micrococcaceae spp.*	
LL-2	*Lactobacillus curvatus*	
F-2	*Lacobacillus farciminis* *Staphylococcus carnosus* *Staphylococcus xylosus*	
LHP	*Pediococcus acidilactici* *Pediococcus pentosaceus*	Extra fast cultures targeted for fermentation temperatures 80-100° F (26-38° C).
CSB (pellets)	*Pediococcus acidilactici* *Micrococcaceae ssp.*	
F-PA	*Pediococcus acidilactici*	
HPS (pellets)	*Pediococcus acidilactici*	Very fast cultures targeted for fermentation temperatures 90-113° F (32-45° C).
FAST-301	*Lactobacillus sakei* *Staphylococcus xylosus* *Staphylococcus carnosus*	This is the fast version of TRADI-302. Acidification features as mentioned under F-SC-111.
BFL-F02	*Pediococcus pentosaceus* *Staphylococcus carnosus ssp.*	This is the fast version of BFL-T03. Acidification features as mentioned under F-1.
BFL-F04	*Lactobacillus sakei* *Staphylococcus carnosus ssp.* *Staphylococcus carnosus ssp.*	The sucrose positive *Lactobacillus sakei* shows a very good growth potential and is able to suppress the growth of a lot of indigenous bacteria. The combination of the two new developed *Staphylococci* gives a very good color formation and a more intensive, but mild aroma development. The special combination of the strains shows a fast pH drop and leads to a firm texture.
BFL-F05	*Lactobacillus sakei* *Staphylococcus carnosus ssp.* *Staphylococcus carnosus ssp.*	Same features as F-SC-111, but this new developed culture gives a stronger and more intensive fermentation flavor.
SM-194	*Pediococcus pentosaceus* *Lactobacillus sakei* *Staphylococcus xylosus* *Staphylococcus carnosus* *Debaromyces hansenii*	Multi application culture that combines all positive features of the different strains. *Lactobacillus sakei* with very good growth potential and the ability to suppress the growth of a lot of indigenous bacteria. *Pediococcus pentosaceus* by its mild lactic acid taste and the accelerated pH drop at higher temperatures. The combination of two different *Staphylococci* for more intensive color formation and mild aroma development. And the yeast *Debaromyces hansenii* on top to obtain a more "Mediterranean" flavor.

4.3.3 Starter cultures for enhancing flavor and nitrate reduction

Sausages fermented with a chemical acidifier such as Gdl or encapsulated acid instead of lactic acid bacteria, generally require *Staphylococci* or *Micrococcaceae spp.* to obtain an acceptable flavor and color. Those single strain cultures are recommended in all sausage products in need of extra flavor or nitrate reductase activity. *S. carnosus* is more salt tolerant than *S. xylosus* and convey a more intense flavor in fast-fermented products.

Culture	Bacteria included	Characteristics
CS-300	*Staphylococcus carnosus ssp. Staphylococcus carnosus*	The combination of the two different *Staphylococci* leads to intensive color formation and color stability. Furthermore it gives a mild and round aroma. The high concentration of both *Staphylococci* gives high nitrate reductase activity.
S-B-61	*Staphylococcus carnosus*	For a good color formation and color stability and additional flavor development.
S-SX	*Staphylococcus xylosus*	For a good color formation and color stability and additional flavor development. Especially suitable in case of too much and undesired acidification taste.

4.3.4 Starter cultures for surface coverage

Mold present on traditional sausages prevents mytoxin formation by wild molds. It allows for uniform drying and contributes positively towards flavor.

Culture	Bacteria included	Characteristics
Mold 500	*Debaromyces hansenii Penicillium nalgiovense*	Moderate to medium growth. Sparse, short coverage with marbled appearance. Rich Italian style flavor formation for long ripened, dry, fermented sausage. Moderate suppression of indigenous flora.
Mold 600	*Penicillium nalgiovense*	Fast growing and strong suppression of wild flora. Dense, medium fluffy and uniform coverage. Traditional white coverage. Pronounced mushroom flavor.
Mold 700	*Penicillium nalgiovense ssp.*	Fast growing and suppressing wild flora. Dense, short and very white coverage. Avoids the traditional talcum stage. Neutral flavor.
Mold 800	*Penicillium candidum Penicillium nalgiovense*	Fast growing and strong suppression of wild flora. Dense, medium to very fluffy coverage. Generates a fresh camembert aroma/strong mushroom flavor and a typical scent of moss. Good growth potential in dry and unstable conditions.

59

| Mold 900 | Penicillium nalgiovense ssp. Penicillium nalgiovense | Early coverage and a very white and powdery look. Suitable for marbled appearance. Nice South European Felino-like aroma. Flexible toward varying growth conditions. |

4.3.5 Starter cultures for bio-protection

Bactoferm™ F-LC is a patented culture blend capable of acidification as well as preventing the growth of *Listeria*. The culture produces pediocin and bavaricin (kind of "antibiotics") and that keeps *Listeria monocytogenes* at safe levels. Low fermentation temperature < 77° F (< 25° C) results in a traditional acidification profile whereas high fermentation temperature 95-113° F (35-45° C) gives a US style product.

F-LC is meat culture with bioprotective properties for the production of fermented sausages with a short production type where a higher count of *L.monocytogenes* bacteria may be suspected. Bactoferm™ F-LC has the ability to control *Listeria* at the same time as it performs as a classic starter culture for fermented sausages. *Use dextrose* as this culture ferments sugar slowly.

Culture	Bacteria included	Characteristics
F-LC	*Staphylococcus xylosus* *Pediococcus acililactici* *Lactobacillus curvatus*	Culture for acidification and prevention of *Listeria*. Applicable at wide temperature range. *Pediococcus acililactici* and *Lactobacillus curvatus* give a controlled, modern pH drop with a mild acidification flavor. The used *Staphylococcus xylosus* gives a good color formation and stability and a very round and mild flavor.
B-LC-20	*Pediococcus acililactici*	Adjunct culture for prevention of *Listeria* for use on top of existing starter cultures.
B-LC-35	*Pediococcus acililactici* *Lactobacillus curvatus* *Staphylococcus xylosus*	*Pediococcus acililactici* and *Lactobacillus curvatus* give a slow, but controlled pH drop with a mild acidification flavor. The used *Staphylococcus xylosus* gives a good color formation and stability and mild flavor.
B-LC-48	*Lactobacillus curvatus*	Homofermentatitve. Grows well in temperatures down to 4° C and survives freezing. Removes oxygen, produces bacteriocin and suppresses growth of spoilage and pathogenic bacteria.
B-2	*Lactobacillus sakei*	Homofermentatitve. Grows well in temperatures down to 2° C and survives freezing. Removes oxygen, produces inhibitory organic acids and suppresses growth of spoilage and pathogenic bacteria.

The following cultures are easily obtainable on Internet and will produce any type of fermented product:

T-SPX, LHP, F-LC, F-RM-52, Mold 600.

4.4 How To Choose The Correct Culture

In order to choose the correct culture the following advice may be used as general guidelines:

1. What style of sausage is produced?
   - Traditional South and North European: choose cultures in paragraph 4.3.1.
   - North European fast fermented: choose cultures in paragraph 4.3.2.
   - US style: choose the *extra fast* and *very fast* cultures in paragraph 4.3.2.

2. A very short on-set of fermentation is needed.
   - Choose a frozen culture instead of a freeze-dried culture.
   - Increase the amount of culture.

3. The salt-in-water percentage in the fresh mince is:
   - > 6% : avoid F-1, LP, T-SP and T-SPX.

The above statement applies to products containing a large amount of salt.

4. The type of sugar is:
   - *Glucose: all cultures will ferment.*
   - Sucrose: avoid T-RM-53, T-SC-150, F-RM-52 and F-SC-111. These cultures contain *Lactobacillus sakei*, which does not ferment sugar well. This fact can be used to our advantage by adding sugars which will not be fermented, yet they will remain in the sausage contributing to a sweeter taste.

5. Nitrate is added as a color forming agent to the mince.
   - Choose cultures in paragraph 4.3.1. and 4.3.2 and adjust the process correspondingly to traditional/slow fermentation.
   - Add extra *Staphylococci* or *Micrococcaceae* spp. from paragraph 4.3.1 to enhance nitrate reductase activity.

6. A product with an intense flavor.
   - Choose traditional technology and cultures from paragraph 4.3.1.
   - Add extra *Staphylococci* or *Micrococcaceae* spp. from paragraph 4.3.3. to enhance flavor formation.

4.5 Lag Phase

Before culture can react with meat, it needs some time to get used to a new environment, it must go through what is known as "lag phase." It has been in a deep freeze sleep and now must wake up and recover. It can be compared to a patient recovering from the effect of anaesthesia. He needs some time to shake off the effects of his induced sleep and be himself again. Mixing freeze-dried cultures with chlorine free cold water for 15-30 minutes before use allows them to "wake up" and to react with meat and sugar faster when introduced into the meat.

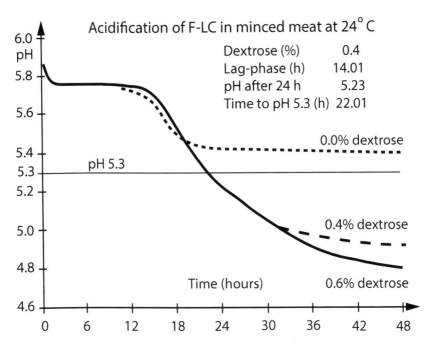

Fig. 4.2 Acidification of Bactoferm™ F-LC in a minced meat at 24° C (75° F).

As can be seen on the graph the lag phase of F-LC culture at 75° F (24° C) is about 14 hours. The lag phase is the time bacteria need to shake off the effects of freezing and to grow in numbers to start producing any significant amount of lactic acid. For a culture this time can be faster or slower depending on the temperature which regulates bacteria activity. There is a small increase in acidity (around pH 5.4, see 0.0% dextrose curve) even though dextrose was not added due to glycogen (sugar) present in meat. 0.4% and 0.6% dextrose curves have the same slope of pH drop for the first 32 hours and they both reach pH 5.3 in 22 hours. After 32 hours 0.4% dextrose curve becomes flat as there is no more sugar to support fermentation.

It can be seen on the graph in Fig. 4.3 that at 98° F (37° C) LHP culture needs only 6 hours to start a full production of lactic acid. The fermentation process is completed in 12-18 hours. Of course at 80° F (27° C) its lag phase will be longer and the pH curve flatter. At 80° F (27° C) it may need 36 hours to develop the same pH drop as it did at 98° F (37° C) in 18 hours. Cultures come in two forms: frozen cultures or deep freeze-dried cultures. Freeze-dried cultures need a few more hours to shake off the effects of the lag phase, the fact that may be of importance for a commercial plant, but hardly for a hobbyist. All cultures sold online are deep-freeze type and it is doubtful that a hobbyist could obtain frozen type cultures, unless he comes up with a large order.

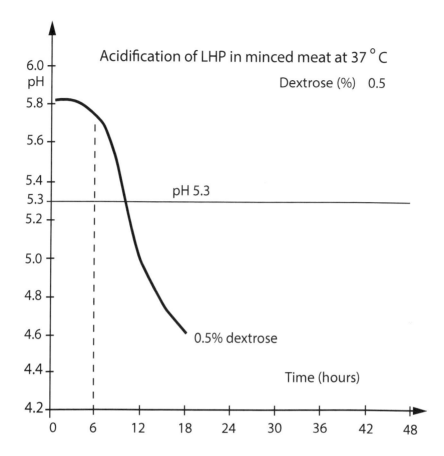

Fig. 4.3 Bactoferm™ LHP pH curve.

The lag phase can be shortened by:

- using frozen culture instead of a freeze-dried culture.
- increasing the amount of culture.
- increasing the temperature.

Increasing the dosage of the culture introduces more bacteria into sausage mince. They will compete for moisture and nutrients with each other so they may grow slower, however, the fact remains that a larger number of bacteria will start fermenting sugar and a faster pH drop will be obtained.

Very fast-fermenting cultures go through a much shorter lag phase, from 30 minutes to a few hours, depending on fermentation temperature. During lag phase there is little fermentation taking place, lactic acid bacteria just get comfortable and they start growing in numbers. Then they suddenly go into action feeding on sugar and producing lactic acid.

63

When freeze-dried cultures are used it is recommended to disperse them in water. There are about 10 million bacteria in one gram of culture. Adding 25 grams of powdered culture to 200 kg (440 lbs) of meat makes uniform distribution quite challenging. Therefore, it is advisable, especially at home conditions, to mix ½ teaspoon of culture in ½ cup (150 ml) of chlorine free water and then pour it down over the meat. Cultures distributed by Internet online companies are of the freeze dried type.

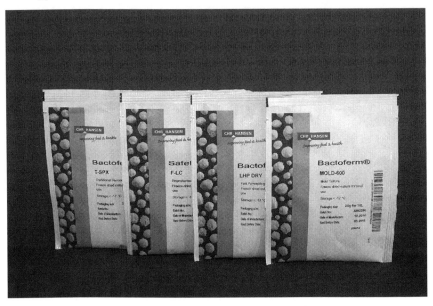

Photo 4.1 The Chr-Hansen cultures presented in the above photo are included in the recipes in this book: T-SPX, F-LC, LHP and Mold 600.

Technical information sheets provide the recommended temperatures for fermentation, however, bacteria will also ferment at lower temperatures, just more slowly. For example, T-SPX is listed at 78-100° F (26-38° C), optimum being 90° F (32° C). T-SPX will ferment as well at 68-75° F (20-24° C) which is not uncommon for "European" style sausages, and 48 hours or more is not atypical.

Taking under consideration the fact that fermented sausages have been made for thousands of years, the starter culture technology is very young indeed. Meat inspectors like them as they increase the safety of products. Manufacturers like them as they allow making sausages much faster and with predictable quality. Home sausage makers should love them as starter cultures make making fermented sausages at home practical, easy, safe and of a predictable quality. As some sausages, notably slow-fermented ones, take many weeks or even months to produce, it is a great loss to waste so much time and investment due to insufficient know-how or one's negligence.

Chapter 5

Additives and Ingredients

Nitrates

Adding nitrites to meat will improve flavor, inhibit growth of dangerous bacteria, tenderize the meat, and develop the pink color widely known and associated with smoked meats. For any aspiring sausage maker it is a necessity to understand and know how to apply cure #1 and cure #2, as those two cures are used worldwide though under different names and with different proportions of nitrates and salt.

Cure #1 (also known as Instacure #1, Prague Powder #1 or Pink Cure #1). Cure #1 is a mixture of 6.25% *sodium nitrite* and 93.75% of salt.

Cure #2 (also known as Instacure #2, Prague Powder #2 or Pink Cure #2) is a mixture of 6.25% *sodium nitrite,* 4% of *sodium nitrate* and 89.75% of salt.

Both cure #1 and cure #2 contain a small amount of FDA approved red coloring agent that gives them a slight pink color thus eliminating any possible confusion with common salt and that is why they are sometimes called "pink" curing salts.

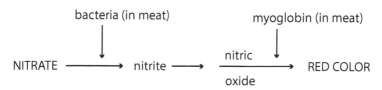

Fig. 5.1 Curing with nitrate.

In the past we used potassium nitrate exclusively because its derivative, sodium nitrite was not discovered yet. *Sodium Nitrate (NaNO₃) does not cure meat directly* and initially not much happens when it is added to meat. After a few hours curing bacteria naturally present in meat start to react with nitrate which releases *sodium nitrite* ($NaNO_2$) that will start the curing process. If those bacteria are not present in sufficient numbers the curing process may be inhibited. Bacteria are lethargic at low temperatures so production of nitrite will be slow, unless curing mixture containing potassium nitrate is kept at 44-46° F (6-8° C). This however, allows spoilage bacteria to grow and shortens the shelf life of the product.

Cure #1 does not depend on microbial action as it contains sodium nitrite. It can react with meat immediately and at refrigerator temperature. For these reasons cure #1 is added to fast-fermented sausages. Cure #2 is applied to slow-fermented products, as nitrite starts an immediate reaction with meat and nitrate guarantees a steady supply of nitrite during long term drying.

The maximum allowable sodium *nitrite* limit for Dry Cured Products (625 ppm) is four times higher than for Comminuted Products (156 ppm). Comminuted products are regular fresh or smoked sausages. The reason that there are much higher allowable nitrite limits for dry cured products is that sodium *nitrite dissipates rapidly in time and* the dry products are *air dried for a long time*. Those higher limits guarantee a steady supply of nitrite in time. That positively contributes to the safety of the product and its color. When the product is ready for consumption it hardly contains any nitrite left. It is said that commercially prepared meats in the USA contain about 10 ppm of nitrite when bought in a supermarket. You could add only sodium nitrite (cure #1) to slow fermented products, however, keep in mind that due to its speedy action, it is advisable to apply more than the 156 ppm allowable limit for regular sausages.

Glucono-delta-lactone (Gdl) is manufactured by microbial fermentation of pure glucose to gluconic acid, but is also produced by the fermentation of glucose derived from rice. In the presence of water it hydrolyzes (breaks down) to gluconic acid, it is non-toxic and completely metabolized in our bodies. Gdl can be found in honey, fruit juices, wine and many fermented products. It is a natural food acid (roughly has a third of the sourness of citric acid), and contributes to the tangy flavor of various foods. Since Gdl lowers the pH, it also helps preserve the food from deterioration by enzymes and microorganisms. Glucono-delta-lactone is often used to make cottage cheese, tofu, bakery products and fermented sausages. Adding 0.1% (1 g/kg of meat) Gdl lowers pH by 0.1 pH. Example:

- Initial meat pH = 5.8, adding 0.4% Gdl lowers pH to 5.4
- Initial meat pH = 5.9, adding 1.0% Gdl lowers pH to 4.9

The addition of sugar will lower pH of the meat during fermentation but adding Gdl will lower the pH *much faster.* Gdl works well at 71-75° F (22-24° C), but will work even faster when the temperature is increased. Decreasing temperature may only slow it down, to stop the reaction we have to freeze the meat which is not practical. Gdl is usually added at 0.2-0.8% (2-8 g/kg). As it is a natural acid, adding more than 1% (10 g/kg of meat) may cause unpleasantly bitter and sour flavor. *Once Gdl is added to the sausage mass it will start lowering its pH* regardless of whether the sausage mix is left in a pan or stuffed into a casing. The reaction will continue for as long as there is remaining Gdl and free water inside of the sausage.

In the USA, Gdl is GRAS, Generally Recognized As Safe, as per 21 CFR 184.1318 for use in food with no limitation other than current good manufacturing practice as a curing and pickling agent, leavening agent; as *pH control agent* and as sequestrant. Gdl is cleared by the Meat and Poultry Inspection Division as an acidifier in meat and poultry products at the following amount:

0.5% - 8 oz of Gdl (0.5%) to 100 lb meat or meat by products.
1.0% - 16 oz (1 lb) of Gdl to 100 lb meat (Genoa salami only).

In the EC, glucono delta-lactone, E 575, is approved *quantum satis* (as needed) unless otherwise restricted for use as an acidity regulator and a sequestrant.

It should be noted that Gdl was a great acidulant in the past, however, with the recent entry of easy to administer cultures, its popularity will definitely diminish. By introducing fast-fermenting culture with the right amount of sugar we can achieve the same results yet produce product with a better flavor.

Citric acid is a weak organic acid found in citrus fruits. It is a natural preservative and is used to add an acidic taste to foods, soft drinks and wine. In lemons and limes it can account for as much as 8% of the dry weight of the fruit. It acts about *three times faster* than Gdl (1 g of citric acid added to 1 kg of meat lowers the ph of meat by about 0.3 units) and in higher doses it will contribute to a sour taste.

Potassium sorbate is very effective in preventing the growth of mold. Sausages are either immersed into or sprayed with a solution of potassium sorbate. Although in the USA many processors use a 2.5% solution of potassium sorbate in water for the prevention of surface mold growth on dry cured salami, the scientific studies (ref. 8) have concluded that the best results are obtained with 15-20% solution.

Ascorbic acid (vitamin C), erythorbic acid, or their derivatives, sodium ascorbate and sodium erythorbate. Those additives speed up the chemical conversion of nitrite to nitric oxide which in turn will react with meat myoglobin to create a pink color. They are normally added at 0.5-0.7 g per kilogram of the sausage mix. Ascorbic acid should not come in direct contact with nitrite as the reaction produces fumes. For this reason, ascorbic acid is added at the beginning to the sausage mix and nitrite with salt at the end of the mixing process.

Non-fat dry milk is often added to fermented sausages as it contains about 50% lactose (slow fermenting sugar). By binding water, milk powder leaves less free water for lactic bacteria to grow thus slowing down the fermentation process.

MSG (Monosodium glutamate) is produced by the fermentation of starch, sugar beets, sugar cane, or molasses. Although once stereotypically associated with foods in Chinese restaurants, it is now found in many common food items, particularly processed foods. MSG can be added at up to 1% (10g/kg) to enhance the flavor of poor quality sausages made with a larger proportion of skins and connective tissue.

Guar gum is a free-flowing, off-white powder produced from guar beans. Guar gum is a very potent water-thickening agent.

Mustard flour binds water well and is often added to spreadable sausages at 1.0-1.5% to extend spreadability.

Salt

When making fermented sausages use between 2.5-3.3% salt. This salt combined with sodium nitrite (cure #1) is your first line of defense against undesirable bacteria. Almost all *regular* sausage recipes (fresh, smoked, cooked) contain 1.5-2 % of salt which is added to obtain good flavor. These amounts are *not high enough* to provide safety against bacteria in uncooked fermented products and *there is no room for a compromise.*

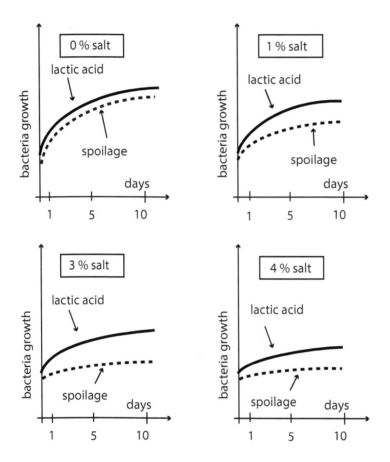

Fig. 5.2 Bacteria growth at different salt levels, no culture used. *The compilation of the above data is based on the research paper "Microbiology of Lebanon Bologna" by James L. Smith and Samuel A. Palumbo, Applied Microbiology, Oct 1973, p.489-496.*

From the above figure it be derived that:

- At 0% (no salt) *all* bacteria will easily grow and the meat will spoil. The spoilage curve follows the lactic acid curve.
- At 1% salt lactic acid bacteria will grow a bit slower, however, there is a noticeable decrease in the growth of spoilage bacteria.
- At **3%** lactic acid bacteria are still growing well, but the growth of spoilage and dangerous (pathogenic) bacteria is seriously inhibited. Pathogenic (dangerous) bacteria will follow the spoilage bacteria curve which becomes flatter.
- At 4% salt lactic acid bacteria are *hardly growing*, spoilage bacteria are inhibited as well. Both curves are almost flat.

When adding salt to fermented sausages try to think of salt not as a flavoring ingredient, but as a barrier against undesirable bacteria. Starter cultures assure proper fermentation, but to inhibit undesirable bacteria in the beginning of the process the salt level should remain high (2.5-3%).

Sugar

Fresh meat contains very little glucose (0.08-0.1%), which is not enough for lactic acid bacteria to produce any significant amount of lactic acid. At least 0.3% dextrose should be introduced into a fast-fermented sausage. In specific products (e.g. American pepperoni), limiting the added sugar to 0.5-0.75% achieves adequate fermentation with no residual carbohydrate present after fermentation.

In general increasing sugar levels up to 1% decreases pH proportionally. *A lower pH is obtained with increasing temperature at the same sugar level.*

Sugar in %	Final pH
0.3	more than 5.0
0.5 - 0.7	less than 5.0
1.0	4.5

Slow-fermented sausages require less sugar (0.1-0.3%) as their safety is achieved by drying and not by increasing acidity.

Dextrose (Glucose)

Lactic bacteria process different sugars differently. *Only glucose can be fermented directly into lactic acid by all lactic bacteria.* The molecular structures of other sugars must be first broken down into monosaccharides (simple sugars like glucose or fructose) and then newly obtained simple sugars (glucose) can be metabolized by lactic acid bacteria.

The fastest pH drop is obtainable with glucose which is the simplest form of sugar that serves as a building block for most carbohydrates. Glucose also known as *dextrose* is sugar refined from corn starch and is approximately 70% as sweet as sucrose (common sugar). As lowering pH is the main hurdle against bacteria growth in the initial stage of production of all fermented sausages, adding dextrose alone or in combination with other sugars should be a common practice.

Dextrose equivalent (DE) is the relative *sweetness* of sugars, compared to dextrose, both expressed as a percentage. For example, a maltodextrin with a DE of 10 would be 10% as sweet as dextrose (DE = 100), while sucrose (common sugar), with a DE of 120, would be 1.2 times as sweet as dextrose. For solutions made from starch, it is an estimate of the percentage reducing sugars present in the total starch product.

Dextrose (glucose) - 100 DE
Sucrose (sugar) - 120 DE
Maltodextrins - 3-20 DE

Sucrose (also called saccharose) is our common table sugar. It is made from sugar cane or sugar beets, but also appears in fruit, honey, sugar maple and in many other sources. Sucrose is composed of 50% glucose and 50% fructose and is *the second fastest acting sugar.* It can be used with Gdl in medium-fermented sausages or in slow-fermented sausages.

Fructose is known as the fruit sugar. It is frequently derived from sugar cane, sugar beets, and corn. The primary reason that fructose is used commercially in foods and beverages, besides its low cost, is its high relative sweetness. It is the sweetest of all naturally occurring carbohydrates. In general, fructose is regarded as being 1.73 times as sweet as sucrose. Honey consists of 50% fructose and 44% glucose.

Maltodextrin is a food additive that can be derived from any starch. Maltodextrin has wide range of applications as a food additive. It is usually sweet or without any flavor. Maltodextrin is popular among body builders and athletes who take it along with whey protein, as it is a simple carbohydrate that converts quickly to energy. Dextrines ferment slow and their use is recommended for slow-fermented sausages.

Maltose - malt sugar is made from germinating cereals such as barley which is an important part of the brewing process. It's added mainly to offset a sour flavor and to lower water activity as its fermenting qualities are poor.

Lactose - also referred to as milk sugar, makes up around 2–8% of milk (by weight). Lactose ferments slower than glucose. It is composed of glucose and galactose. Lactose milk sugar is about 20% as sweet as sugar. Non-fat dry milk contains about 52% of lactose. Lactose binds water very well.

Maltose and lactose are less important as primary fermenting sugars but may be used in combination with common sugars to bring out extra flavors.

Raffinose - little or no sweetness, occurring in the sugar beet, cottonseed, etc., and breaking down to fructose, glucose, and galactose on hydrolysis.

Galactose - makes up half of lactose, the sugar found in milk.

Starch - ferments slow, but can be used in slow-fermented sausages.

Relative Sweetness Scale - Sucrose = 100	
Sucrose	100
Fructose	140
High Fructose Corn Syrup	120-160
Glucose (Dextrose)	70-80
Galactose	35
Maltose	30-50
Lactose	20

The rate and the extent of the pH drop may be manipulated by a careful administration of different sugars. By using a combination of dextrose and slowly acting sugars, a rapid but small pH decrease can be achieved at the beginning of the fermentation stage and a slower rate of pH drop can be achieved in the later stages of the fermentation period. This kind of control is instrumental in producing quality traditionally fermented products which are made with nitrate.

The following table displays effectiveness of some of the above sugars in lactic acid production.

Carbohydrate (1%)	Lactic acid produced (%)	Final pH
Glucose	0.98	4.08
Saccharose	0.86	4.04
Maltose	0.72	4.24
Maltodextrin	0.54	4.54
Galactose	0.31	4.83
Raffinose	0.08	6.10

Lactic acid production and final pH achieved by *Lactobacillus pentosus* during growth in MRS-broth at 30° C (86° F) for 12 hours.

Data of Chr. Hansen

The fast but *moderate* drop in pH provides safety against undesirable bacteria, yet is not low enough to inhibit the growth of beneficial *Staphylococcus* which is needed for color and flavor formation.

In most cases different sugars are combined, some are metabolized by lactic bacteria to produce lactic acid and others contribute to the development of flavor. For example, if we combine dextrose with maltose when making a fast-fermented sausage, dextrose will be completely consumed by lactic acid bacteria, but a part of maltose will remain unfermented adding a degree of sweetness to the sausage.

Sugar introduction also helps offset the sourly and tangy flavor of fast and medium-fast fermented sausages and acts as a minor hurdle in lowering water activity.

Flavorings

The main flavor component in slow-fermented sausages is the meat itself which is augmented by the aromatic flavors produced by the flavor forming bacteria (*Staphylococcus* and *Kocuria*). Fermentation followed by an extensive drying period provides time and proper conditions for lactic and curing bacteria to start many reactions, some not yet fully understood, which at the end create those distinctive flavors. Spices bring food wonderful flavors, but they are very volatile and spice flavor disappears quite rapidly. For this reason they play a lesser role in slow-fermented sausages which require many months of drying. In fast or medium-fast fermented sausages which are produced within 1-3 weeks, there is not enough time for bacteria to fully develop meat flavor. The high acidity (low pH) of those sausages will inhibit the action of flavor forming bacteria anyhow. In those sausages, spices play an important role as their flavor remains strong and they contribute to off setting a sourly flavor of fast fermented products.

Besides using different combinations of sugars to influence sausage flavor, many alcoholic beverages such as rum, red wine, sherry, brandy, cointreau or even beer are used. Popular flavoring is honey or fruit syrup. One can make his own favorite combinations of flavorings by mixing about 20% of fruit or whole spices with 80% of spirit (vodka, rum, red wine) and leaving it in a closed container for about 3 days. Then about 0.4% (4 g/kg) of filtered liquid (or plain spirit) may be added to minced meat. Some popular combinations (in percent):

rum-raspberry syrup 50/50
rum-honey 50/50
rum-bay leaves 90/10
rum-garlic (chopped) 90/10
red wine-garlic (chopped) 90/10
red wine-bay leaves 90/10

Spice wine: 100 g red wine, 5 g bay leaf, 5 juniper berries, 1/2 cinnamon stick, 1/2 clove. Place all ingredients in a closed glass jar and leave for 3 days. Filter and use.

You can use any quality liqueur of your choice such as Curacao (bitter orange), Cointreau (orange), Cherry Liqueur, Drambuie (whiskey), Allasch (Caraway), Dom Benedictine (herbs), Brandy or Cognac. Most of those brands are too expensive to end up in commercial products, but you deserve the best. Keep in mind that most liqueurs contain sugar or honey and both of them will contribute to lower pH. However, in fast fermented sausages the process may be so short that lactic acid bacteria may not have time to convert those sugars into acidity. In slow fermented sausage sweet combinations will increase acidity so using sweet liqueurs or wines should be avoided as they will increase acidity. Dry wines, rum or brandy are better choices.

Spices

South European sausages are more heavily spiced than North European or American types. The most plausible explanation is that those sausages are dried longer so larger amounts are added as spices are very volatile and lose their aroma rapidly. The most popular spices in the manufacture of fermented sausages are *pepper and garlic*. Other popular spices such as allspice, marjoram, thyme, rosemary, fennel, anise, cinnamon, fenugreek, cloves, mace, mustard, nutmeg, ginger, cardamom, coriander, oregano, and sage are normally added at around 0.1-0.2% (1-2 g/kg). Spices like garlic, paprika and caraway are added in different amounts depending on preference. Paprika is a known colorant and will contribute to the red color of a sausage.

Pepper. Ground pepper is the spice that is added to all fermented sausages. It is available as whole seeds but you have to grind them. It comes in two forms:

- black pepper - unripe seeds of the plant with the skin left on
- white pepper - ripe seeds with the skin removed

It is available as coarse grind, sometimes called butcher's grind or fine grind. A recipe will call for a particular grind but the final choice will be up to you. Some recipes will call for whole pepper corns. The dividing line is whether you want to see the pepper in your product or not. Otherwise it makes no difference and you can replace black pepper with the same amount of white pepper, although the black pepper is a bit hotter. Without a doubt *black pepper is the most popular spice* added to fermented sausages.

Mace and Nutmeg can leave a bitter taste when more than 1.0 gram per 1 kg of meat is used. As a rule they are not used in fresh sausages as their aroma is easily noticeable.

Garlic can be used fresh or granulated. Although the flavor of fresh or granulated garlic is basically the same, fresh garlic has a much stronger aroma.

Paprika is a well known colorant and will give the sausage an orange tint.

Red pepper contains more sugar than other spices and is thought to support fermentation.

Thyme is similar to marjoram but stronger.

Vinegar though not a spice is used in some sausages like white head cheese or Mexican chorizo.

- It is safer not to use fresh herbs (oregano, onion, parsley) when making *fermented sausages* as they may contain unknown bacteria.
- Dark spices such as nutmeg, caraway, cloves, and allspice can darken the color of the sausage.
- Meat plants use commercially prepared extracts that have a much stronger flavor.
- Similarly to the case of coffee beans, the advantage of grinding seeds before use is a fresher aroma.

Spice	Dosage in g/kg
Allspice	1.5
Cardamon	2.0
Chillies	0.5
Cinnamon	2.0
Cloves	1.5
Coriander	2.0
Fennel	2.0
Garlic paste (fresh)	5.0
Garlic powder	1.5
Ginger	2.0
Juniper	2.0
Marjoram	3.0
Mace	1.0
Nutmeg	1.0
Onion (fresh)	10.0
Onion powder	3.0
Paprika	2.0
Pepper-white	2.0
Pepper-black	2.0
Thyme	1.0

Above - basic guidelines for spice usage as practiced by commercial sausage manufacturers.

How many grams of spice in one flat teaspoon	
Allspice, ground	1.90
Bay leaf, crumbled	0.60
Basil, ground	1.40
Caraway, seed	2.10
Cardamon, ground	1.99
Cinnamon	2.30
Cloves, ground	2.10
Coriander, seed	1.80
Fennel, whole	2.00
Garlic powder	2.80
Ginger, ground	1.80
Mace, ground	1.69
Marjoram, dried	0.60
Marjoram, ground	1.50
Mustard seed, yellow	3.20
Mustard, ground	2.30
Nutmeg, ground	2.03
Onion powder	2.50
Oregano, ground	1.50
Paprika, ground	2.10
Pepper-black, ground	2.10
Pepper-white, ground	2.40
Thyme, crumbled	0.60

The numbers are based on spice data published by the American Spice Trade Association. The above data are a point of reference for your calculations and you can adjust the amount of spices the way you like.

To weigh spices and starter cultures accurately digital scales are recommended. They are small, up to 1/100 g accurate and inexpensive.

Chapter 6

Safety Hurdles

The start of fermentation is nothing else but a war declaration by bacteria residing inside the meat and the stuffed sausage becomes the battlefront. Fermented sausages and air dried meats are at an extra risk, as in many cases they are not submitted to the cooking/refrigerating process. There is less risk involved when we make a fresh sausage which will be cooked and eaten within a day or two. Cooked or smoked/cooked products are microbiologically stable as the heat kills bacteria and the product is kept under refrigeration. Raw meat dry sausages are not cooked, yet they must be safe to eat.

When is a Fermented Product Considered Shelf Stable?

In order to be considered shelf stable, products with Aw 0.90 or less, and pH 5.3 or less, must also contain a minimum 100 ppm (part per million) nitrite or nitrate salt calculated at the moment of formulation. Products that do not meet the requirements for being shelf stable must be kept refrigerated and labelled with these instructions. For example, a raw fermented sausage that has a pH of 5.3 and Aw greater than 0.90 does not meet the criteria of a shelf stable product.

Type	Aw	pH
Very perishable	> 0.95	> 5.2
Perishable	0.95 - 0.91	5.2 - 5.0
Shelf stable	< 0.90	< 5.3
	single hurdle enough	4.6
	0.85	single hurdle enough

To prevent the danger of *Clostridium botulinum* in fermented products that are classified as shelf stable, nitrite/nitrate should be added at a *minimum of 100 ppm along with a minimum of 2.5% salt.* Regardless of what precautions are taken, some bacteria will always be present and will start multiplying rapidly in the first hours of fermentation. Then as the lactic bacteria start feeding on sugar, the sausage becomes more acidic and unwanted bacteria stop growing. During this time moisture evaporates from the sausage, and that makes life for bacteria even more difficult as they need free water to survive. Although moisture evaporates from the sausage, salt remains inside which makes the sausage even saltier to bacteria. The scale starts slowly tipping in our favor and there comes a moment, when the sausage is safe to consume. The manufacture of fermented sausages at home conditions creates formidable hazards because:

- Temperatures in the kitchen will be much higher than in a commercial meat plant, even with a fully running air conditioning system.
- The temperature of the sausage mince may be higher than recommended.
- Home sausage making equipment process meats very slowly, increasing the temperature.
- Mixing and stuffing are not performed under a vacuum which may affect color and make fats rancid later.
- Fermenting and drying chambers are in most cases without proper temperature, humidity and air speed controls.
- Lack of proper testing equipment (pH, Aw) and the list goes on...

The only way fermented sausages can be successfully made at home is to exactly *follow the good manufacturing practices*. The kitchen becomes a little meat plant, and Suzie or Paul must become not only proficient sausage makers, but also competent meat technologists. This can be easily accomplished by reading and re-reading the chapters of this book. Once sufficient knowledge of the subject is acquired, microorganisms will become a part of the sausage making procedure, they will be accepted as something that we better get along with if we want to make a good product. We will realize that not only is there nothing to be afraid of bacteria, but that they can be a helpful partner. The rest will fall into the proper place. And remember... we have been making those products for thousands of years and books were not even around.

Types of Hurdles

A sophisticated alarm system consists of many layers: perimeter protection, motion detectors, sirens and central station connection. Fermented sausages are like a sophisticated alarm - they need many levels of security measures to stop intruding undesirable bacteria. To prevent the growth of unwanted bacteria we employ a combination of steps known as *hurdles*:

- Processing meats with a low bacteria count at low temperatures.
- Adding salt.
- Adding nitrite/nitrate.
- Lowering pH of the meat to < 5.3.
- Lowering Aw (water activity) by drying to < 0.91.
- Using bio-protective cultures.
- Smoking.
- Cooking.
- Spices.
- Cleanliness and common sense.

Using a combination of different hurdles is more effective than relying on one method only. For example the first hurdle is an application of salt and sodium nitrite which slows down spoilage and keeps pathogenic bacteria at bay. This first hurdle is a temporary one and if we don't follow up with additional hurdles, such as increasing acidity and lowering water content the product will spoil.

Meat Selection

Meat of a healthy animal is clean and contains very few bacteria. Any invading bacteria will be destroyed by the animal's immune system. Once the animal is slaughtered these defense mechanisms are destroyed and the meat tissue is subjected to rapid decay. Although unaware of the process, early sausage makers knew that once the animal was killed it was a race between external preservation techniques and the decomposition of the raw meats to decide the ultimate fate of the issue. Most bacteria are present on the skin and in the intestines. The slaughtering process starts introducing bacteria into the exposed surfaces. Given time they will find their way inside anyhow, but the real trouble starts when *we* create a new surface cut with a knife. This creates an opening for bacteria to enter the meat from the outside and start spoiling it. We must realize that they don't appear in some magical way inside of the meat, they always start from *the outside and they work their way in.*

Meat Surface Area and Volume Relationship

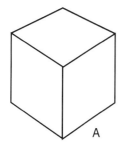 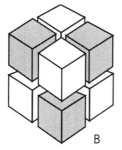

Fig. 6.1 Relationship of surface area and volume.

A. Cube A is 1 inch on each side and has a volume of 1 cubic inch and the surface area of 6 square inches.

B. Three complete cuts (two vertical and one horizontal) produce eight small cubes with a volume of 0.125 cubic inch.

Total volume remains the same - 1 cubic inch, but total *surface area has doubled* and is 12 square inches.

This is what happens when the meat is cut, *the surface area increases.* Now imagine what happens when the grinder cuts meat through a 1/8" (3 mm) plate. It creates an infinite number of small particles which are exposed to air.

And spoilage bacteria need air to live. The more cuts, the more air and free water available to bacteria and the more spoils of meat. This is the reason why *ground meat has the shortest shelf life.*

In a large piece of meat the outside surface serves as a natural barrier preventing access to bacteria. *They have a long distance to travel to reach the center of the meat.* Meat muscles are surrounded with a connective tissue which also *acts as a protective sheath and so does the outside skin.* Duties like cutting meat, grinding, mixing or stuffing all increase meat temperature and should be performed at the lowest attainable in the kitchen temperatures. If working at higher temperatures try to process meats as fast as possible and then place them in a refrigerator. *Take only what you need.*

Some bacteria are present on our hands, others live in our nose and throat so personal hygiene is of utmost importance. In addition, each meat processing facility develops its own microbiological flora in which bacteria live on walls, ceilings, machinery, tools etc. This is the reason why meat plants have to be continuously sanitized and cleaned. All those bacteria are just waiting to jump on a piece of meat and start working in.

Going into details on selecting meats according to their pH or using terms like PSE, DFD or MDM meats is beyond the scope of these pages and will make them confusing to read. What we want to stress is that meat must be as fresh as possible with the lowest count of bacteria possible. Commercial producers try to keep this number between 100 and 1000 per gram of meat but a home based sausage maker must make sure that:

- *Meat is very fresh and always kept cold.*
- *Facilities and tools are very clean.*
- *Working temperatures are as low as possible.*
- *Take only what you need rule always applies.*

If the above conditions are not met, bacteria will multiply and will compete for food with cultures inhibiting their growth. The acidity of the meat influences its ability to hold water, and meats with pH > 6.0 can bind water better than meats with pH < 6.0. This moisture helps bacteria to multiply. Selecting meat with lower acidity (5.7-5.8) provides more safety, as it creates less favorable conditions for the growth of undesirable bacteria.

It also shortens the fermentation time needed to drop pH to a safe level. By adding different amounts of Gdl to the sausage mass commercial processors can adjust the pH level of meat. This will be performed when making fast or medium-fast fermented sausages. There is little we can do about a selected meat's bacteria count when buying it in a local supermarket, but we have to keep it refrigerated at home. Meat must not be processed above 12° C (54° F), for an extended time, as the growth of *Staphylococcus* occurs at 15.6° C (60 °F).

Temperature Control

It is crucial to maintain *the lowest possible temperature* during the first processing steps, such as meat selection, cutting, grinding, mixing and stuffing. During those periods, meat is hopelessly unprotected and left at the mercy of spoilage and pathogenic bacteria. Until salt and nitrite are added the only defense against meat spoilage is the low initial bacteria count of fresh meat, and the low processing temperature. Common sense is of invaluable help and we must:

*   Take only what is needed - process only as little meat as you can.
*   Keep processed meats refrigerated.
*   Use partially frozen meat and fats when grinding.
*   Do not use warm equipment (last minute equipment washing).
*   Work at the lowest possible temperature - set air conditioning thermostat to the lowest value. If no climate control is available, meat should be processed in the early hours of morning or in the evening.
*   Consider making sausages in cooler months of the year.

Typical temperatures of cooling units:

Home refrigerator	Butcher's cooler
36° - 40 F° (2° - 4° C)	32 F ° (0° C)
Home freezer	Butcher's freezer
0° F (-18° C)	-25° F (- 32° C)

When making fresh or cooked sausages, one may relax some of the above recommendations and still produce a fine sausage. Most regular sausages are fully cooked which kills all bacteria and makes the sausage safe to consume. Many fermented sausages are raw meat sausages that will never be cooked, so obviously they have to be submitted to different and more stringent rules. Once the sausage is placed in a fermentation/drying room, the temperature is increased. After fermentation the sausage will start drying and some types will dry for three months or longer. Different stages of drying call for different temperatures. Although the optimal temperature of fermenting and drying is usually provided by a recipe, it will not make much difference if the temperature is a few degrees higher or lower from the recommended value. Only industrial drying chambers with computer controlled controls allow a precise adjustment of temperature, humidity and air speed.

Salt

Bacteria hate salt and different bacteria strains possess different degrees of resistance. For example, *Lactobacillus* lactic acid bacteria as well as curing bacteria *Staphylococcus* and *Kocuria,* show more resistance to salt than spoilage or pathogenic types. By competing for nutrients with spoilage and pathogenic bacteria they prevent them from growing.

The more salt applied to the meat the stronger fence is created against unwanted bacteria. But to stop them from growing by salt alone, the salt levels will have to be so high that the product will not be edible. Such a product will have to be soaked for long time in running water in order to be consumed. What's more, applying salt at more than 4% will inhibit lactic bacteria from producing lactic acid and as a result little fermentation will take place. Well, if stopping them with salt entirely is not a practical solution then how about making life for them just miserable? And this is exactly what we do by adding between 2.5% – 3% salt into the minced meat.

Nitrate

Nitrite prevents *Clostridium botulinum,* the most toxic substance known to man from growing and releasing toxin. Although cases of food poisoning by *Cl.botulinum* are rather rare, they have one thing in common - they are fatal. In addition nitrite also suppresses *Salmonella.*

Lowering pH (increasing acidity)

When using acidification as a main safety hurdle, most fast-fermented sausages are microbiologically stable when pH 5.3 or lower is obtained within a prescribed time. Depending on the culture and fermentation temperature this can be easily accomplished within 7-36 hours for a fast-fermented sausage and 48-72 hours for a medium-fermented type.

In slow-fermented sausages the acidity of meat increases very slowly and *never reaches the point that might guarantee the safety of the sausage.* These sausages depend on drying to become microbiologically stable.

The introduction of more sugar leads to a lower pH and stronger acidification. About 1 g (0.1%) of dextrose per 1 kg of meat lowers pH of meat by 0.1 pH. This means that 10 g of dextrose added to meat with an initial pH value of 5.9 will lower pH by one full unit to 4.9. Sugar levels of 0.5% - 0.7% are usually added for reducing pH levels to just under 5.0.

Adding 1 g (0.1%) of Gdl per 1 kg of meat lowers the pH of meat by 0.1 pH. It shall be noted that the addition of sugar already lowers the pH of the meat and adding Gdl will lower the pH even more. As it is a natural acid, adding more than 8 g may cause a bitter and sour flavor. In slow-fermented salami pH does not drop generally lower than 5.3 but the sausage is microbiologically stable due to its low moisture level (Aw 0.87-0.88). Most American semi-dry sausages exhibit pH of 4.8 or even lower.

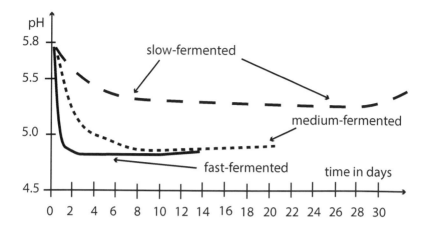

Fig. 6.2 Decrease in pH in slow, medium and fast-fermented sausages

Once the pH reaches 5.3 or less, *Staphylococcus aureus* and other pathogens are kept in check and further lowering pH or drying the sausage at low temperatures will make it microbiologically stable.

Lowering Aw (removing moisture)

Just adding 3% salt reduces the initial water activity level to 0.97. The sausage starts to lose moisture from the time it enters the fermentation room and continues to do so through the drying process. In about 3-6 days the Aw drops to about 0.95 and the sausage is more stable as some pathogenic bacteria (*Salmonella, Bacillus*) stop multiplying. Drying too fast at the beginning of fermentation may inhibit lactic acid bacteria from producing acid. Most microorganisms do not grow below Aw 0.91, with a few exceptions, notably *Staphylococcus aureus* which remains active until 0.86. Molds of course show great resistance to low moisture levels. *The activity of most spoilage and pathogenic bacteria stops when Aw of 0.89 is reached.* Aw drop is little affected by pH or number of bacteria, and is more linear in nature. Stated simply, the drying process is time dependent and factors that affect drying will also influence a decrease in water activity.

"The higher Aw, the lower pH is needed to protect sausages against undesirable bacteria and vice versa"

81

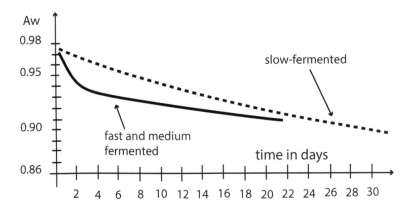

Fig. 6.3 Decrease in Aw in fast, medium and slow-fermented sausages.

Bio-protective Cultures

Bio-protective cultures like Bactoferm™ F-LC may be added for production of fermented sausages with a short production type where a higher count of *Listeria monocytogenes* bacteria may be suspected. Bactoferm™ F-LC has the ability to control *Listeria* at the same time as it performs as a classic starter culture for fermented sausages. The culture produces pediocin and bavaricin (kind of "antibiotics"), which keep *Listeria monocytogenes* at safe levels. These proteins, generally known as bacteriocins, act as a defense mechanism against competitive flora by attacking competitors. This is known as *competitive exclusion* - use of desirable competitive microorganisms to inhibit undesirable microorganisms.

The addition of any commercial culture provides a safety hurdle as those millions of freshly introduced bacteria compete for food (moisture, oxygen, sugar, protein) with a small number of bacteria residing in meat, preventing them from growing. It may be called a biological competition. Keep in mind that all cultures, although in varying degree, go through a lag phase, which is generally longer for slow fermenting types and lasts 6-14 hours, the shorter time corresponding to higher temperatures.

Smoking is covered in detail in Chapter 7.

Cooking

Cooking is a very effective way to kill bacteria but it is hard to imagine classical traditionally made salamis that will be cooked as this will alter their texture, taste and flavor. Fast-fermented sausages such as summer sausage, Thuringer, and cervelats are made very fast and cooking provides a recognized and FDA approved measure of safety. By cooking their products, commercial producers avoid fights with meat inspectors and cover themselves with a strong wall of protection in case something goes wrong. Keep in mind that the fermentation process can be stopped at any time (if no chemical acidulants were added) by submitting sausages to heat treatment. Cooking fermented sausages makes them definitely safer as the heat will kill bacteria. On the downside, this heat also kills bacteria which are instrumental in developing meat flavor. For example, raw semi-dry products exhibit higher sensory values than cooked products. The texture of a cooked sausage will suffer too as the individual specs of fat so typical in these sausages will melt down during heat treatment and will not be visible anymore. The texture of the sausage will become creamier.

The partially cooked sausage may be additionally dried to lose some of its weight, but the drying process must be performed at proper drying temperatures 53-59° F (12-15° C). Many recipes ask for cooking sausages to 137° F (58° C) as the risk of trichinosis is eliminated at this temperature. Commercially grown pigs are disease free in the USA and they have been disease free in Europe for a long time, where *every slaughtered pig is inspected for trichinosis* anyhow. In the USA *it is assumed* that a pig due to strictly controlled diet is trichinae free. Freezing pork also prevents the possibility of contracting trichinosis, and such meat can be used in sausages that will not be cooked. If cooking is required it makes sense to fully cook meat to FDA recommended 160° F (72° C) internal meat temperature. This way all bacteria will be effectively killed and there won't be any reason to worry about *Salmonella, E.coli* and others.

Spices

Throughout history, spices were known to possess antibacterial properties and cinnamon, cumin, and thyme were used in the mummification of bodies in ancient Egypt. It is hard to imagine anything that is being cooked in India without curry powder (coriander, turmeric, cumin, fenugreek and other spices). *Spices alone cannot be used as a hurdle against meat spoilage* as the average amount added to meat is only about 0.1% (1 g/1 kg). To inhibit bacteria, the amounts of spices will have to be very large and that will alter the taste of the sausage. Rosemary, mace, oregano and sage have antioxidant properties that can delay the rancidity of fat. Marjoram promotes the rancidity of fats. Black pepper, white pepper, garlic, mustard, nutmeg, allspice, ginger, mace, cinnamon, and red pepper are known to stimulate *Lactobacillus* bacteria to produce lactic acid.

Latest research establishes that spices such as *mustard, cinnamon*, and *cloves* are helpful in slowing the growth of molds, yeast, and bacteria. Most cases of illness associated with *Campylobacter* are caused by handling raw poultry or eating raw or under cooked poultry meat and *only garlic* offers some protection. During the last few years a number of studies were undertaken to investigate its antibacterial and antiviral properties. It is widely believed that garlic contributes positively to our cardiovascular and immune systems and a number of on-the-shelf drugs have entered the market. Detailed research was done on the antioxidant and antimicrobial effects of garlic in chicken sausage (ref. 24) and the conclusion follows:

This study concluded that fresh garlic, garlic powder and garlic oil provide antioxidant and antimicrobial benefits to raw chicken sausage during cold storage (38° F, 3° C) and the effects are concentration dependent. Among the garlic forms studied, fresh garlic at a concentration of 5% demonstrated the most potent effect, but such a high concentration may not be acceptable by many people because of its strong flavor. However, the addition of fresh garlic at 30 g/kg or garlic powder at 9 g/kg, did not result in a strong flavor and at the same time, they produced significant antidioxidant and antibacterial effects and extended the shelf life of the product up to 21 days.

What is very significant is that for centuries Thai fermented pork sausage "Nham" and Balinese fermented sausage "Urutan" have been made with 5% of fresh garlic that corresponds to 50 g/kg - the amount found to be effective in the above study.

Use of fresh spice in fermented products is generally not a good idea. Fresh spices being moist may contain bacteria, insects, and molds, which will be introduced into the sausage and may affect the process.

Cleanliness and Common Sense

Home made sausages are subject to the ambient temperature of the kitchen and a dose of a common sense is of invaluable help:

- Take only what you need from the cooler.
- When a part of the meat is processed put it back into the cooler.
- Keep your equipment clean and cold.
- Work as fast as possible.
- Try to keep meat always refrigerated.
- Work at the lowest possible temperature.
- Wash your hands often.

For a hobbyist application of safety hurdles is of crucial importance as home owners do not own a full range of comminuting equipment such as powerful grinders and bowl cutters. Meat plants can process frozen meat and fat in a bowl cutter, but a manual grinder will struggle with such a load. Commercial stuffers can fill casings under a vacuum so no air will be present inside the sausage, a hobbyist will use a needle to remove air bubbles.

The biggest difference is of course a fermentation and drying chamber. Commercial units come equipped with temperature, humidity and air speed control. A home owner will often use a modified refrigerator which can be equipped with basic controls and will work as well as industrial units. To make it short a homeowner faces more technological challenges than a commercial producer, however, he can do things that a producer will not dare try:

- produce different sausage on a daily basis.
- experiment with recipes.
- modify recipe to his liking.

Chapter 7

Smoking Fermented Sausages

There are two distinctive methods of smoking meats:

1. Cold smoking, usually at 71° F (22° C) or less.

2. Hot smoking, anything from 71° F (22° C) and up.

The dividing line which separates both methods is the temperature when meat or fish proteins start to cook. Throw an egg on a cold frying pan and start raising the heat. At a certain point the white of the egg which actually looks like a clear jelly starts changing color and becomes cooked egg white. The technical term is *coagulation of protein*, this is when the product starts to cook. In meat this usually happens at around 85° F (29° C); there is a rapid loss of moisture and the texture of the meat becomes hard. This will prevent a further smoke penetration and the removal of moisture.

Mystery of Cold Smoking

The majority of hobbyists think of cold smoking as some mysterious preservation technique that will produce a unique and superb quality product. What makes matters worse is that they start to experiment with different smoke temperatures and establish their own rules which then spread around and are repeated by newcomers into the field of smoking meats. In most German, Polish or Russian meat technology books the upper limit for cold smoking is 71° F (22° C). Let's put some facts straight:

- cold smoking is not a preservation method, it will not preserve meat unless the meat will be dried.
- the higher amount of salt is added to meat that would be smoked to inhibit the growth of spoilage bacteria.
- cold smoking is an additional safety hurdle that helps to achieve microbiological safety of meat.

Cold smoking was nothing else but a drying method whose purpose was *to eliminate moisture so that bacteria would not grow.*

This technique developed in North Eastern European countries where the climate was harsh and winters severe. When meats were cold smoked for 2-3 weeks, yes, the meat became preserved, but it was drying that made the meat safe. If the same meat was dried at 54° F (12° C) without any smoke present, it would be preserved all the same.

The pigs were traditionally slaughtered for Christmas and the meat had to last until the summer. Noble cuts were cooked or salted, but trimmings were made into sausages that were dried which was not an easy task to accomplish with freezing temperatures outside. The only way to heat up storage facilities was to burn wood and that produced smoke. They were two choices:

- hang meats 5 feet above a small smoldering fire OR
- burn wood in a firebox that was located outside. The firebox was connected with the smokehouse by an underground channel that would supply heat and smoke at the same time.

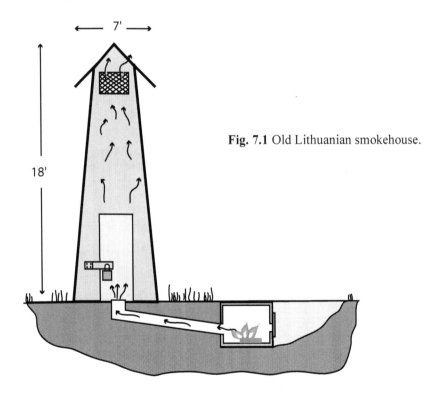

Fig. 7.1 Old Lithuanian smokehouse.

As the temperature had to be higher than freezing temperatures outside, the slowly burning fire provided suitable temperatures for drying. It is common knowledge that fire produces smoke so the meats and sausages were dried and smoked at the same time. They were just flavored with cold smoke which not only helped to preserve the product but gave it a wonderful aroma. In addition it prevented molds from growing on the surface. Those advantages of applying smoke were not ignored by our ancestors and smoking became an art in itself. The meat, however, was preserved by drying and the benefits of smoke flavor was just an added bonus.

A large smokehouse was also a storage facility where smoked meats hung in a different area where they continued to receive some smoke, although on a much smaller scale. This prevented any mold from growing on the surfaces of hams or sausages, as molds need oxygen to grow.

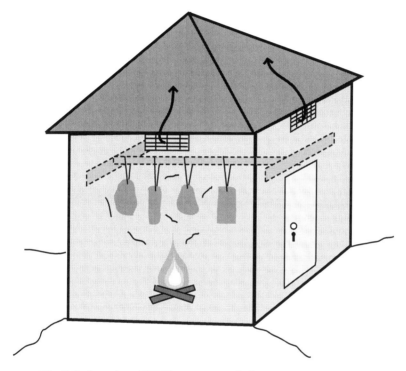

Fig. 7.2 American XVIII century smokehouse.

It was established that meats dried best when the temperatures were somewhere between 10-15° C (50–60° F) and although the temperature of the smoke leaving the firebox was higher, it would be just right by the time it made contact with meat. Whole logs of wood were burnt. The fire was allowed to die out as people went to sleep. The meats hung until the morning and the fire would be re-started again. So when you see an old recipe saying that ham or sausage was smoked for 2 weeks, well it really was not, as it probably received smoke for about 1/3 of the time. Those meats were not cooked, they were dried and could be considered fermented products.

Italians and Spaniards were blessed with a climate that provided cool prevailing winds at right temperatures. There was no need to burn wood to warm up the drying chambers. As a result products did not acquire a smoky flavor. For this reason people in the Mediterranean basin are not particularly fond of smoked products, and people in Germany, Poland, Russia, Lithuania love them, but don't generally like uncooked air dried products. The majority of all processed meat products in Northern Europe are of smoked variety.

There is little difference about Italian salami, Hungarian salami or Polish Cold Smoked Sausage. Italian salami is dried without smoke and Hungarian salami or Polish sausage were dried with cold smoke. *The product was drying out and the smoke happened to be there.* Preservation was on people's mind rather than creating cold smoked flavor. Very few products are cold smoked today, notably cold smoked salmon known as "lox." The texture of cold smoked products is firmer and they can be sliced paper thin. The taste is a different story, you must acquire a liking for cold smoked products. In the past people already knew what we know today, that hot smoked products taste better. Cold smoking was our answer to the lack of refrigeration in the past. Do you think we would have bothered to smoke meats for weeks if refrigeration had been present? No, we would hot smoke them for a few hours and then they would end up in the refrigerator.

Cold smoking is performed with *a thin smoke,* 52-71°F (12-22°C), 70-80% humidity, from 1 - 14 days, and a good air ventilation to remove excess moisture. *Cold smoking is not a continuous process,* it is stopped a few times to allow fresh air into the smoker. Often recipes call for 3-4 days of cold smoking, but that does not mean that the smoking is continuous. Applying a heavy continuous smoke for such a long period (even at a low temperature) may impart a bitter taste to the product.

Cold smoking slows down the spoilage of fats, which increases the shelf life of meat. The product is drier and saltier with a more pronounced smoky flavor. The color varies from yellow to dark brown on the surface and dark red inside. *Cold smoked products are not submitted to the cooking process.* Cold smoking assures us of total smoke penetration inside of the meat. The loss of moisture is uniform in all areas and the total weight loss falls within 5-20% depending largely on the smoking time.

It is obvious that you cannot produce cold smoke if the outside temperature is 90° F (32° C), unless you can cool it down, which is what some industrial smokers do. In tropical areas like Florida you are limited to the winter months only and the smoking must be done at night when temperatures drop to 40 - 60° F (4-16° C) or even lower. The question arises to how to continue cold smoking when temperature increases to 80° F (27° C) at day time? Well, do not smoke, move meat to the area of 50° F (10° C) or refrigerate. Then when the temperature drops in the evening, start smoking again.

Photo 7.1 & 7.2 Using the weather to his advantage, Waldemar Kozik has no problems with cold smoking sausages in Catskill Mountains of New York.

Smoking Slow-Fermented Sausages

It should be pointed out that *when making slow-fermented sausages only cold smoke should be applied.* In order not to unbalance ongoing fermentation, the temperature of the smoke should approximate the temperature of the fermentation chamber. For the same reason cold smoking will be applied to semi-dry sausages which will be fermented but not cooked. Applying smoke which is much cooler than the fermentation temperature will slow down fermentation. Applying smoke which is much hotter than the fermentation or drying temperature will create favorable conditions for the growth of undesirable bacteria. All raw fermented sausages which are not subjected to heat treatment must be smoked with cold smoke.

When making traditional slow-fermented sausages we apply fermentation temperatures around 66° F (18° C) and even less when drying. To match these values we have to apply cold smoke that falls more or less in the same temperature range. *Cold smoking is basically drying with smoke.* Think of cold smoke as a part of the drying/fermentation cycle and not as the flavoring step. *If the temperature of the smoke is close to the fermentation temperature, there is very little difference between the two.* The sausage will still ferment and the drying will continue. If we applied heavy smoke for a long time, that would definitely inhibit the growth of color and flavor forming bacteria which are so important for the development of flavor in slow-fermented sausages. *As drying continues for a long time and cold smoking may be a part of it, it makes little difference whether cold smoke is interrupted and then re-applied again.*

The drying temperature falls into 54-64° F (12-18° C) range and cold smoke applied at 64° F (18° C) or less fits nicely into this range. To sum it up, the length of cold smoking is loosely defined, but the upper temperature should remain below 72° F (22° C). Smoke which is applied early in the fermentation stage will definitely inhibit the growth of lactic acid bacteria to some degree, especially *if the diameter of the sausage is small.* In such a case it will be wiser to wait until fermentation is over before the smoke is applied. Applying smoke during the fermentation period creates a barrier to the growth of *Staph. aureus* at the surface of the product where toxin production may be a problem.

Application of smoke prevents growth of mold on sausages, however, this will not last indefinitely, so the procedure may have to be repeated. As mold can already grow in the first days of fermentation it is recommended to apply a thin cold smoke at the early stage of production. If mold appears before smoking was performed, or shortly after, the sausage should be rinsed and wiped off and then smoke may be applied again.

Smoking Fast-Fermented Sausages

Semi-dry sausages, which are of fast-fermented type, are fermented at higher temperatures. These sausages can be smoked with warmer smoke as they are subsequently cooked.

Warm smoking 77-122° F, (25-50° C) can be applied to semi-dry sausages which will be cooked. If sausages are fully cooked, 154-160° F (68-71° C), the **hot smoke** 140-176° F (60-80° C) may be administered. Smoke may be applied late during the fermentation stage (preferably after) *when the surface of the sausage is dry.* Applying heavy smoke early during the fermentation stage is not the best idea as smoke contains many ingredients (phenols, carbonyls, acids etc.) which may impede reactions between meat and beneficial bacteria, especially in the surface area. After hot smoking/cooking, shower sausages with hot water (removes grease and soot), then with cold water and then transfer them to storage. At home, the sausages are normally smoked/cooked outside and they are cold showered only. This prevents them from shrivelling and shortens the meat's exposure to high temperatures.

Wood for Smoking

Any hardwood is fine, but soft evergreen trees like fir, spruce, pine, or others cause problems. They contain too much resin and the finished product has a turpentine flavor to it. It also develops a black color due to the extra soot from the smoke, which in turn makes the smoker dirtier, too. This wood will burn quickly and cleanly, but will not be suitable for smoking.

We don't use wet wood for cold smoking because we want to eliminate moisture, not bring it in. Cold smoke warms the surface of the meat up very finely, just enough to allow the moisture to evaporate. Creating cold smoke for two days with wet wood will never dry out the meat.

Wet chips or sawdust seem to produce more smoke but this is not true. The extra amount of smoke is nothing else but water vapor (steam) mixed with smoke. This does make a difference when hot smoking at 105-140° F, (40-60° C) and the smoke times are rather short. That extra moisture prevents the sausage casings from drying out during smoking, however, wet chips are not going to be wet for very long; the heat will dry them out anyhow. The type of wood used will largely depend on the smoker used and the location of the fire pit.

With a separately located fire pit it makes little difference what type of wood is burned as this design can take a lot of abuse and still provides efficient and comfortable smoke generation. Most people that use these types of smokers don't even bother with chips or sawdust and burn solid wood logs instead.

Photo 7.3 Chopping oak wood.

Photo 7.4 Burning whole logs of wood is a comfortable way of generating cold smoke when smoking continues for a long time.

Chapter 8

Fermented Sausages

History of Fermented Sausages

Meat preservation was always the primary concern for our ancestors and although they managed to hunt even the largest of animals, most of the meat was left to rot away. Before 2200 B.C., the Chinese discovered that salting meat was an effective way of preserving it. By 1500 B.C., the Egyptians were using this technique and the Greeks and Romans were salting meats before the Christ era. Plenty of salt was rubbed into hams which were left out on racks for a few weeks. As the hams were left to dry out, more moisture was removed which made them microbiologically stable. Of course there was more to it but basically Spanish hams were made that way for hundreds of years.

The next breakthrough came when it was discovered that salts which came from different mines exhibited various qualities. Some salts contained impurities that would impart a nice pink color to the meat. In addition, the meat would develop a different and pleasant flavor, and it would last longer, all of which were much in demand. At that moment nitrate curing was born and that preservation method continues even today.

The Italian name for sausage was "salsus" which was derived from the Latin word "sal" for salt. First salamis were pounded with mortar until a meat paste was obtained, then the paste was stuffed into casings and dried. Low quality salami sausage was the basic staple of Roman soldiers as it had a high nutritional value and kept for a long time. That fact had partly contributed to the effectiveness of the Roman military machine. Much later Napoleon said: "The army marches on its stomach." Meat that was pounded into thinner slices and then left in the sun for drying would be preserved for future use. Then we started to add spices, which had contributed to a longer shelf life of the product and added an extra aroma which often made up for poor sausage quality. In some countries even today a fermented sausage is stuffed into an unusual casing or wrapped up in banana leaves. Sausages were stuffed into casings with fingers through a horn or any funnel resembling device. Even today, fermented sausages that have the best flavor are those which are slow-fermented with nitrate the same way it was done hundreds of years ago.

Traditionally, the production of fermented meats relied on bacteria present at the butcher's premises. The facility developed its own microbiological flora in which microorganisms lived all over the establishment. Meat brought from outside had already been infected with bacteria. In some establishments the slaughter of the animal was performed right on the premises which also contributed to new bacteria infecting the meat. Summing it up, there was no shortage of microorganisms and this combination of bacteria from the meat and from the premises often created favorable conditions for making fermented sausages. Such plants developed different bacterial flora and produced sausages of particular qualities. In the past, meat facilities were not sanitized so scrupulously as the ones of today which helped create more favorable conditions for the bacteria to survive. These conditions were unique to each establishment and it was impossible to duplicate them anywhere else. By the same token, sausage makers were unable to produce a fermented sausage in two different locations that would be of the same quality.

Many places in Italy developed a specific flora which was instrumental in producing a high quality product of a peculiar taste and flavor. Suddenly such establishments developed fame and a brand name for making wonderful meat products. They probably were not better sausage makers than their counterparts working in different locations. They were lucky to have their shop located in their area which was blessed by mother nature for making fermented sausages. They did not have much clue to what was happening, but passed this empirical knowledge to their sons and it worked like magic.

Until the second half of the XX century, the manufacture of fermented sausages was covered in a shroud of secrecy. One of the secrets was known as back slopping, which was reusing a part of the sausage mass from the previous batch. Such inoculation helped to produce a sausage of the same quality as the one previously made. Unfortunately, any defects that were acquired in following productions would be passed along and the method is seldom used today. Climatic differences were a significant factor in the development of different methods of smoking, drying, and preserving meat products. The best time of year was when temperatures were cooler and mildly humid. In the summer, higher temperatures and lower humidity did not favor the production of high quality sausages. The South had a drier climate with steady winds and the best air-dried hams originated there (Spanish Serrano, Italian Parma). In the North the weather was less predictable with cooler temperatures and higher humidity. Those conditions were ill suited for making air-dried products and smoking became the preferred method. For those reasons Mediterranean countries produced slow-fermented sausages that were only dried and countries in Northern Europe produced fermented sausages which were smoked and dried.

Modern production is independent of outside conditions and parameters such as temperature, humidity and air speed are computer controlled. This latest technology combined with a universal use of bacteria cultures permit producing fermented sausages of constant quality at any time of the year. Even so the manufacture of fermented products is still a combination of an art and technology. In the past there was no need for any classification as all sausages were dry products.

Thus, the technology of making salamis, chorizos and other products depended on air-drying and not on increasing the acidity of meat as practiced today.

All fermented sausages can be smoked or not, but as a rule South European varieties are usually not smoked. North European sausages are almost always smoked. Most semi-dry sausages in the USA are smoked.

Mold covered salami appeals to many customers. Countries in which molded sausages are commonly expected are: Italy, Romania, Bulgaria, Spain, Hungary, France, and Belgium. Northern and Eastern European countries: Germany, Poland, Russia, England, Sweden, Finland, Denmark prefer sausages without mold, largely due to the fact that the majority of meats and sausages made in those countries are of smoked variety and the application of smoke prevents mold formation. In America mold covered sausages are popular mainly in California, especially in the San Francisco Bay area.

Fermented sausages are often called *raw* fermented sausages, however, this holds true only for sausages which were never submitted to heat treatment. Basic classification:

- Dry (slow-fermented), smoked or unsmoked, little acidity, traditional cheesy flavor - Salami, Chorizo, Salami, Italian Pepperoni.

- Semi-dry (fast or medium fermented), acidic flavor, usually smoked and cooked after fermentation - Lebanon Bologna, Summer Sausage.

	Dry	Semi-dry
Fermentation	slow without cultures or slow with cultures	fast with fast-fermenting cultures
Fermentation temperature	20-24° C (68-75° F)	26-46° C (78-115° F)
pH drop	5.0-5.5	4.8-5.4
Smoking	varies from country to country	usually yes
Moisture loss	30% or more	10-20%
Cooking	no	often partially cooked
Flavor	cheesy, aromatic	sourly, acidic

Style	Fermentation Temperature	Time to pH of 5.3	Aw	Time
South European	18-24° C 60-75° F	longer than 40 hours	less than 0.90	3 weeks or longer. Nitrate added.
Milano salami, Naples salami, Italian pepperoni, Spanish Chorizo, French saucisson				
North European	22-26° C 70-80° F	less than 30 hours	more than 0.90	less than 3 weeks. Nitrite added.
Danish salami, German Mettwurst				
American	above 32° C 90° F	less than 15 hours	more than 0.90	2-3 weeks or less. Nitrite added.
American pepperoni, summer sausage				

American methods rely on rapid acid production through a fast fermentation in order to stabilize the sausage against spoilage bacteria. In European countries milder fermentation temperatures are used and the drying, instead of the acidity, is the main safety hurdle against undesirable bacteria.

Any fully cooked sausage is considered to be shelf stable and safe to eat. Dry sausages are not cooked at all and must conform to new requirements which forces a sausage maker to apply a new set of rules which require understanding of basic microbiology. To be considered shelf stable or ready-to-eat, a *raw* fermented sausage must exhibit the following characteristics:

Sausage type	pH plus Aw	In addition some moisture must be removed
Dry	pH 5.3 or less plus Aw 0.90 or less	25 - 50%
Semi-dry	pH 5.3 or less plus Aw 0.90 or less	15 - 25%
Generally, the sausages are stable when pH is below 5.3 and Aw below 0.90		

Sausages are also shelf stable when	**pH 4.6**	*single hurdle enough*
	single hurdle enough	**Aw 0.85**

European Certificates of Origin

Throughout Europe there is a huge assortment of great foods. When a product acquires a reputation extending beyond national borders it can face competition from other products which may pass themselves off as the genuine article and take the same name. Our hats go off to the French who invented the idea in the 1930's to protect their regional wines. The system used in France from the early part of the twentieth century is known as the appellation d'origine contrôlée (AOC). Items that meet geographical origin and quality standards may be endorsed with a government-issued stamp which acts as an official certification of the origins and standards of the product to the consumer. In 1992, the European Union created the following systems to promote and protect food products:

Photo 8.1 Protected Designation of Origin (PDO) - covers the term used to describe foodstuffs which are produced, processed and prepared in a given geographical area using recognized know-how.

Example: Italy - Prosciutto di Parma.

Photo 8.2 Protected Geographical Indication (PGI) - the geographical link must occur in at least one of the stages of production, processing or preparation.

Example: France - Boudin blanc de Rethel.

Photo 8.3 Traditional Speciality Guaranteed (TSG) - does not refer to the origin but highlights traditional character, either in the composition or means of production.

Example: Spain - Jamon Serrano.

This system is similar to the French Appellation d'Origine Contrôlée (AOC) system, the Denominazione di Origine Controllata (DOC) used in Italy and the Denominación de Origen system used in Spain. The law (enforced within the EU and being gradually expanded internationally via bilateral agreements of the EU with non-EU countries) ensures that only products genuinely originating in that region are allowed in commerce as such.

The purpose of the law is to protect the reputation of the regional foods and eliminate the unfair competition and misleading of consumers by non-genuine products, which may be of inferior quality or of different flavor. These laws protect the names of wines, cheeses, hams, sausages, olives, beers, and even regional breads, fruits, and vegetables. As such, foods such as Gorgonzola, Parmigiano Reggiano, Asiago cheese, Camembert de Normandie and Champagne can only be labelled as such if they come from the designated region. To qualify as Roquefort for example, cheese must be made from the milk of a certain breed of sheep and matured in the natural caves near the town of Roquefort in the Aveyron region of France where it is infected with the spores of a fungus (Penicillium roqueforti) that grows in those caves.

Italy has a long history in the production of traditional fermented sausages and almost every part of the country offers many great products, some of which have been awarded Protected Designation of Origin and Protected Geographical Indication certificates. In order to preserve the original taste and flavor these products are made without starter cultures and sold in local markets. European Certificates of Origin don't come easy and only a few countries were able to obtain them for meat products. Countries which were granted most Certificates of Origin for Fermented Meat Products are: Italy, Hungary, Spain, Portugal, France, Germany. The complete list can be obtained from the European Commission/ Agriculture & Rural Development,
http://ec.europa.eu/agriculture/quality/schemes/index_en.htm

How Fermented Sausages Differ From Others

Making a regular sausage is amazingly simple; the meat is ground, salt and spices are added, and the mass is stuffed into a casing. If this is a fresh sausage, the process ends right there and the sausage goes into the refrigerator. Then it is fully cooked before serving. Or the sausage is smoked first and then cooked and consumed. This is a simple, fast and relatively safe process if basic safety precautions are in place. On the other end it takes a lot of effort to produce a high quality traditional fermented sausage. There is a serious investment in time and a lot of care is needed by the sausage maker. It is almost like planting a tomato plant in the garden, a lot of pruning and watering is needed within the next three months. Or like making wine, it has to ferment, clarify, mature, and only then it is ready to be consumed. A lack of heat treatment is what separates fermented sausages from others, another difference is their cheesy or tangy taste.

The noticeable difference in flavor between South European, North European and American femented sausages is not as much due to spice combinations, but to different manufacturing methods which are used for making sausages. These methods influence the choice of starter cultures, fermentation temperatures, amounts and types of sugars, and the resulting pH drop. Another huge factor is the presence or absence of color and flavor forming *Micrococcaceae* bacteria, which are responsible for the sausage aroma.

Production Methods for Making Fermented Sausages

There are three methods of making fermented sausages:

- Chance contamination - traditional method without starter culture.
- Back slopping - traditional method without starter culture.
- Starter cultures - modern method.

Chance Contamination

The traditional method where the sausage mix is either kept for a few days at 41° F (5° C), stuffed and fermented *or* it is stuffed, kept for a few days in a cooler and then fermented. The procedure is called the *chance* contamination because we *take a chance* that everything will proceed according to the plan. That much for science. Today we know that the reason for this cold storage was to give time for naturally occuring lactic and curing bacteria to grow. With today's rigid safety standards and scrupulous sanitizing, the amount of surrounding bacteria is certainly lower which creates a deterimental factor for bacterial fermentation. Refrigerator temperatures provide less opportunity for bacteria to grow, but given time they would. And if everything proceeds according to the plan there will be enough lactic acid bacteria to start a healthy fermentation. Unfortunately, not only lactic bacteria but all other microorganisms will grow as well and if the product will not spoil it would have definitely a shorter shelf life. However, we can still make great products this way as long as we create favorable conditions for beneficial bacteria and an unfavorable environment for spoilage and pathogenic ones.

Back Slopping

Back slopping relies on reintroducing a part of the sausage mix (around 5%) from the previous successful production. A part of the sausage mix is taken *after the fermentation step and prior to any heating or drying* and frozen for later use. This will inoculate a new batch of sausages with a proven quality meat paste which contains living bacteria. As those bacteria produced a high quality sausage before, we may expect that they would introduce the same qualities into a new production. In other words the quality of the new sausage batch should be as good as the previous one. The contamination problem still remains as it is impossible to predict what spoilage and pathogenic bacteria are present in a new batch of sausages. A new production can be contaminated with unknown bacteria and the problem will become evident only after a few back slopping cycles. By that time the whole premises might be contaminated with a new and undesired strain of bacteria. A commercial producer making a thousand pounds of sausages a day cannot rely on wild bacteria to produce constant quality products. And any possible risks that may be even remotely present must be eliminated. Parameters such as pH of meat material, sausage pH, water activity Aw, temperature, air speed and bacteria count must be carefully monitored. Starter cultures make the production of fermented products much simpler and safer.

Starter Cultures

A recipe can be downloaded from the Internet and with some luck, one may produce quality salami at home, however, the next time one attempts to make the same sausage, it may turn out completely different, even if the same ingredients were included. Starter cultures solve the problem, they are inexpensive, easy to use and there is no excuse for not using them. Any fermented sausage made at home, regardless of its type, should include starter culture. This increases the chances of making a successful product and provides a safety hurdle against the growth of undesirable bacteria.

Basic Sausage Making Steps

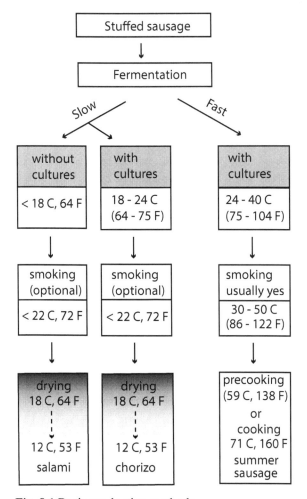

Fig. 8.1 Basic production methods.

It is assumed that a reader is already familiar with the basic sausage making process. The purpose of the following section is to highlight procedures which are of crucial importance to making fermented sausages.

Although the first steps of sausage making such as meat selection, curing, grinding, mixing and stuffing initially seem to be the same, however, they have to be tuned to new safety requirements. All tasks involved in the manufacture of fermented sausages must always be performed in such a way that meat safety is *never compromised.* A mistake in any of the processing steps can later spoil the sausage or bring harm to the consumer. The processing steps which are unique to making fermented sausages are fermenting, ripening and drying and they are covered in a detail.

Meat Selection

Pork and beef are the most popular meats for making fermented sausages. Only the best raw materials are chosen for making dry or semi-dry sausages. Any blood clots and glands must be removed as these may accumulate undesired bacteria. Those bacteria will then multiply during the curing or fermentation step and will affect the quality of the product. Meats must be well trimmed of gristle and sinews which will remain tough in the finished product.

Such defects are less apparent in finely minced sausages but will strike out in coarsely ground sausage. The fact that fat has a lower acidity is not of grave concern as it accounts for the minor parts of a sausage and the initial pH of the sausage mass is the average of all meats. Typical pH values of raw meats:

Raw material	pH
Pork	5.7 - 5.9
Pork back fat	6.2 - 7.0
Emulsified pork skins	7.2 - 7.8
Beef	5.5 - 5.8
Chicken breast	5.6 - 5.8
Chicken thigh	6.1 - 6.4

Meat flavor increases with the age of the animal. The characteristic flavors of a particular animal are concentrated more in the fat than in the lean of the meat. Freezing and thawing has little effect on meat flavor, however, prolonged frozen storage can effect meat's flavor due to rancidity of fat. Rancidity is off-flavor created by meat's reaction with oxygen which is accelerated by exposure of meat to light.

Offal meat such as liver or kidneys is not used for making fermented sausages.

Fat

A firm texture is desired in dry or semi-dry sausages so the fresh chilled pork back fat is selected as it is firm and dry and does not show signs of rancidity even after prolonged ripening periods. Many semi-dry sausages are partially or even fully cooked, so soft fats will melt easily affecting the texture of the sausage. Softer inter-muscular fatty tissues should not be used as it cannot be cleanly chopped to clearly defined particles. The slices would have a somewhat blurred unclear appearance. Soft fat also increases the risk of early rancidity.

Hard fat is preferred and pork *back fat* is the material of choice. It is much firmer than other fats, it is white and tastes the best. Fat contains little water (10-15%) so a fatty sausage requires less time to dry out.

Soft fat is a poor choice for making sliceable sausages but it is a good choice for making spreadable sausages (Mettwurst, Teewurst), especially the ones with a fine grind. Soft fat smears easily and may adhere to the inner casing surface, clogging up the pores and affecting drying. It can coat meat particles which fat film what will affect the drying process.

Beef fat has a higher melting temperature than pork but is yellowish in color which affects the appearance of the product where discrete particles of fat should be visible. There are some that may object to pork fat on religious grounds and beef fat (tallow) will have to do.

Chicken fat is very soft and melts at such low temperatures that it is of no practical use.

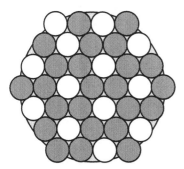

Fig. 8.2 Meat and fat particles of the same size - cut through the same grinder plate.

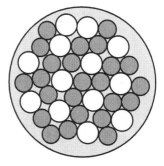

Fig. 8.3 Sausage lost 30% of its original weight. Meat particles lost most of the water, the fat less. This is why the fat stands out more.

Fat Rancidity

Rancidity is the process which causes a substance to become rancid, that is having an unpleasant smell or taste. Development of rancidity is a slow process, that is why we usually don't sense the problem as meat spoils before rancidity has a chance to occur. The spoilage can be prevented by freezing the meat, however, rancidity will appear in about 3 months. The meat will be safe to consume but it will carry off-flavor. Because dry sausages can be stored for a year or more, the fat they carry might start to develop some rancidity. Fat rancidity cannot be avoided, but it can be slowed down by selecting the freshest fat material and conducting drying/ripening process at <20° C and 75-80% humidity. The following ingredients are credited with slowing fat rancidity: nitrates, ascorbic acid (vitamin C), tocopherol, spices like rosemary, thyme, sage and smoke application.

Melting temperature of some fats		
Pork	28 - 40° C	82 - 104° F
Beef	40 - 50° C	104 - 122° F
Lamb	44 - 55° C	110 - 130° F
Chicken	24° C	75° F

In large metropolitan areas it may be difficult to get back fat and ethnic butcher stores may be the only place to carry it. Many supermarkets carry heavily salted pork fat which needs to be de-salted in cold water before use. If no back fat is available, use meats which contain more fat and grind them together. Instead of struggling with fat smearing when processing meats at warm temperature it is better to use cuts that contain a higher proportion of fat.

Fermented Sausages Made From Other Meats

Fermented sausages can be made from pork, beef, lamb, goat, venison, poultry or a combination thereof. In Germany fermented sausages are often made from equal amounts of pork and beef, in Poland pork is more popular. Hungarian and Italian sausages contain mostly pork. Naturally fermented and dried meats are made all over the world and particular climatic zones often dictate what animals can grow there. Lamas have adapted well to the high Andes of South America and will be popular meat in Bolivia and Chile. Sheep and goats generally prosper well in mountainous locations. High altitudes establish the vegetation that will grow at those levels which will attract only animals that like such a diet. Ostrich is commonly consumed in South Africa.

Chicken. Making a sausage from chicken meat only presents some problems as chicken meat exhibits high pH (breast 5.6-5.8, thigh 6.1-6.4.) and high Aw. Both factors create favorable conditions for bacteria growth. *Campylobacter jejuni* is a typical pathogen found in poultry meat. Chicken fat contains more water and less collagen structure than other fats which makes it soft and semi-liquid at room temperature. When submitted to heat treatment, chicken fat will melt inside the sausage creating oily pockets. To improve a sausage composition some pork fat should be added.

Fish. Fermented fish products are popular in countries such as the Philippines, Japan, and China. The products are not as much as fermented sausages but fermented fish paste and fish sauce which are used for general cooking. Rice is used as a filler and the source of carbohydrates for fermentation. Two known products are Balao Balao (fermented rice and shrimp) and Burong Isda (fermented rice and fish). There was research done on making fermented fish sausages and the customer acceptance in order of preference follows below:

- fish-pork, the highest score
- fish-beef
- fish-chicken

Non-fish beef-pork sausage was rated the highest of all. Fish flesh does not contain myoglobin so there will not be development of a pink color even in the presence of nitrate. The final flavor is always fishy even when other meats were added.

Venison. Sausages made of venison are commercially made in Canada and Alaska. Venison is lean meat so it should be mixed with pork back fat, hard fat trimmings or have some fatty pork or beef added. A proportion of 60% venison to 40% other meats is a good choice.

Wild game. Game meat (except deer) is at risk of being infected with trichinosis and should be submitted to freezing before use. Freezing may not kill larval cysts in bears and other wild game animals that live in *Northwestern U.S. and Alaska*. That meat has to be cooked to 160° F (71° C) internal temperature or cured according to the US government standards.

There are a few factors that influence the selection of the meat:

Local custom. People in Alaska might use caribou, moose, reindeer or bear meat. Norway is known for using different meats such as moose, reindeer, mutton, lamb, goat, horse, offal (heart, liver) and blood. Norwegian fermented sausages such as Faremorr, Sognemorr gilde, Stabbur and Tiriltunga contain beef, lamb and horse meat and are heavily smoked.

Religion. In many countries people stay away from pork, depriving themselves from eating the best quality products.

Economics. The consumption of higher value meats is reserved to the upper class and those less fortunate have to look at other combinations of meats. Sausages are made from sheep, goats, camels, horses and other meat but those materials will hardly appeal to the majority of Western consumers. Chicken is the most popular meat consumed worldwide as it is easy to raise and can be eaten by the average family at one sitting.

Curing

We have been curing meats for smoked and fermented sausages for centuries without understanding the process, We simply knew that cured meats developed a nice pink color, had better flavor and lasted longer. We knew that when meat was cured it was easier to produce consistent quality salami.

Curing is usually the step that precedes natural fermentation and its purpose is to increase the number of beneficial bacteria. Ground meat, salt, sodium nitrite, little sugar are mixed together and placed in a cooler for 72-96 hours, depending on the size of meat particles. The temperature should be around 38 - 40° F (4-5° C) to keep meat from spoiling yet providing favorable conditions for lactic, color, and flavor forming bacteria to grow. If a sausage mass (*without salt and nitrite*) were placed in a refrigerator, all types of bacteria would multiply resulting in meat spoilage. *Adding sufficient amounts of salt with nitrite/nitrate is the factor which directly influences the success of the following fermentation.*

Adding about 3% salt significantly slows down the growth of undesirable bacteria yet still permits beneficial ones (lactic acid and curing) to multiply. Beneficial lactic acid, color and flavor forming bacteria tolerate increased salt levels much better than spoilage and pathogenic bacteria. As a result spoilage is delayed but beneficial bacteria grow in numbers which will increase the chances of successful fermentation. Although increasing the salt level to 4% will prevent even more spoilage and pathogenic bacteria from growing, it will also inhibit the growth of lactic acid bacteria and this will adversely affect their growth during curing and fermentation. In the past when nitrate was used, if the curing temperature was low, there was very little nitrate curing taking place. *Micrococcus* and *Staphylococcus* curing bacteria were still sleepy at such low temperatures to strongly react with nitrate and little nitrite was released. Subsequently, not much color curing took place. Nevertheless both lactic acid and curing bacteria increased in numbers and that gave a jump start to the following fermentation process that was performed at a higher temperature.

The disadvantage of this curing process which would often last for 10 days, was the fact that *not only beneficial bacteria, but all others* such as spoilage and dangerous ones increased in numbers as well. This questions the effectiveness of the curing step as the procedure is performed at cool temperatures. Let's assume that we have 100 lactic acid bacteria in 1 gram of meat to be cured. At 40° F (4° C) they might double in 12 hours under perfect conditions. That means that after 48 hours we end up with 1,600 lactic acid bacteria ready to start fermentation. At the same time we have raised plenty of spoilage bacteria. Starter culture will bring the same number of the *desired* type of bacteria in an instant without adding any unwanted ones.

A detailed research study was performed on the microbiology of curing in regard to semi-dry fermented sausages (see reference 3) and the results were as follows:

"Little or no microbial activity was detected during the generally practiced 2-4 day holding period of the sausage prior to smoking."

Microbial activity occurred mainly during the heating and smoking period. Reduction of nitrate occurred generally during the first 2 to 16 hours of smoking and heating, while acid production was initiated usually after 8-16 hours". Increasing bacterial count by curing is the guessing game which can be completely eliminated by introducing starter culture. The sufficient numbers of lactic and curing bacteria are introduced on day one what prevents the unnecessary growth of spoilage and pathogenic bacteria. The meat enters the fermentation stage directly.

Curing Methods Compared

Traditional Method. Nitrate, no starter cultures. Sausage mass was placed for about 48 hours in a refrigerator and then stuffed into casings.		Modern Method. Nitrite/nitrate, starter cultures. Sausage mass is stuffed into casings without delay.	
Advantages	Disadvantages	Advantages	Disadvantages
Some growth of naturally occurring lactic acid (*Lactobacillus*) and curing bacteria (*Micrococcus, Staphylococcus*), protein swelling, tiny pH drop.	Unknown number and nature of bacteria, growth of spoilage and pathogenic bacteria, little curing color development (too cold for curing bacteria to process nitrate), sausage mass firming up resulting in harder stuffing.	Introduction of large numbers of lactic acid (*Lactobacillus, Pediococcus*) and curing bacteria (*Micrococcus, Staphylococcus*) of known quality. Easier to control and more predictable fermentation and drying. Color development at low temperatures. Easy stuffing.	Starter cultures may not be available in some parts of the world.

As mentioned earlier, the curing step is seldom practiced today as every manufacturer adds starter cultures for better control of the process. Nevertheless, *curing is still a fine and recommended procedure for making of any kind high quality smoked meats and sausages.*

Pan Curing

Original way to cure meat was as follows:

1. Meats were manually cut into 2" cubes, salt, sugar and nitrite were added and thoroughly mixed. Then meats were packed tightly (to remove air) about 6-8" high into pans.

2. Meats were covered with a clean cloth to prevent air from discoloring the meat and to allow gases to escape.

3. Pans were placed in a refrigerator for 3-4 days.

This time could be shortened to 48 hours by grinding meats as smaller particles cure faster.

106

Back fat is salted only as it does not contain myoglobin and no color formation will occur. However, nothing will happen if fat is mixed with salt and sodium nitrite (cure #1). Sodium nitrite will simply not react with fat.

Grinding. Commercial producers use bowl cutters for mincing meat as these machines allow cutting meat and fat down to very fine particles. A big advantage of a bowl cutter is that all ingredients can be introduced to the rotating bowl and cutting and mixing can be accomplished in the same machine. Bowl cutters work at high speeds and generate large amounts of heat which during the manufacture of regular or emulsified sausages is controlled by adding about 30% of ice into the meat. The introduction of so much water *cannot be permitted* when making fermented sausages so the temperature of the sausage mass must be carefully monitored when bowl cutters or food processors are employed.

Photo 8.4 Bowl cutter.

Grinders also generate some heat so *to produce a clean cut the meat must be cold or partially frozen*. Cutting/grinding temperatures are -2-1° C (28-30° F) for meats and -3-2° C (27-26° F) for fats. There should be easily distinguishable meat and fat particles. This can be achieved when:

- the cutting knife is sharp.
- the meat and fat are cold.

107

If the fat is not cold the smearing will occur. Meat particles will be surrounded with fat film and the drying will be slower. The degree of chopping is dictated by the recipe and local preference. Traditional Italian, Spanish and French dry sausages are chopped coarsely with 6-12 mm plate, but the majority of slow-fermented sausages are ground through 2-5 mm plate. Spreadable fermented sausages are ground with a fine plate as a small grind contributes to better spreadability. Keep in mind that that the smallest particles a grinder can produce is around 3 mm (1/8") even when the meat has been partially frozen. Obtaining 2 mm particles requires a bowl cutter.

Mixing. During the production of regular sausages spices are often mixed with water in a blender and then added to meat. This helps to distribute all ingredients more evenly and makes mixing and stuffing sausages easier. *In fermented sausages the addition of water to the sausage mass should be avoided as this creates favorable conditions for the growth of bacteria and will prolong drying.* Some recipes call for wine or vinegar which seems to contradict the above statement. Both of those liquids are very acidic in nature and although they bring extra water they make up for it by increasing the acidity of the sausage mix which inhibits bacteria growth. The temperature of the sausage mix should be between 32-40° F (0-5° C). If this temperature increases, the sausage mix should be cooled down in a refrigerator before proceeding to the stuffing step. Commercial mixers work at vacuum and at around 34° F (1° C), however, mixing at home will be done at higher temperature. When mixing meat with ingredients, it is best to follow this sequence:

1. Minced meats, starter culture, nitrite/nitrate, spices.
2. Minced fat.
3. Salt.

Starter cultures should not be mixed with salt, nitrite or spices *in advance* as unpredictable growth of culture bacteria may occur (all they need is a bit of moisture from spices). As a result starter cultures with different characteristics will be introduced into the sausage. As starter cultures are mixed with a *little* amount of water it makes sense to pour them over the meat trying to distribute them evenly. It is advisable to use gloves when hand mixing meats with ingredients as many of us carry pathogenic bacteria (*Staphylococcus aureus*) on our hands. The same bacteria reside in our throat and nasal passages so coughing and sneezing is out of the question.

Stuffing. Sausage mass can firm up very fast and should be stuffed firmly without much delay. This becomes an even bigger problem when Gdl is used. It is important not to leave any air pockets inside as they can: discolor the meat, show up as little pores later and provide oxygen to spoilage bacteria. In addition, oxygen affects the development of curing color and promotes rancidity in fats.

Spoilage bacteria *(Pseudomonas spp.)* need oxygen to survive and applying vacuum during mixing and stuffing is an effective way to inhibit their growth. At home a precaution must be made so that the sausage mix is stuffed firmly and any air pockets which are visible in a stuffed casing are picked with a needle. To remove air commercial producers perform mixing and stuffing under a vacuum at around 32° F (0° C). The stuffed sausages should enter the fermentation stage as soon as the sausages reach room temperature. Natural and synthetic casings are used as long as they allow moisture and smoke to go through. They must be able to cling to meat and shrink with it as it goes through the drying process. Natural casings are salted and they must be soaked for at least 30 minutes in cold water and then rinsed. To further reduce the possibility of any contamination by bacteria you may rinse casings briefly (in and out) with vinegar.

Conditioning. In commercial plants meat and fats are supplied in a frozen state. The process of grinding, mixing and stuffing is undertaken at a low temperature. As a result the stuffed sausage is very cold. If such a cold sausage is placed in a warmer fermenting room, the condensation will appear on the surface of the casing. To prevent this, the sausage must remain in the fermentation chamber at a prevailing temperature at low humidity (60%) and without air speed until the moisture evaporates. This might require many hours depending of course on sausage diameter. Then when the surface of the sausage becomes dry, the fermentation starts at the required temperature, humidity and air speed. At home conditions the manufacturing process will be performed at higher temperatures so condensation should not occur and the conditioning step will not be needed.

Fermentation. *The main purpose of the fermentation is to increase the microbiological safety of the sausage by increasing the acidity of the meat.* It is a biological process that preserves the meat and provides a distinctive flavor. Fermentation does not improve the taste of the sausage, on the contrary, fast fermented sausages develop a sour and tangy taste. Fermentation is performed by increasing the temperature of the sausage after stuffing. This triggers an increased activity of all types of bacteria and it is our task to keep this process under control.

There is no golden rule which will cover fermentation parameters such as temperature, time and relative humidity. This can vary from one manufacturer to another. Many manufacturers don't own climate controlled fermentation chambers and use chambers which depend on weather conditions that prevail during a particular season. As weather changes from year to year, sausages which are made in the same season may be subjected to different temperatures, humidities, and winds the next year and this makes constant quality of the product difficult to control.

Fermentation is covered in detail in Chapter 3.

Drying is covered in detail in Chapter 1.

Smoking is covered in detail in Chapter 7.

109

Cooking. This process is optional and depends on a type of a sausage that is being made. Partial or full cooking is applied to fast-fermented semi-dry sausages. Slow-fermented dry sausages are not cooked.

Storing. Sausages should be kept in a dark room which will prevent color change and fat rancidity. A little air flow (0.05-0.1 m/sec) keeps the air fresh and inhibits the formation of mold. The temperature is set to about, 50-60° F (10-15° C). The humidity should remain at around 75% as a lower humidity will increase drying and the sausage will lose more of its weight. Higher humidity and temperature may create favorable conditions for the development of mold. If any mold develops it can be easily wiped off with a solution of water and vinegar. Then the sausage can be cold smoked for a few hours which will inhibit the growth of a new mold. Molds need air to live so they are present only on the surface and in most cases there is nothing wrong with the meat itself.

Sausage Appearance, Texture and Flavor

The type of the sausage that will be produced generally dictates the manufacturing process which decides the taste and flavor of the sausage. In semi-dry sausages fermentation temperature and the amount of sugar will influence the acidity of the sausage, the flavorings will contribute to its flavor. In slow-fermented sausages the time and drying will be the major factors. Sausage appearance depends on many factors:

- choice of casing
- casing color
- meat color
- texture
- lean to fat particles ratio
- particles size

Most of these factors are established during the processing stage, however, flavor and taste components are decided by the fermentation and ripening.

Sausage Color

Sausage color depends on the meat selected, amount of nitrite added, number of curing bacteria, ratio of lean meat to fat and the length of drying. The color of *fresh meat* is determined largely by the amount of *myoglobin* a particular animal carries. The more *myoglobin* the darker the meat. Going from top to bottom, meats that contain more *myoglobin* are: horse, beef, lamb, veal, pork, dark poultry and light poultry. The amount of *myoglobin* present in meat increases with the age of the animal. Different parts of the same animal, take the turkey for example, will display a different color of meat. Muscles that are exercised frequently such as legs need more oxygen. As a result they develop a darker color unlike the breast which is white due to little exercise. This color is pretty much fixed and there is not much we can do about it unless we mix different meats together.

110

The color of *cooked* (uncured) meat varies from greyish brown for beef and grey-white for pork and is due to denaturation (cooking) of *myoglobin*. The red color usually disappears in poultry at 152° F (67° C), in pork at 158° F (70° C) and in beef at 167° F (75° C). The color of *cured* meat is pink and is due to the reaction between nitrite and *myoglobin*. The color can vary from light pink to light red and depends on the amount of *myoglobin* a particular meat cut contains and the amount of nitrite added to the cure. In cured meat nitrite reacts with myoglobin and creates nitrosomyoglobin which is responsible for a deep red color. As the meat is heated the color is permanently fixed and becomes a typical pink color of cured meats. *Slow-fermented dry sausages are never cooked, however, the red color of nitrosomyoglobin becomes stabilized by drying.* Dark spices like nutmeg, caraway, cloves, and allspice can darken the color of the sausage. Paprika is a known colorant and will impart a reddish color into the sausage. Smoked paprika is added to Spanish dry sausages making them orange-red.

Sausage Texture and Flavor

In a good salami meat and fat particles should be easily distinguishable. This can be accomplished if the smearing is avoided and raw materials are processed in a very cold state. The choice of meat, fat and processing steps such as cutting, grinding and mixing will initially decide the texture of the sausage, however, fermentation and drying will influence the texture and the flavor even more.

The flavor is harder to define as it usually consists of two components: the taste and the flavor. The taste part can be described as salty, bitter or sour, however, the flavor fraction is harder to define as it contains an immense number of aroma components. The complex flavor of fermented sausages have been described in many ways: popcorn, crackers, mushroom, earthy, garlic, onion, sweaty socks, vomit, butter, fruity, rose, orange, honey, soap, clean laundry, leather, paint, rubber, leather, horse, olives, sourdough and others.

Fast-fermented (semi-dry) sausages. Fermentation process is fast and pH drop is large, the latter contributing to a firmer texture. As the pH drops below pH 5.3 the forces that bind water become weaker and the water is easily released making the sausage firmer. This is known as "iso-electric point" and happens around pH 4.8. This means that a significant amount of drying can take place during the fermentation stage if enough acidity has been produced. More water will be removed during the following smoking step. The firmer texture greatly improves sliceability which is a desired feature in all but spreadable fermented sausages. As fast-fermented sausages usually lose only 10-15% of their original weight, the proper drying step may not be needed at all.

The flavor of fast-fermented sausages will be sourly as there is no ripening stage. *Staphylococcus* flavor producing bacteria will not survive high acidity levels and are *not even included* in fast acting starter cultures. As a result a fast-fermented sausage stands no chance to develop any complex flavors associated with dry sausages.

Slow-fermented (dry) sausages. *Time makes dry sausages.* Time is the main factor that develops complex flavor in dry sausages. Time is the luxury that a commercial plant can hardly afford, but a hobbysit has plenty of it. The conclusion is simple; high quality slow-fermented product can easily be made at home that will out shine the typical commercially made products.

Slow-fermented dry sausages exhibit little acidity which means that thay have been made with very little or no sugar at all. As a result the sausage never reaches pH 4.8 iso-electric point that promotes removal of moisture. There is very little drying in the fermentation stage and it may be said that sometimes when sugar has not been added, there is no fermentation stage at all. The stuffed sausage simply enters the fermentation-drying stage. As there was little moisture removal during the fermentation stage, the texture of the sausage is anything but firm. In simple terms the slow drying process is responsible for the hard texture of the dry sausage.

As fermented sausages are characterized by very little acidity the flavor is never sourly. This also means that *Staphylococcus* flavor producing bacteria which are sensitive to acidity, are never threatened and can continue reacting with meat proteins and fat particles developing hundreds of different aromatic flavors. If you look at the composition of T-SPX slow-fermenting starter culture you will see that *Staphylococcus xylosus* flavor forming bacteria is included.

The flavor of fermented sausages improves during storage due to a slight pH increase. This is a result of bacterial activity (proteolysis) and action of yeasts and molds which consume lactic acid.

It should be pointed out that as the sausage slowly dries out it loses moisture, but not the original amount of salt which remains inside. That will change the proportion of salt in regards to the weight of the meat and the sausage should taste saltier. The truth is that this is hardly noticeable due to the bacterial action on proteins and fats which somehow covers up this saltiness.

Dry sausages carried in American supermarkets are commonly heat treated. They might be called salami or pepperoni, but have very little in common with the original products. Quote from Federal Register: Feb 27, 2001 (Vol 66. # 39): *Cattle and sheep may carry E. coli O157:H7 in the intestinal tract at the time of slaughter. However, among commercially-prepared meat products, only those that contain beef have been implicated in a number of foodborne illnesses associated with this pathogen.*

Many smaller plants either stopped making their traditionally fermented sausages, removed *beef* from the recipe, or added a *cooking step* to avoid fighting with meat inspectors who were enforcing government regulations. As a result the huge industry of semi-dry sausages has developed and it is hard to find a true dry fermented sausage.

US Standards For Making Fermented Sausages

In the USA the FSIS of the United States Department of Agriculture requires that the shelf-stable dry sausages be nitrite cured, fermented, smoked, reach a final pH of 5.0 or less, and have a moisture/protein ratio of 1.9:1 or less.

Dry sausages are products that, as a result of bacterial action or direct acidulation should reach a pH of 5.3 or less and are then dried to remove 25-50% of the moisture, resulting in a moisture/protein ratio complying with the standards.

Semi-dry sausages are products that as a result of bacterial action or direct acidulation should reach a pH of 5.3 or less and are then dried to remove 15% of the moisture, resulting in a moisture/protein ratio of 3.1:1 or less. Some semi-dry sausages receive a pasteurization treatment following the fermentation period and become shelf stable. Since the pH is lowered during the fermentation period, the degree-hour concept applies only to the time required to reach a pH of 5.3.

Fermented and acidulated sausages (citric acid, lactic acid or GDL added) shall attain a pH of 5.3 or lower *within the proper time frame* (defined in temperature-degrees below) in order to control the growth of pathogenic bacteria such as *E. coli 0157:H* and *Staphylococcus aureus*. *During fermentation of sausages to a pH 5.3, it is necessary to limit the time during which the sausage is exposed to temperatures exceeding 60° F (15.6° C),* otherwise the product will spoil, even though the recommended pH was attained. This time frame is temperature dependent and these are the following criteria:

Time in F degree-hours **above 60° F** (16° C)	Max. chamber temperature
less than 1200	less than 90° F (32° C)
< 1000	90 - 100° F (32 - 38° C)
< 900	greater than 100° F (38 °C)
Degrees are measured as the excess over 60° F (15.6° C), the critical temperature at which staphylococcal growth effectively begins.	

Constant Temperature Fermentation

F Degree-hours **above 60° F** (16° C)	Chamber Temperature		Maximum hours to pH 5.3
	° F	° C	
1200	75	24	80
1200	80	27	60
1200	85	30	48
1000	90	32	33
1000	95	35	28
1000	100	38	25
900	105	41	20
900	110	44	18

The above table provides maximum hours that a product may be fermented at given **constant** fermentation temperature (measured in ° F) to obtain pH 5.3. For example, at 80° F (27° C) constant temperature a sausage must reach pH 5.3 within 60 hours or less. Those hours can also be calculated for any temperature and the following examples demonstrate how.

Example A: Sausage fermented for 48 hours at the constant temperature 86° F (30° C) to pH of 5.3.

For the calculation time in degrees over 60° F (16° C) is taken and:
Degrees: 86 - 60 = 26
Hours: 48
Degree-hours (above 60° F) = 26 x 48 = 1248 degree hours. The result **fails** the guidelines of 1200 degree-hours by 48 hours. The time has to be decreased by 2 hours:
Degree-hours = 26 x **46** = 1196 degree-hours. Process A **passes** guidelines of 1200 degree-hours.

Example B: Constant temperature 90° F for 40 hours with a pH decline to 5.3
Degrees: 90 - 60 = 30
Hours: 40
Degree-hours: 30 x 40 = 1200 degree-hours
Process B **fails** the guideline limit of 1000 degree-hours.

Variable Temperature Fermentation

In many cases fermentation proceeds at different temperatures and for each temperature setting, a separate degree-hours are calculated and then added together. In testing each process, each step-up in the progression is analyzed for the number of degree-hours it contributes, with the highest temperature used in the fermentation process determining the degree-hour limitation. Degree hours is calculated *for each temperature* during fermentation.

Example C:

F Degree hours above 60° F	Chamber ° F	Adjusted Temperature	Degrees Result	Maximum hours to pH 5.3
10 hrs	75	75 - 60 =	15	10 x 15 = 150
10 hrs	85	85 - 60 =	25	10 x 25 = 250
14 hrs	95	95 - 60 =	35	14 x 35 = 490
			Total degree-hours:	890

In the above example a product was fermented at three different temperatures (75, 85 and 95° F) for a total time of 34 hours.

114

The total sum of the calculated degree-hours is 890 hours which is less than the maximum of 1000 hours for 90 - 100° F temperature range.

Process C **passes** the guidelines.

Example D:

F Degree hours above 60° F	Chamber ° F	Adjusted Temperature	Degrees	Maximum hours to pH 5.3
10 hrs	75	75 - 60 =	15	10 x 15 = 150
12 hrs	85	85 - 60 =	25	12 x 25 = 300
18 hrs	98	98 - 60 =	38	18 x 38 = 684
			Total degree-hours:	1134

Process D **fails** the guideline because the limit is set at 1000 degree-hours for these times and temperatures and the process has taken 1134 degree-hours to reach pH 5.3

Understanding these tables is of utmost importance as one can set his own fermentation temperatures and times without blindly relying on unproven recipes and be in strict compliance with government standards. Besides, it provides a great deal of satisfaction knowing that the process is safe and that we are in total control.

8.12 Canadian Fermentation Standards (MH MOP, Chapter 14.10.3 (15) - Fermented Meat Products).

As most of the world uses the metric system we are enclosing Canadian Food Inspection Agency standards for fermentation times which are based on degrees Centigrade. Those standards are based on degree/temperatures and the same starting temperature of 60° F (15.6° C) is used. At this temperature 60° F (15.6° C) *Staphylococcus aureus* starts to grow and produce toxins.

Degree/Hours are the product of time as measured in hours at a particular fermentation temperature multiplied by the degrees over 60° F (15.6° C).

Degree/hours = time (hours) x temperature in excess of 60° F (15.6° C).

Fermented sausages must reach pH 5.3 or lower within a certain time, depending on temperature. The reason being that at pH < 5.3 *Staphylococcus aureus* growth is inhibited.

Time in C degree-hours above 15.6° C (60° F)	Maximum chamber temperature
less than 665	less than 33° C, (90° F)
< 555	33-37° C (90 - 100° F)
< 500	greater than 37° C, (100° F)

Constant Temperature Fermentation

The table below provides the maximum hours that a product may be fermented at a given **constant** fermentation temperature (measured in ° C) to obtain pH 5.3. For example at 86° F constant temperature a sausage must reach pH 5.3 within 46.2 hours or less. Those hours can also be calculated for any temperature and the following examples demonstrate how.

C degree-hours limit for the corresponding temperature	Chamber Temperature		Maximum hours to pH 5.3
	° F	° C	
665	68	20	150.0
665	71.6	22	103.4
665	75.2	24	78.9
665	78.8	26	63.8
665	82.4	28	53.6
665	86	30	46.2
665	89.2	32	40.5
555	91.4	33	31.8
555	93.2	34	30.1
555	95	35	28.6
555	96.8	36	27.2
555	98.6	37	25.9
500	100.4	38	22.3
500	104	40	20.5
500	107.6	42	18.9
500	111.2	44	17.6
500	114.8	46	16.4
500	118.4	48	15.4
500	122	50	14.5

Example A: Fermentation room temperature is a constant 26° C. It takes 55 hours for the pH to reach 5.3.
Degrees above 15.6° C: 26 - 15.6 = 10.4
Hours to reach pH of 5.3: 55
Degree/Hours calculation: (10.4) x (55) = 572 degree/hours
The resulting degree/hours limit (less than 33° C) is 665 degree/hours.
Conclusion: Process A **passes** the test because its degree/hours is less than the limit.

116

Example B: Fermentation room temperature is a constant 35° C. It takes 40 hours for the pH to reach 5.3.

Degrees above 15.6° C: 35 - 15.6 = 19.4

Hours to reach pH of 5.3: 40

Degree/Hours calculation: (19.4) x (40) = 776 degree/hours

The corresponding degree/hours limit (between 33 and 37°C) is 555 degree/hours.

Conclusion: Process B **fails** the test because its degree/hours exceeds the limit.

Example C: Fermentation room temperature is a constant 25° C. It takes 60 hours for the pH to reach 5.3.

Degrees above 15.6° C: 25 - 15.6 = 9.4

Hours to reach pH of 5.3: 60

Degree/Hours calculation: (9.4) x (60) = 564 degree/hours

The corresponding degree/hours limit (less than 33° C) is 665 degree/hours.

Conclusion: Process C **passes** the test because its degree/hours is less than the limit.

Variable Temperature Fermentation

In many cases fermentation proceeds at different temperatures and for each temperature setting, separate degree-hours are calculated and then added together. In testing each process, each step-up in the progression is analyzed for the number of degree-hours it contributes, with the highest temperature used in the fermentation process determining the degree-hour limitation. Degree hours is calculated for each temperature during fermentation.

Example D: It takes 35 hours for a product to reach a pH of 5.3 or less. Fermentation room temperature is 24° C for the first 10 hours, 30° C for second 10 hours and 35° C for the final 15 hours.

Time in C degree hours above 15.6° C (60° F)	Chamber ° C	Adjusted Temperature	Degrees Result	Maximum hours to pH 5.3
10	24	24 - 15.6 =	8.4	8.4 x 10 = 84
10	30	30 - 15.6 =	14.4	14.4 x 10 = 144
15	35	35 - 15.6 =	19.4	19.4 x 15 = 291
			Total C degree-hours:	519

The highest temperature reached = 35° C

The corresponding degree/hour limit = 555 (between 33 and 37° C)

Conclusion: Process D **passes** the test because its degree/hours is less than the limit.

117

Example E: It takes 38 hours for a product to reach a pH of 5.3 or less. Fermentation room temperature is 24° C for the first 10 hours, 30° C for second 10 hours and 37° C for the final 18 hours.

Time in C degree hours above 15.6° C (60° F)	Chamber ° C	Adjusted Temperature	Degrees Result	Maximum hours to pH 5.3
10	24	24 - 15.6 =	8.4	8.4 x 10 = 84
10	30	30 - 15.6 =	14.4	14.4 x 10 = 144
18	37	37 - 15.6 =	21.4	21.4 x 18 = 385.2
			Total C degree-hours:	613.2

The highest temperature reached = 37° C
The corresponding degree/hour limit = 555 (between 33 and 37° C)
Conclusion: Process E **fails** the test because its degree/hours exceeds the limit.

Quote from The Canadian Food Inspection Agency "Meat Hygiene Manual of Procedures" - Chapter 4

(iv) Disposition of lots which have not met degree/hours limits:

The inspector in charge must be notified of each case where degree/hours limits have been exceeded. Such lots must be held and samples of product need to be submitted for microbiological laboratory examination after the drying period has been completed. Analyses should be done, at least for *Staphylococcus aureus* and its enterotoxin, and for principal pathogens such as *E. coli O157:H7, Salmonella, Listeria monocytogenes*, etc.

If the bacteriological evaluation proves that there are fewer than 104 *Staphylococcus aureus* per gram, that neither enterotoxin nor other pathogens are detected, then the product may be sold provided it is labelled as requiring refrigerated storage. In the case of an *Staphylococcus aureus* level higher than 104 per gram with no enterotoxin present, or if other pathogens are present in very low numbers the product may be used in the production of a compatible cooked product but only if the heating process destroys all of the pathogens present.

In the case where *Staphylococcus aureus* enterotoxin is detected in the product, irrespective of the level of viable Staphylococcus aureus cells, the product shall be destroyed.

Safety Options And Examples of Validated Processes

Prior to 1994 there were no specific rules controlling the manufacture of fermented sausages in the USA. Then at the end of 1994 about two dozen cases of *E.coli 0157:H7* poisoning were reported in the Pacific Nort West and in Northern California. This outbreak of *E.coli 0157:H7* poisoning was attributed to the consumption of dry sausages. More cases associated with *E.coli 0157:H7* followed in Australia (1995) and Canada (1998, 1999). To date, outbreaks of *E.coli 0157:H7* linked to the consumption of dry/semi-dry fermented sausages have been associated with *beef meat ingredients*.

The USDA panicked and following the 1994 US outbreak, a set of stringent regulations were introduced and aimed at commercial producers. In 1966 the final protocol was drafted which requires commercial producers of dry and semi-dry fermented sausages to follow 1 of 5 safety options:

1. Utilize a heat process as listed in 9 Code of Federal Regulations, 318.17 - achieve a 5-log kill using a heat process (145° F, 63° C) for 4 minutes (5-log kill is the time required to destroy 90% of the organisms present).

2. Include a validated 5 log inactivation treatment.

3. Conduct a "hold and test" program. This option requires finished product testing and is expensive.

4. Propose other approaches to assure 5-log kill.

5. Initiate a hazard analysis critical point (HACCP) system that includes raw batter testing and a 2-log inactivation in fermentation and drying.

All those options must address *Salmonella, Trichinella* and *Staphylococcus*. FSIS expanded the *Staphylococcus aureus* monitoring program to include *E.coli 0157:H7*. Since some fermented products are fully cooked, it should be reiterated that thorough cooking destroys *E.coli 0157:H7*, post process contamination must be avoided. At the same time, it has been concluded that *Salmonella* may also be found in the resulting product.

These regulations created a nightmare for little producers and some stopped making fermented products altogether, others removed beef from recipes and others reluctantly started to cook the sausages.

It is strongly advisable that the reader becomes familiar with the first two options as they can be easily adapted to home conditions.

Options 3-5 require in house laboratory testing and will be utilized by commercial meat processors.

Option 1. Include as part of the manufacture of the sausage, one of the following heat processes which is recognized as controlling E.coli 0157:H7.

Minimum Internal Temperature		Minimum processing time in minutes after the minimum temperature has been reached
°F	°C	
130	54.4	121 min
131	55.0	97 min
132	55.6	77 min
133	56.1	62 min
134	56.7	47 min
135	57.2	37 min
136	57.8	32 min
137	58.4	24 min
138	58.9	19 min
139	59.5	15 min
140	60.0	12 min
141	60.6	10 min
142	61.1	8 min
143	61.7	6 min
144	62.2	5 min
145	62.8	4 min

Option 2. Use a manufacturing process (combination of fermentation, heating, holding and/drying) which has already been scientifically validated to achieve a 5 log kill of E. coli 0157:H7.

The following processes have been scientifically validated as achieving a 5-log kill or greater reduction of *E. coli 0167H:7*.

Fermentation chamber temperature		pH at the end of fermentation process	Casing diameter	Subsequent process (dry, hold or cook)	Reference
° F	° C				
70	21	> 5.0	< 55 mm	heat (1 hr @ 110° F and 6 hours @ 125 ° F)	1
90	32	< 4.6	< 55 mm	hold @ 90° F for > 6 days	1
90	32	< 4.6	< 55 mm	heat (1 hr @ 110° F then 6 hrs @ 125° F)	1
90	32	< 4.6	56 - 105 mm	heat (1hr @100° F, 1 hr @ 110° F, 1 hr @ 120° F, then 7 hrs @125° F)	1
90	32	> 5.0	56 - 105 mm	heat (1hr @100° F, 1 hr @ 110° F, 1 hr @ 120° F, then 7 hrs @125° F)	1
96	36	< 5.0	< 55 mm	heat (128° F internal product temperature x 60 minutes) and dry (at 55° F and 65% relative humidity to a moisture protein ratio of < 1.6;1)	2
110	43	< 4.6	< 55 mm	hold @ 110° F for > 4 days	1
110	43	< 4.6	56 - 105 mm	hold @ 110° F for > 4 days	1
110	43	> 5.0	56 - 105 mm	hold @ 110° F for > 4 days	1

Ref. 1: Nicholson, R., et al, *Dry fermented sausages and Escherichia coli 0157:H7*. National Cattlemen's Beef Association, Research Report Number 11-316, Chicago, Illinois, 1996.

Ref. 2: Hinkens, J.C., et al, *Validation of Pepperoni Processes for Control of Escherichia coli 0157:h7*, Journal of Food Protection, Volume 59, Number 12, 1996, pp.1260-1266.

121

Examples of Validated Processes

Because there are many different combinations of factors that impact the safety and stability of fermented sausages, it is hard to come up with one validation study that will apply in each case. A commonly used process that has been validated is to achieve a pH < 5.0, followed by a heat process to achieve 128° F (53.3° C) internal temperature for 1 hour.

Summer Sausage - the sausage is fermented with a starter culture at 110° F, (43.3° C) until the pH is 4.7 or lower, then cooked to 152° F (66.7° C) internal meat temperature. The final pH 4.4, Aw 0.964.

Pepperoni - the sausage is fermented with a starter culture at 102° F, (38.9° C) until the pH is 5.7 or lower, then cooked to 128° F (53.3° C) internal meat temperature. The final pH 4.7, Aw 0.896.

In the majority of cases fermented sausages are made from a combination of pork and beef. Using safety option 1 or 2 takes care of *E.coli 0157:H7* and *Salmonella*. Cold temperature, cleanliness and proper sanitation procedures take care of *Listeria monocytogenes*. Nevertheless, pork must be taken care of as it may be contaminated with *trichinae*. If pork meat was not previously frozen according to the government standards for destruction of *trichinae* (see Appendix), it must be heat treated:

Heat treatment to ensure destruction of Trichinella in pork		
Minimum internal temperature		Minimum time in minutes
° F	° C	
130	54	60
131	55	30
133	56	15
135	57	6
136	58	3
138	59	2
140	60	1
142	61	1
144	62	1
145	63	instant

It can be noted (Option 1, page 120) that the heat treatment of the sausage for destruction of *E. coli 0157:H7* will take care of *trichinae* as well.

Chapter 9

Slow-Fermented Sausages

Production of Slow-Fermented Sausages

The technology of making dry sausages relies on drying. The water content of finished dry sausages is below 35% which correspond to Aw 0.90. When stored at 60° F (15° C), 70-75% humidity, such a sausage will last for at least one year.

A curing process normally precedes fermentation when cultures are not added. Then a sausage mass is re-mixed, stuffed into casings and introduced to a fermentation chamber. The optimum temperature is around 68° F (20° C) as it stimulates the growth of lactic acid bacteria while suppresing the growth of spoilage bacteria. Lactic acid bacteria start metabolizing sugar slowly and the acidity in the meat starts to build up. This gives curing and flavor forming bacteria time to develop flavor so typical of traditionally fermented dry sausages. As little sugar is added the final pH drop is small so there is very little total acidity. This acidity combined with ongoing drying creates a hostile environment for the growth of spoilage and pathogenic bacteria.

This traditional method perfected in hundreds of years was not chosen for its outstanding qualities, but it was the only way we knew about making sausages that could be stored at room temperature. Our ancestors would be more than happy to use starter cultures and Gdl to produce stable sausages in as little as 3 days, but the technology was not available then.

The pH drop in finished sausages varies from 5.0 to 5.5, therefore it is difficult to determine when the fermentation stops and when the drying begins. For all practical purposes the process may be thought of as one long drying step. German books define it as "Reifung" and although exact translation means *maturing* or *ripening* in reality it covers steps such as fermentation, drying, and color and flavor development.

Flavor

Complex flavor of dry sausage is being developed in all stages of the process: fermentation, drying, ripening and even in storage. The true salami flavor of a slow-fermented sausage depends mainly on the breakdown of sugars, fats and proteins during the fermentation and drying processes. These reactions are products of microbiological action of color and flavor forming bacteria.

A small amount of sugar will not produce enough acidity to develop a sourly flavor. In true Hungarian salami the addition of starter cultures and sugars are not permitted in order to eliminate any possibility of the acidic taste of the sausage.

General Guidelines

Salt. Use 3.0% salt to prevent growth of undesirable bacteria. Keep in mind that the salt content in percent in the finished sausage will be higher than in the sausage mix, as the sausage loses a substantial amount of water during the process. Salt content in the finished sausage can be around 4.0-4.5%, however, this increased saltiness is somehow hard to sense in dry products.

Sodium nitrite. Sodium nitrite can be applied to regular smoked sausages at 150 ppm (parts per million) which corresponds to 2.5 g (1/2 tsp) of cure #1 per 1 kg (2.2 lb) of meat. For slow-fermented sausages cure #2 is the best choice. The maximum amount of sodium nitrite allowed by law for dry meat products is 625 ppm because sodium nitrite dissipates in time rather quickly and dry products take a long time to produce. When the product is finished only a small amount of residual nitrite remains.

Do not decrease the amount of salt or nitrite as these provide the only protection against spoilage and pathogenic bacteria, especially during the initial stage of the process.

Sugar. The amount of sugar (if used) is usually small (0.1-0.3%), just enough to provide enough acidity to protect meat against spoilage bacteria in the initial stage of the process. A smart solution will be to use the following sugar combination:

1/3 of dextrose (glucose) at 0.1% (1 g/1 kg of meat).
2/3 of sucrose (table sugar), at 0.2% (2 g/1 kg of meat).

Dextrose will be *immediately* metabolized by bacteria and a small pH drop will be obtained. This amount of acidity, however small, provides an immediate safety protection for the meat. During that time bacteria is also breaking sucrose into dextrose and fructose so even more acidity will be produced, however, bacteria need some time to extract dextrose from sugar.

Curing. This step takes place when no starter cultures are added.

- cut meats into 1" (2.5 cm) pieces, mix with salt, cure and sugar, pack tightly in a container, cover with clean cloth and leave in refrigerator for 72-96 hours. Grind meat with a correct plate, mix with spices and stuff into casing OR
- grind meats with a correct plate, mix with salt, cure, sugar and spices, pack tightly in a container, cover with parchment and leave in refrigerator for 48 hours. Re-mix meat mass (it firms up during curing) and stuff into casing.

124

Conditioning

If stuffed sausages are taken from a cooler or are stuffed at very low temperatures, they have to go through a *conditioning stage* to allow moisture to escape. They are placed at room temperature, prevailing humidity, no air draft, until there is no moisture on the surface.

Fermentation

Fermentation is covered in detail in Chapter 3. Making a traditional slow-fermented sausage at home without starter cultures is not recommended as this is a complicated process which requires great operating skills.

Fermentation without starter culture. Cure meat-see Chapter 8. Place sausages for 3-8 days in a fermentation room at 64-72° F (18-22° C). It is understood that some sugar has been added. The higher the temperature, the shorter the fermentation time and the greater danger of spoilage when no starter cultures are added.

Fermentation starts basically from the moment the sausages are placed in the drying/ripening chamber at around 68° F (20° C) and 95% humidity. Both, the temperature and the humidity are gradually decreased every day or two. Once it has been decided that the fermentation has been accomplished, the sausages enter long drying/ripening process at <60° F (<16° C) and 75-80% humidity. As mentioned earlier it is nor easy to determine when fermentation ends and when drying begins when a small amount of sugar is added. The sausages are considered dry when they lost 30-40% of their original weight.

Fermentation with starter culture.

There is no need to cure meat. Follow instructions which come with a starter culture. T-SPX is a very popular culture for making slow-fermented sausages. When applied at 64-75° F (18-24° C) the culture will produce great dry sausages, low in acidity and rich in aromatic flavor so typical of Southern European sausages. You can even use F-LC culture which can ferment al low or high temperatures.

Maximum recommended temperature for slow-fermented sausages made *with sugar and starter culture* is:

75° F (24° C) when pH drops to <5.3 within 72 hours.
85° F (29° C) when pH drops to <5.3 within 48 hours.

Remember, however, that slow-fermented sausages are made with a little sugar so the pH usually remains at pH 5.8 or higher. Ensuing removal of moisture guarantees security.

	Slow Fermented (Dry) Sausages	
	With culture	**Without culture**
Fermentation temp.	20°-24° C, 68°-76° F	16°-20° C, 62°-68° F
Ferm. humidity %	90 → 85	90 → 85
Fermentation time	3-5 days	3-8 days
Drying temperature	16° → 12° C, 60°-54° F	16° → 12° C, 60°- 54° F
Drying humidity %	80 → 75	80 → 75
Drying time	3-4 months	3-4 months
Sugar	Sucrose	Sucrose
Curing agent	Nitrate, or nitrite plus nitrate (cure #2)	Nitrate, or nitrite plus nitrate (cure #2)
Final pH	5.2-5.6	5.2-5.6
Expected final Aw	0.88	0.88
Weight loss	>30%	>30%
		Prior to fermentation, meat is cured.

Most slow-fermented sausages are ready in 3-4 weeks, however, the ripening process will continue during additional drying and storing. There is very little difference between the two, as both processes, drying and storing take place at 50-60° F (10-15° C).

A typical traditionally produced salami process

Pork pH 5.9 Beef pH 5.8	Temp.	Humid-ity %	Air Speed m/sec	Time	pH	Aw
Conditioning	20-25° C 68-77° F	60-70	none	1-6 hrs		
Fermenting	18-25° C 66-77° F	95-92	0.8-0.5	2-4 days	5.6-5.2	0.96-0.94
Drying	22-18° C 72-66° F	90-85	0.5-0.2	5-10 days	5.2-4.8	0.95-0.90
Drying	< 15° C < 60° F	80-75	0.2-0.1	4-8 weeks	5.0-4.6	0.92-0.85
When the sausage achieves acidity pH of 5.2 or lower and water activity Aw 0.89, it is considered microbiologically stable and safe to consume.						
Storing	15-10° C 60-50° F	80-75	0.1-0.05	after 8 weeks of drying →	pH increase up to 5.4	0.89-0.85
During the storage period the pH will increase, the sausage will be less acidic and its flavor will be more mellow and more cheesy.						

Day	Process	Temp.		Humidity %	Air speed m/sec
		° C	° F		
1	fermentation *	24	75	95	0.8
2		22	72	95	0.6
3		22	72	93	0.5
4		22	72	93	0.5
5		20	68	90	0.4
6		20	68	90	0.4
7	drying	18	64	88	0.3
8		18	64	88	0.3
9		18	64	85	0.2
10		18	64	85	0.2
11		18	64	80	0.1
12		18	64	80	0.1
13........	drying continues until desired weight loss is obtained (1-2 months)	16-12	60-54	80-75	< 0.1
	storing	10-15	50-59	75-80	< 0.1
* Fermentation can last for 2 days at 24 → 22° C or 3 days at 20° C. Conditioning (if needed) may precede fermentation.					

Drying. Sausages are transferred to the drying room 54-62° F (12-16° C), 65-75% humidity. Dry sausages require 30-40% moisture loss which should be accomplished in 6-8 weeks. When sausage loses 30% of its weight its Aw is around 0.86. Drying times are influenced by the sausage recipe composition and casing diameter. The larger diameter of the sausage the longer the drying process. Drying starts from the moment the sausage is stuffed, even at refrigerator temperature. Keep in mind that slow-fermented dry sausage stuffed into 24 mm casing will lose at least 30% of its moisture when it is ready for distribution and its diameter will become accordingly smaller. Such a fermented sausage is usually defined as meat stick and can be dried within a week. A sausage stuffed into 60 mm casing will be at its best after 3 months of production time. Typical ripening times:

Salami - French Ménage, 55-60 mm, ripened for 28-32 days
Salami - Italian Turista, ripened for 14-21 days
Spanish Salchichón, ripened for 14-18 days,
French Varzi and Italian Crespone Milano, both 90-100 mm, ripened for 60-70 days.

During ripening the sausage acquires its aromatic flavor. There is no specific time that defines the end of ripening and the process continues through drying and storing stages.

Check the bottom end of the sausage for the following symptoms:

Sausage end	Drying conditions
Flexible	good
Dry	humidity too low or air speed too fast
Wet	humidity too high or air speed too slow

Note: research that was done on flavor of traditionally produced dry sausages concluded that sausages made with nitrate exhibited superior quality to those that were made with nitrite only. A panel of professional testers-judges has made this finding (ref.13).

Smoking. If a smoky flavor is desired, you may apply a thin cold smoke at 64° F (18° C) or lower after fermentation has ended or during drying. The length of smoking time depends on the diameter of the casing and the color desired. Unsmoked dry sausages are often called *air-dried.*

In order to produce quality dry sausages follow these three basic rules:

1. Keep fermenting and the first stage of drying around 64-68° F (18-20° C).
2. Control humidity in such a way that the casing of the sausage is not overly wet or dry.
3. Apply cold smoke at 59-68° F (15-20° C).

Storing Sausages

After drying or smoking sausages are hung in a dark storage room at 50-60° F (10-15° C), 75-80% humidity where the process of color and flavor development will continue. Sausage will keep on drying what will additionally contribute to its stability. A weak draft should be present (0.05-1.0 m/sec)

Molds

Mold is desired on many traditionally made dry sausages. The distinction must be made between the wild mold which is produced by unknown strains of mold present in the air and the cultured mold grown in a laboratory and packed as starter culture. The wild mold can be grey, green or black while the cultured mold will be white or creamy. It goes without saying that the sausage covered with questionable color of mold should be discarded. The fault lies partly with the operator not paying attention to the process as mold needs plenty of moisture to grow. That of course is due to high humidity and insufficient air speed. More moisture is produced than being removed, the equilibrium is shaken and the mold appears. In these conditions the sausage becomes slimy to the touch and the mold starts to appear. This can easily be corrected by wiping the mold off a with a cloth soaked in salt solution or vinegar. Mold needs oxygen to survive and that

128

is why it is present on the surface only. The inside of the sausage should be fine.

Smoking is an effective method of mold control, however, it will prevent mold for a certain time only. If mold reappears, it should be wiped off again, cold smoke should be applied for 3-4 hours and the sausage can keep on drying. If smoking is not employed, mold can be prevented by spraying or dipping sausages in 15% solution of potassium sorbate which is usually applied after 2-3 days.

Planned growing of cultured mold offers two benefits:

1. It creates a secondary skin which slows down drying. Slower drying provides more time for curing and flavor producing bacteria to develop more intense color and flavor.

2. At the end of the drying process molds start to consume lactic acid which lowers acidity and develops a milder flavor. It may be considered a reversed pH drop. Mold covered sausages exhibit more complex and aromatic flavor.

The smoke should not be applied to molded sausages as soot and unburnt smoke particles will adhere to white mold and the result will be a black unsightly surface. If both the smoky flavor and white mold are desired, the acceptable method is to cold smoke back fat before grinding.

There are mold starter cultures made by Chr-Hansen, for example Mold-600 which promote the desirable mold growth. A solution of culture mold and water is applied onto the surface of the casing where it will grow in the form of a white mold through the drying/ripening process.

Molds can be applied to sausages by dipping them into a mold-solution straight after filling, or the solution can be sprayed later on again if mold growth is unsatisfactory. It is a good idea to spray solution on smokesticks and carts as well, however, be advised that it might be difficult to get rid of mold from the drying chamber later on. It is recommended to have a separate chamber for sausages that will be covered with mold. Home improvised drying chambers such as refrigerators are easy to sanitize with a bleach solution so recurring mold should not be the problem. Molds need at least 75% humidity to grow. Higher temperatures also favor their growth.

When *Penicillium* mold cultures are used, they are applied to sausages just before the sausages enter the fermentation room. If mold develops and it is not desired, it can be easily wiped off with a cloth saturated with a salt solution or vinegar. Commercial producers dip sausages into 10-20% solution of potassium sorbate which effectively prevents mold growth, but the fact must be mentioned on the label. Wild growing mold on the sausage surface is of dubious nature and poses the risk to the sausage. Its color can be white, grey, yellow, brown, or black and the length and density may vary. Generally white or white-grey molds are fine but it is still a wild mold, and it would be much wiser to use mold growing starter cultures.

Talc and Rice Flour

Molds often don't grow uniformly and uneven surface coverage may be expected. Sprinkling sausages with talc powder or rice flour is a commonly used fix.

Dips

Dips are decorative edible solutions, based on gelatin that are applied to the surface of the sausages. They must adhere to the surface fast and well and they should be elastic enough to shrink with the sausage. The sausages must be mature and dry in order not to shrink too much in time.

Preparation

- If the sausage was kept in a refrigerator it should be brought to room temperature.
- The casing is fully removed to expose the meat. If it is oily it should be wiped off with a paper towel. The casing is discarded.
- A mixture of desired spices, crushed peppers, herbs, dried fruits, nuts or shredded cheese is prepared. The mixture is spread on the table.
- Gelatin is mixed with water at around 122-140° F (50-60° C). The gelatin solution is poured into a narrow and long pan.
- The sausage is immersed into gelatin solution.
- The sausage is rolled all around over the decorative mixture.
- The sausage is hung for 30 minutes to allow gelatinized mixture to adhere.
- The procedure is repeated (immersion, rolling, hanging).
- The sausage is placed in a storage room.

Heating and Drying. Slow-fermented sausages are usually dried only but they can be submitted to heat treatment as well. The product can be partially cooked to 120-140° F (49-60° C) or fully cooked to 155-160° F (68-71° C), both methods provide a means of destroying pathogens potentially present in meat. Applying heat too *early* is not recommended as *heat will kill the color and flavor forming bacteria* and no more flavor development will take place. When submitted to heating after fermentation the sausage initially dries fast, but then the drying slows down due to surface drying and skin formation. Sausages not submitted to high temperatures exhibit more of a "raw" taste and firm bite with a definite fat and lean meat differentiation. Fully cooked sausages exhibit a hard bite and little fat and lean definition due to fat melting.

Chapter 10

Fast-Fermented Sausages

Semi-Dry Fermented Sausages

The semi-dry fermented sausages are coarse ground fermented products that can be made in a traditional way or they can be made with starter cultures. *They are made safe by acidification to pH 5.3 or less.* In addition they must lose 15-25% of moisture. The moisture can be removed by drying/smoking or cooking.

In today's terms semi-dry sausages are sausages which are fast or medium fast fermented. In both cases acidification is the main method of production and the pH drop (4.6-5.2) determines the safety of the sausage. The weight loss is about 15-20%. As these are fast-fermented products, dextrose is added to the meat mixture to encourage a fast pH drop.

Fast conversion of sugar into lactic acid by lactic acid bacteria is directly responsible for the tangy or sour taste in fast fermented sausages. The lower pH the more sourly flavor. The faster acidity is achieved, the faster the sausage becomes microbiologically stable and can be distributed to stores. This technology is popular in North Europe and especially in the USA.

In fast-fermented sausages about 1-2 days are needed to drop pH to 4.8 and in medium-fermented sausages about 2-3 days. Such a rapid pH drop cannot be obtained through traditional fermentation so a high temperature fast acting starter cultures are employed. Fermentation time will depend on the starter culture used, fermentation temperature, the amount and type of sugar and extra additives such as Gdl or citric acid.

After fermentation, these sausages are smoked with warm smoke of 90-110° F (32-43° C). The smoking period lasts 2-4 days at temperatures favorable for bacterial growth which usually is the fermentation temperature or slightly higher. Some manufacturers hold the sausage at 70-80° F (21-27° C) for 16-24 hours before smoke is applied. As the smoking continues, the temperature in the smokehouse is slowly raised, for example up 10° F every two hours, which heats the core of the sausage and makes the cooking process shorter. This is done gradually and depending on the diameter of the casing and the color desired, the process may take up to 12 hours or longer. Keep in mind that those temperatures cook the meat and the texture of the sausage will be different to the sausage that was cold smoked and never cooked.

In the USA, semi-dry sausages are fermented and cooked but usualy not dried. The only weight loss is due to the moisture loss during fermentation and cooking. Another common procedure consists of heating sausages in a smokehouse (no smoke applied) for 8-16 hours followed by a variable period of heating and smoking.

Unlike dry sausages, semi-dry sausages are usually pre-cooked to 60° C (140° F) in a smokehouse after fermenting and smoking. This eliminates any possibility of pork being infected with trichinosis. Because of ever tightening safety concerns and with the blessing of our meat inspectors, many commercially produced semi-dry products such as summer sausages are *fully cooked* to 160° F (72° C). An example is fast fermented pepperoni (which once used to be the classical slow-fermented dry sausage) used for pizza toppings.

Although not recommended, semi-dry sausages can be made without starter cultures:

- Cure meats for semi-dry sausages for 2-4 days with salt, sugar, nitrite/nitrate and spices at 35-40° F (2-4° C). Use 2.5-3% salt.
- Mix and stuff into casings.
- Ferment until pH < 5.3 is obtained within recommended time.
- Dry or cook.

Without starter cultures such a large pH drop may be hard to achieve within the prescribed times, and if no heating treatment is planned, chemical acidulants such as Gdl or citric acid must be added to make the sausage safe. Drying makes little sense as it is not going to improve the flavor or texture of the sausage and will only result in a loss in weight.

Smoking. Semi-dry sausages are usually smoked at 72-90° F (22-32° C) with a medium heavy smoke.

Cooking. Quite often semi-dry sausages are partially cooked at 122-140° F (50-60° C) to inhibit bacterial development.

Storing. After cooking sausages can be stored by hanging them at 50-54° F (10-12° C) which will dry them even more. A semi-dry sausage left drying for a sufficient amount of time will lose more moisture and become the dry sausage, but its sourly flavor will remain. As explained earlier dry sausages owe their characteristics to the flavor forming bacteria (*Staphylococcus* and *Kocuria*) which can not survive the sudden drop in pH to below 5.0. This low pH and the absence of flavor producing bacteria explains the tangy and sour taste of semi-dry products.

Semi-dry sausages are made today with starter cultures that guarantee the desired pH drop will be obtained in the planned time period.

Fast-Fermented Sausages

These are the youngest group of sausages and the use of very fast fermenting starter cultures makes their production possible. The safety of these sausages depends mainly on a fast pH drop and heat treatment as there is not enough time to lower the water activity Aw to the safe level. *Fast-fermented sausages are the easiest ones to make at home* and the starter cultures can be ordered online. Summer sausage is a well known American fast-fermented sausage. The flavor of the sausage is largely influenced by the final pH, type of sugars used and introduction of spices.

Characteristics	Fast-fermented
Fermentation temperature	24°- 40° C (76°-104° F)
Fermentation humidity %	92-90
Fermentation time	1-2 days
Cooking	Yes
Curing agent	nitrite
Sugar	dextrose
Flavor	tangy, sourly
Final pH	4.6 - 5.0
Weight loss %	< 15
Starter cultures	yes
Production time	7-14 days

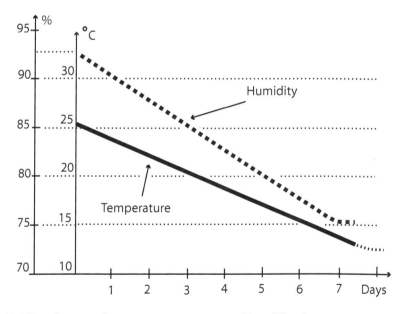

Fig. 10.1 Fast-fermented sausages, temperature and humidity decrease.

In industrial drying chambers temperature and humidity levels are lowered on a daily basis. The above graph is a good approximation of those conditions, there is about a 2 degrees drop in temperature every day.

At home conditions in small drying chambers such as an old refrigerator, the temperature can be easily controlled, but humidity control is often improvised and is accomplished by placing a dish filled with water inside. A humidity sensor is needed to display readings and the larger the surface area of the dish, the more water will evaporate.

Medium Fast-Fermented Sausages

Medium-fast fermented sausages fall between fast-fermented and slow fermented sausages. Sausages become stable due to the combined effect of pH drop and drying even without subsequent heat treatment. The flavor of the sausage is tangy and is influenced by spices, sugars and to some degree by flavor producing bacteria (*Staphylococcus* and *Kocuria*). Most semi-dry sausages (fast and medium-fast fermented) are smoked during the fermentation stage which elevates the temperature in the fermentation chamber to about 90-110° F (32-43° C). Then they are partially or fully cooked.

Characteristics	Medium-fast fermented
Fermentation temperature	24°- 38° C (76°-100° F)
Fermentation humidity %	92-90
Fermentation time	2-3 days
Drying temp.	22°-16° C
Drying hum. %	85-75
Drying time	3-4 weeks
Curing agent	nitrite
Sugar	glucose
Flavor	tangy, sourly
Final pH	4.8 - 5.0
Weight loss %	<30
Starter cultures	yes
Production time	21-28 days

In fast fermented and medium-fast fermented sausages pH reduction is the main hurdle against bacteria which is accomplished by using cultures, adding sugar, glucono-delta-lactone (Gdl) and citric acid. There is some risk when using Gdl or citric acid in sausages produced at home, as too fast of a drop in pH may be achieved which will result in a sourly flavor that has to be compensated in some other way. Achieving such a low level of pH in such a short time produces a product with a noticeable tangy flavor which, however, may be offset by using a combination of different sugars.

Time needed to decrease pH value of the sausage to 5.0		
Fast-fermented	Medium fast-fermented	Slow fermented
0.5-2 days	2-4 days	does not drop below 5.2

Dextrose, which is recommended for fast-fermented sausages is completely metabolized by all lactic bacteria and after fermentation ends, little of it remains to flavor the sausage. Adding additional slow fermenting sugars such as corn syrup or lactose will impart some sweetness to the product as there will not be sufficient time for the lactic bacteria to break down these sugars. There is little need to worry about mold on the surface, as there is not sufficient time for it to grow. If the sausages were stored in a humid condition, there would be such a possibility but fast or medium-fast fermented sausages are normally consumed soon.

Without starter cultures it will be very risky to attempt making fast-fermented (semi-dry) sausages which will not be subsequently cooked. The safety of this type of sausages relies heavily on a fast pH drop to 5.3 or less in about 48 hours. Without starter cultures such a fast pH drop is difficult to achieve unless Gdl is introduced.

Gdl

Commercial producers add chemicals such as Gdl (glucono-delta-lactone) or citric acid into a sausage mass to rapidly increase the acidity of the meat and to create an extra margin of safety. Unfortunately, this introduces a sourly flavor to the sausage so typical in fast-fermented salamis. Gdl is cleared by the Meat Inspection Division for use at 0.5% which comes to 5 g per 1 kg (2.2 lb) of meat. When Gdl is added acidification (release of gluconic acid) occurs at 70-74° F (21-23° C).

It is possible to produce a fast-fermented sausage without starter cultures or sugar by adding Gdl alone. About 1 g (0.1%) of Gdl per 1 kg of meat lowers the pH of meat by 0.1 pH. Adding 1% will lower the pH of the meat from 5.7-5.9 (initial value) to 4.7-4.9 making the sausage safe. This will, however, make the sausage very sour and will have to be offset by adding flavorings. Keep in mind that the sausages start to taste sourly when pH 5.0 is reached. Adding more will make the sausage very sour and somewhat bitter. Sausages produced with Gdl alone exhibits inferior color and sourly flavor. A much better solution is to use Gdl (2 g per 1 kg of meat), sugar (3 g/kg) and fast fermented culture together. Once Gdl has been added, the meat has a tendency to solidify so the mass should be stuffed without delay.

Sodium nitrite (cure #1) should be used because pH drop occurs so fast that curing bacteria do not have sufficient time to react with nitrate which is present in cure #2 and no nitrite will be produced.

Storing Sausages

After drying or smoking sausages are hung in storage room at 50-60° F (10-15° C), 75-80% humidity where the process of color and flavor development will continue. Sausage will also keep on drying what will additionally contribute to its stability.

Spreadable Fermented Sausages

These are cold smoked, uncooked *raw meat sausages* that must be refrigerated. The process of making raw sausages ends with the cold smoking stage. When cultures became available, the processors started to use them for precise control of fermentation. The product now could be fully acidified (pH <5.0) by adding more sugar and/or Gdl. When properly packed and stored at 40° F (4° C) spreadable sausage has an acceptable shelf life of up to 30 days. The shelf life of spreadable sausages compared to dry or semi-dry fermented sausages is much shorter and that is the reason that American supermarkets do not stock them. Disregarding this little shortcoming, they are great sausages and as the name implies can be spread on bread. In Germany and Poland they are a popular item. This can be attributed to a large number of neighborhood butchers who cater to the local clientele. Although such a sausage may have a relatively short life, it can be made in smaller quantities depending on demand. There is a bigger sausage diversity in European stores which may be explained by a long tradition.

Coarse ground spreadable sausages like Mettwurst are ground through 3-8 mm plate and fermented at 95% humidity and have an air speed of about 0.8 m/sec dropping down about 0.1 m/sec every two days.

Finely ground spreadable sausages like Teewurst are ground through 2 mm plate and fermented at about 90% humidity. It is easier to produce a good spreadable sausage when 50% of fat has been added.

Acidity

The pH drop should fit into 5.1-5.4 range. Acidity is obtained by adding Gdl, sucrose or lactose, starter cultures and a proper choice of fermenting temperature. To offset the salty/sourly flavor around 0.2% of maltose or malto-dextrin may be added. Maltose can be added at up to 0.4% (4g/kg) as only a fraction of maltose can be converted into lactic acid by lactic acid bacteria. As pH becomes lower, the sausage texture becomes firmer which decreases its spreadability. In simple terms the less acidity sausage has, the easier it is to spread.

General Guidelines

Materials. The majority of spreadable fermented sausages are made of pork, but other fatty meats like beef or lamb may be used. The level of fat must be quite high (40-50%) as this adds to spreadability. For the same reason the soft fat like belly fat should be used. When not enough soft fat is available about 1-2% of vegetable oil may be added, however, take into account the amount of intramuscular fat the meat contains. Vegetable oil offers two benefits:

- oil is transparent so the sausage seems to be leaner.
- oil is less prone to rancidity.

136

Salt is applied at around 2.5%. Sodium nitrite (cure #1) is added as it reacts immediately with meat. It is not recommended to use potassium nitrate or cure #2 with Gdl as the rapid pH drop will inhibit curing bacteria and no nitrite will be produced.

Gdl drops pH fast, however, it contributes to a harder texture, a feature which is not desired in spreadable sausages. Gdl should be applied below 5 g/ kg, otherwise the taste will be too sourly and metallic, especially when sugar was also added. A better solution is to use Gdl (2 g per 1 kg of meat), sugar (3 g/kg) and fast fermented culture together.

Grinding

Fine grind contributes positively towards spreadability of the sausage.

Drying

Spreadable sausages are dried during the smoking step. An overly dried sausage will be too hard to spread. Once when no moisture appears on the sausage the process may be considered finished. The air speed is slow around 0.1 m/sec. Spreadable sausages do not need to dry much as they are not expected to have a very long shelf life. By having a higher Aw they are moister what positively contributes to spreadability. When Gdl has been added the sausage can be dried at 68° F (20° C), 90% humidity and moderate air flow for one day. Then it can be cold smoked.

Smoking

The manufacturing of spreadable sausages ends with the smoking stage. Any subsequent drying will only affect their spreadability. Sausages are smoked with a thin cold smoke at 64-72° F (18-22° C), 75%. The casings must not be wet when smoke is applied.

Emulsifiers

These two ingredients are often added as they contibute positevely to better spreadability:

Guar gum has almost eight times the water-thickening potency of cornstarch and only a very small quantity is needed for producing sufficient viscosity.

Mustard flour binds water well and is often added to spreadable sausages at 1-1.5 ratio to extend spreadability. Adding mustard flour does not change the flavor of the sausage, on the contrary it slows down the action of lactic acid bacteria what leads to a softer texture. In addition mustard flour retards fat rancidity.

A typical process for making spreadable sausage

Salt, cure #1, dextrose, fast-fermenting culture.

Pork must be trichinae free. If in doubt freeze pork before processing as prescribed by the official regulations.

Days	Temperature	Humidity	Process
1	22° C/72° F	90	Fermentation
2	22° C/72° F	90	Fermentation
3	18° C/64° F	85	Smoking

A very weak air-speed is introduced. Apply a thin cold smoke. For large diameter casings add another day of smoking/drying.

Storing

When done, spreadable sausages should be consumed without delay or refrigerated.

Chapter 11

Cold Smoked, Cooked Fermented and Non-Fermented Sausages

Cold Smoked Sausages

The technology of making North European cold smoked sausages resembles very closely the manufacturing process of making Italian salami or Spanish chorizo. The main difference is that in a cold climate a small fire was warming the sausage chamber, just enough to prevent the sausages from freezing. In the first stages of combustion burning wood produces smoke so a thin cold smoke is always present. After a while no more smoke is produced, however, the wood continues to burn. To sum it up the purpose of burning wood was to keep the facilities warm and the smoke just happened to be there. This establishes a proper definition of cold smoking: *"Cold smoking is drying meat with smoke."* Italians did not need to warm up the premises as the climate was just right for drying sausages with air and smoking was seldom performed.

What follows is the manufacturing process for making Polish cold smoked sausages. At first glance it looks like the process can be applied to any smoked sausages, however, when you look at the temperatures you will see that they are much lower. And this is exactly what separates the traditional production of fermented sausages from other types, those lower temperatures. In the recipe section there are a number of cold smoked sausages with detailed instructions.

1. Cut meat into 25-50 mm (1-2 inch) pieces and mix with salt and cure #1. Leave for 3 days in refrigerator.
2. Grind meat.
3. Mix with spices.
4. Condition for 2 days at 35-42° F (2-6° C) and 85-90% humidity.
5. Smoke with a thin cold smoke at 64° F (18° C) for 1-2 days.
6. Dry at 50-53° F (10-12° C) and 75-80% humidity until sausages lose 15% of the original weight.
7. Store at 53° F (12° C) or lower, 75% humidity.

A fine dry sausage of salami type will be produced. The manufacturing process takes place at such low temperature that lactic acid producing bacteria naturally present in meat will hardly grow and ferment even if an additional sugar was added. The final product will not exhibit any acidity. Drying process will decide whether a semi-dry or dry sausage is produced. If the sausage loses 20-30% of its original weight it will be a semi-dry sausage which can be stored t room temperature. If the sausage loses 30% of its original weight it will be a dry sausage. Make note that the storing conditions are the same as drying requirements which means that the sausage will continue to mature and dry during storage.

Cooked Fermented Sausages

Fully cooked fermented sausages are cooked products that they are fast-fermented and then partially cooked and dried or fully cooked until they are safe to consume. The product is ready to eat and what differentiates it from a regular smoked and cooked sausage is the tangy flavor it has developed during the fermentation stage. This definition makes making fermented sausages fast and safe. All that is needed is a fast-fermenting culture like LHP or F-1, 1 g dextrose and 100° F (38° C) fermenting temperature. Instead of a starter culture Gdl can be added to develop acidity. Such a fermentation process can be accomplished in 12 hours and the sausage can be submitted to thermal treatment. If such a sausage is fully cooked, the manufacturing process becomes very easy as there is little to worry about pH drop or Aw water activity. What we get is a safe to consume sausage with a tangy taste.

Why to cook a sausage that has always been made without cooking?

It is all about money. It is faster, safer, easier and cheaper to create sourly salami without drying the sausage. Drying a sausage is a slow and expensive procedure that make take a week to accomplish, but the same sausage can be fully cooked in 30 minutes. Well it may have a different texture and flavor, but for most people if it is hard and sourly it must be salami. And it matters little whether the slices of pepperoni on top of pizza were traditionally fermented and dried for a month or acidified and cooked in just one day.

Applying a fast-fermented culture at 104° F (40° C) and 1% dextrose will ferment a sausage in 12 hours, then it can be smoked for 4 hours. Starting smoking at 110° F (43° C) and gradually increasing the temperature to 176° F (80° C) will smoke and cook the sausage in one day. The pH drop in a sausage that will be *fully cooked* does not need to be very low, as the cooking step will make the sausage safe. Acidity loses its importance as a safety hurdle and becomes a flavoring step. Due to high cooking temperature the texture of the sausage will suffer as the little specks of fat will melt down and will not be as distinctive anymore. Some purists may frown upon such a technique but to make some fast snack food such as small summer sausage or meat sticks it will work just fine.

There are two types of cooked fermented sausages:

- partially cooked and dried sausages.
- fully cooked sausages, drying not necessary.

Fast-fermented sausages must exhibit a characteristic tangy flavor. This can be produced by:

- one day natural fermentation (very small amount acidity will be produced).
- starter culture and sugar.
- Gdl.

In all above cases the product will be cooked resulting in a short production time.

Partially Cooked and Dried Fermented Sausages

Ingredients for 1 kg of meat:

Salt 20 g, Cure #1 2.5 g, Gdl 5g, fast-fermenting culture L-HP, dextrose 2g, spices.

To avoid smearing use partially frozen meat and fat. Mix ground meats with all ingredients and stuff without delay. Ferment at 72-76° F (22-24° C), 90% humidity for 48 hours. Cold smoke at 73° F (22° C) for 24 hours. Bake in smokehouse at 167° F (75° C) until meat reaches 140° F (60° C) internal temperature. Dry at 53-59° F (12-15° C), 75% humidity for 2 days. Store in refrigerator. You can store it at 53-59° F (12-15° C), 75% humidity which will be continued drying. Two more days of drying will make sausage safe to be kept at room temperature. In order to obtain real salami texture the meat and fat must be very cold, grinder knife must be sharp and mixing performed at low temperature. It will help to mix ingredients in a very cold stainless steel bowl. Production time about 5 days.

Fully Cooked Fermented Sausages

Natural fermentation

Ingredients for 1 kg of meat

Salt 20 g, Cure #1-2.5 g, spices.

Cut meat into 25-50 mm (1-2 inch) pieces and mix with salt and cure #1. Leave for 3 days in refrigerator. To avoid smearing use partially frozen meat and fat. Mix ground meats with all ingredients and stuff into casings. Condition at 64° F (18° C), 90% humidity for 12 hours. Apply cold smoke at 64° F (18° C) for 4 hours. Bake in smokehouse at 176° F (80° C) until meat reaches 158° F (70° C) internal temperature.

With Starter Culture

Salt 20 g, Cure #1 2.5 g, fast fermenting culture L-HP, dextrose 2 g, spices.

To avoid smearing use partially frozen meat and fat. Mix ground meats with all ingredients and stuff into casing. Ferment at 72-76° F (22-24° C), 90% humidity for 48 hours. Smoke at 72° F (22° C) for 12 hours. Bake in smokehouse at 176° F (80° C) until meat reaches 158° F (70° C) internal temperature.

With Gdl

Ingredients for 1 kg of meat

Salt 20 g, Cure #1-2.5 g, Gdl 1% (10 g/1 kg), spices.

To avoid smearing use frozen meat and fully frozen fat. At home conditions use partially frozen meat and fat. Mix ground meats with all ingredients and stuff without delay. Ferment at 75° F (24° C), 90% humidity for 48 hours. Apply smoke at 140° F (60° C) for 2-4 hours. Bake in smokehouse at 176° F (80° C) until meat reaches 158° F (70° C) internal temperature. Shower with cold water to prevent wrinkles.

The sausage will have a tangy taste, meat and fat particles somewhat less defined than in uncooked sausages because of higher processing temperatures which should not exceed 176° F (80° C), otherwise the fat will start melting inside and the texture will suffer.

Non-Fermented Dried Sausages

Some sausages are not fermented or acidified, yet shelf stable. They are made without cultures or acidulants (Gdl, citric acid) and no fermentation takes place. Generally, after stuffing these sausages are partially cooked to 146° F (63° C), and then dried to a water activity of < 0.86 (Aw growth limit for *Staph. aureus*). Due to the higher pH, these products must be dried to a lower water activity than fermented products to achieve shelf stability. Non-fermented dried sausages are also known as non-fermented salamis.

Polish Dry Sausages

A very interesting group of sausages were cold smoked products made in the past in Poland and Russia before the advent of refrigeration. Many of these sausages were naturally fermented cold smoked products which would fully qualify to be called salami. Starter cultures were not around yet so the products were naturally fermented and dried. They were not thought of being salami and people simply called them dry sausages. Fermentation was not even mentioned, but what was significant is that a little amount of sugar was usually added which did trigger a minor acid production. Sugar was added because people knew that potassium nitrate worked much better with sugar, the color was more intense and the flavor was better too. A few decades later it was discovered that sugar was an essential nutrient for curing and lactic acid bacteria. As the amount of sugar was very minute, the final products exhibited none of the sourly flavor so common today. The procedure was as follows:

- Top quality meats were selected and cured for 3-4 days with salt and potassium nitrate at around 42-46° F (6-8° C). Curing bacteria forced potassium nitrate to release sodium nitrite which reacted with meat's myoglobin creating a pink color.

- Sausages were cold smoked for weeks at the time. This allowed natural fermentation and drying to take place inside of the smokehouse. Due to the action of the smoke, there was no mold on sausages and if it developed, it would be wiped off. Drying with cold smoke resulted in a steady removal of moisture and the product became a dry sausage.

- Sausages were left hanging in a smokehouse or in a different chamber and were consummed on a need basic. The sausages kept on drying out and during this "ripening" process were developing salami like flavor.

The processing times and temperatures fall precisely into the principles of making traditional products as practiced in Southern Europe. The only difference was that due to a favorable climate Mediterranean products were dried without smoke in the open air and North European sausages were smoke/dried inside a smokehouse.

We could classify these sausages as:

- Cold smoked sausages - as salami,

- Spreadable fermented sausages called "Metka" sausages. Metka sausages were usually cold smoked and no further processing was performed. They had to be kept in a refrigerator.

Russian Fermented Sausages

During the era of Communism, there was a diverse assortment of meat products in Russia comprising of more than 200 types, varieties, and classes of sausages. The basic classification was as follows: cooked sausages, frankfurters (narrow and thick), semi-smoked sausages, smoked sausages, and other more specialized sausage products. Due to the lack of refrigeration most of those sausages were either dry or semi-dry in order to last at room temperatures. Depending on the quality of the raw material (meat and fat) they were subdivided into: higher class, class 1, and class 2.

Dry sausages		Semi dry sausages	
higher class	class 1	higher class	class 1
pork, Metropolitan, delicatessen, Russian, special, Jewish, cervelat, Tambov, Maikop, tourist, Neva, Uglich, and Braunschweig varieties	Moscow, fancy, Ukrainian, Orsk, mutton sausages	cervelat, Rostov, summer delicatessen	Moscow, fancy, Ukrainian, mutton, Minsk

The smoked sausages were subdivided into raw or hard smoked (*dry sausages*) and smoked and cooked (semi-dry, summer type sausages). The meat was cured with salt and nitrate for 5-7 days at 40° F (4° C), then cold smoked for 3-5 days (below 71° F, 22° C) and then dried for 25-30 days at 54-56° F (12-14° C). Of course no starter cultures were used. In addition they were dry sausages (higher class only-Kazakh dry sausage) made from 35% horse meat, pork, pork fat, and semi-dry sausages made in high class (35% horse meat, pork, pork fat) and class 1 (70% horse meat, pork, pork fat).

Non-Fermented Cooked Dry Sausages

A large number of sausages made after the war was made with preservation in mind. This group will cover any sausage that is smoked, cooked and then air-dried at 50-59° F (10-15° C). This reduces Aw (water activity) to about 0.92 which makes the product shelf stable without refrigeration. The *majority* of sausages which were made after the war in Poland, Germany, or Russia would fit into this category. They were not called salamis but had their own names: Kabanosy, Mysliwska, Krakowska and more than fifty others.

Those sausages were always cured for 3-4 days at refrigerator temperatures, then smoked. Then they were dried and smoked again. Cooking was accomplished by baking in a smokehouse or poaching in hot water. These sausages were simply hung in kitchen pantries and would keep on losing moisture, in time becoming dry sausages. They were consumed as needed. When the war ended, there were no refrigerators and the above method worked very well.

Modifying Recipes

The conclusion can be made that almost any sausage recipe can be converted to the fermented cooked type as long as the meat is fermented first (with or without starter cultures) and then cooked to a safe internal temperature 160° F (71° C). It should be stored in a refrigerator, however, if kept at 50-59° F (10-15° C), 75% humidity, the sausage will start drying out becoming first a semi-dry and later dry sausage. You can take any sausage, stuff it into 75 mm casings, smoke and cook and call it non-fermented salami.

Chapter 12

Equipment

Making fermented sausages presents new challenges which we don't face when making other types of sausages. To control temperature, humidity, and air speed is not easy and requires expensive computer controlled drying chambers.

Commercial producers use huge rooms with air conditioning ducts supplying air at the right temperature, humidity and speed, however, there are no small drying chambers designed for home production of fermented sausages so a hobbyist must use his ingenuity to come up with suitable solutions.

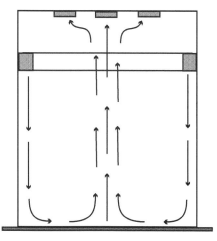

Fig. 12.1 Air flow in a commercial drying chamber.

Refrigerator Drying Chamber

A used refrigerator can be easily adapted for fermenting and drying sausages. Most refrigerators are made with a separate freezer door which is normally located in the upper part of the unit. Well, this section is not needed and will not become part of the system. A one door refrigerator is more practical.

Temperature Control

Without a doubt a precise control of a vast range of temperatures 50-104° F (10-40° C) and 60-95% humidity is not easy. A thermostat of a refrigerator is designed to control temperatures between 32-40° F (0-4° C), but not higher. Such temperatures are not needed during fermenting and drying sausages. There is a commonly available device called a "line voltage thermostat control" which offers an elegant solution. This little device consists of a temperature sensor, switches and adjustable display which can transform an ordinary refrigerator into a wonderful drying chamber.

Line Voltage Thermostat - Single Stage

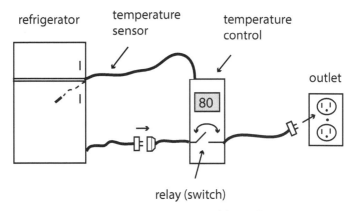

Fig. 12.2 Electronic temperature control in *cooler* mode.

A refrigerator is disconnected from the outlet and is connected with the temperature control which is then plugged into the electrical outlet. The refrigerator's thermostat is not controlling temperature anymore and is taken over by the temperature sensor of the controller. There is no need to drill a hole as the refrigerator door has rubber insulation and the sensor's cable is thin. The microprocessor in the control monitors the temperature through the sensor which is inserted into the refrigerator. When the temperature is warmer than the set point, the processor will energize the internal switch. This allows the refrigerator to draw the current through the controller and start cooling. The drawing is not to scale and the typical unit is about: 6.5" x 2.7" x 2.5". The beauty of this set up lies in the fact that no damage is done to the refrigerator. These units can control coolers, heaters or any electrical device.

The unit depicted in Fig. 12.2 is *a single stage control which means that it can control only one device at a time.* There are two stage units which can control a heater and a cooler from the same control. A line voltage thermostat set to "cooling" mode can only *decrease* temperature lower than the temperature that remains outside the refrigerator.

There are instances when the temperature inside the chamber must be higher than ambient temperature:

- Fast fermented sausages made with starter cultures which require fermentation temperatures of around 86 -113° F (30-45° C).

- Drying chamber is located in a cool climate where temperatures are below 68° F (20° C) for a larger part of the year. Under such circumstances the same line voltage thermostat can be combined with a heater and used in the heating mode.

146

To increase temperature the line voltage control control is switched to "heating mode", the refrigerator is disconnected and the heater is plugged into the temperature control.

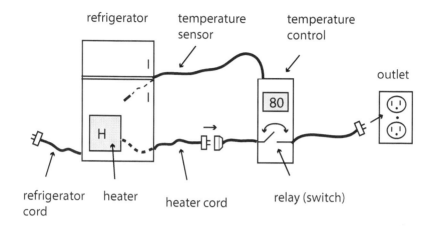

refrigerator   temperature   temperature
           sensor   control

outlet

80

refrigerator   heater   heater cord   relay (switch)
cord

Fig. 12.3 Electronic temperature control in *heater* mode. Refrigerator not working but used as a fermentation/drying chamber.

Any little heating element, ceramic heater, heat lamp or even UL approved light fixture will easily raise the temperature in a small unit such as a refrigerator. Using an ordinary light bulb for an extended period of time is not recommended as prolonged exposure to light creates rancidity in fat. Temperature control can be used in the heating mode during fermentation, which lasts on average about 1-2 days and even less for fast fermented products. Then when a product enters the drying stage, the heater can be removed and the control unit is switched back into the cooling mode.

When ambient temperatures are low and the heating mode is selected, the refrigerator can still be used as a drying chamber, even though it is disconnected from the power supply. In cooler climates it is practical to build a large drying chamber (even a walk in unit) from any materials, as long as a good insulation is included. Not being limited by space, any kind of a free standing heater and humidifier can be placed inside as long as there is electricity close by. These electronic temperature controls are very precise and can maintain the set temperature within 1 degree.

147

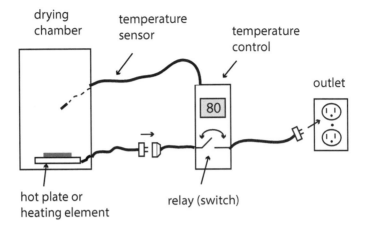

Fig. 12.4 Line voltage thermostat in heating mode. Drying chamber can be any type of an insulated box or unit.

Line Voltage Thermostat - Two Stage

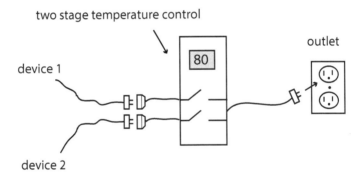

Fig. 12.5 Two stage line voltage thermostat.

The advantage of a two stage thermostat is that two independent devices such as a heater and a cooler or a heater and the fan can be connected to only one temperature control. Two stage temperature control offers more possibilities but comes at a higher cost.

Humidity Control

Humidity control is much harder to accomplish than temperature. All those improvised arrangements such as placing salt covered with water in a shallow pan or bringing more water filled pans into the chamber may increase the humidity level to 50-60%, which is nowhere close to the required humidity during fermentation.

In 1975, folks at Clemson University Clemson, Ohio came up with an interesting idea for the construction and operation of a relatively inexpensive cabinet for sausage fermentation (ref. 9). Temperature could be controlled to plus minus 1° C with a relative humidity of approximately 95%.

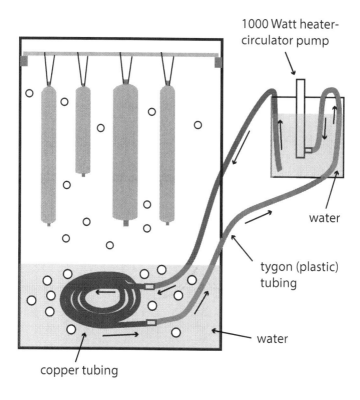

Fig. 12.6 Sausage fermentation cabinet with air temperature controlled via warm water bath heated by external heater-circulator pump.

The above design provides a *constant* high humidity of about 95% which is an ideal setting at the beginning of fermentation. Cabinet air temperatures of 86-100° F (30° and 38° C) were achieved with external water bath settings at approximately 86-125° F (38°-52° C). The capacity of the external tank (heater pump) was 16 liters (7.27 lbs) and the cabinet contained 25 liters of water (11.3 lbs) which covered the coil in the bottom of the cabinet.

149

These are not huge amounts of water (one gallon of water weighs 8.34 lbs) and a separate, large surface area container may be inserted into the cabinet, as long as the copper tubing fits inside and is covered with water. The only problem is that this cabinet has to be exclusively designated as the fermentation chamber as it provides no means for lowering humidity, except switching it off. It is not possible to dry sausages at such high humidity levels. This old but still interesting design can be improved upon by using a fish tank heater and the temperature controller:

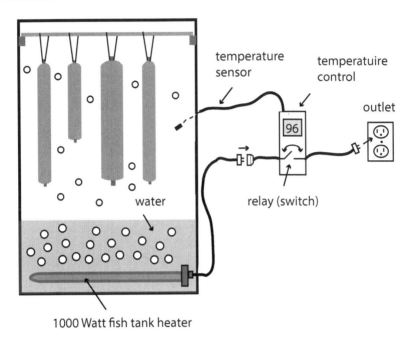

1000 Watt fish tank heater

Fig. 12.7 Sausage fermentation cabinet with air temperature controlled via fish tank water heater and temperature controller.

Unbreakable high wattage submersible titanium heaters come in 500 and 1000 Watts, but they need the temperature controller. Both water designs are simple to make and they lead themselves quite well for fermenting fast-fermented sausages. Slow-fermented sausages can be fermented with such arrangement as well as long as the air temperature will stay at around 68° F (20° C).

There is an even simpler solution for making fast-fermented sausages where humidity will be at a constant 100%. A serious limitation of this design is that no lowering of humidity and *no drying is possible* and this method should be used for *very short fermenting times only.*

To prevent salt migration from the sausage into the water, some salt (½ cup to 1 gal of water) should be added into the water or a higher amount of salt must be added to the sausage mince. Nevertheless this arrangement can be used for making fast-fermented sausages with a fast fermenting starter culture at 104° F (40° C). Under such conditions fermentation can be accomplished in 12 hours and after drying the casing, the sausage can be submitted to smoking, cooking or both. Then it can be dried if additional weight loss is desired.

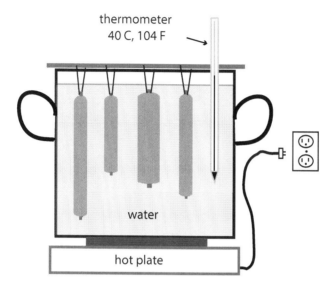

Fig. 12.8 Fermentation in water. No cover necessary.

Adjustable Humidifiers

Air conditioners and refrigerators dehumidify air to about 40-50% relative humidity. This is much too low for making fermented sausages, especially at the beginning of the fermentation stage when 90-95% humidity is required. If a sausage is fermented without humidity control, periodic spraying or immersing it in water will help to provide 100% of humidity on its surface, if only for a short while. The simplest way to control humidity is to install a small digital adjustable humidifier. A good unit should lock to the setting within a few percents. In industrial units increasing humidity is accomplished by steam injection but home units produce a cool vapor mist.

It takes a day or two to get to know your adjustable humidifier. When fermentation starts humidity should be high (> 90%), but set your humidifier lower at about 75% and see what will happen in an hour or two. Evaporating moisture from the sausages will increase humidity inside your fermentation chamber to about 90% or higher. Open the door periodically to let the moisture out (do some fanning with a magazine) and humidity will fall down let's say to 80%. Close the door and check it again to see the humidity level.

151

Were you to set your humidity at 90% or higher, the evaporating moisture from the sausages will soon saturate the chamber and the sausages will be soaking wet. The door should be opened and the chamber dehumidified. When drying sausages do the same, set your humidifier at 60% and see how humid the drying chamber becomes. *As the sausage loses more moisture these changes will be less pronounced* and a point will be reached when humidity in the chamber will be a little higher than the setting of the humidifier.

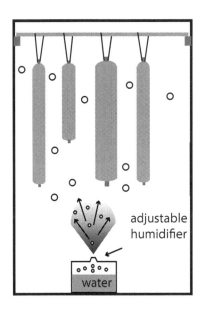

Fig. 12.9 Adjustable humidifier.

Photo 12.1 An improvised set up - refrigerator temporarily used as a fermentation/drying chamber. Digital humidifier providing humidity.

Line voltage thermostat is set to "heat" mode and increases temperature (fermentation stage) by switching on the barbecue starter. When set to "cool" for the drying stage, line voltage thermostat uses the refrigerator as a cooling device. No drilling needed. Smoke sticks attached to screens by carabiner spring clips. An ordinary twine or plastic tie wraps will hold them too.

Humidity control plays an important role in greenhouse production of flowers and vegetables and many clever devices can be obtained from green house equipment suppliers.

In closed chambers such as modified refrigerators, there is no ingress nor egress of the air and the evaporating moisture from the sausages will increase the humidity in the chamber. The fan will just facilitate drying but will move the same moist air around. That is why the door will have to be periodically opened to let this moisture out. If an opening could be made, a fan controlled by a humidistat switched to "dehumidify" mode would remove moist air outside. In commercial chambers the correctly prepared air (temperature and humidity) is blown into the room and sucked out at the other side.

Humidistat

There is a device called a line voltage humidistat which basically works like the temperature control described earlier. When in "humidify" mode the device will increase humidity by switching on the humidifier. When in "dehumidify" mode the same device will switch on the fan to remove moist air from the chamber.

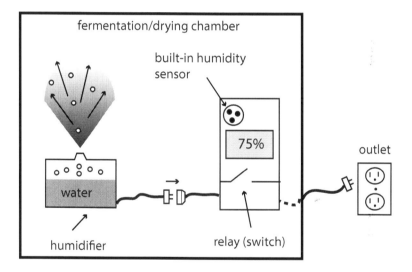

Fig. 12.10 Single stage humidistat.

The in line voltage humidistat depicted above comes with a built-in humidity sensor and must be installed within the drying chamber. There is a humidistat which comes with a remote humidity sensor and a control unit can be mounted outside of the drying chamber.

153

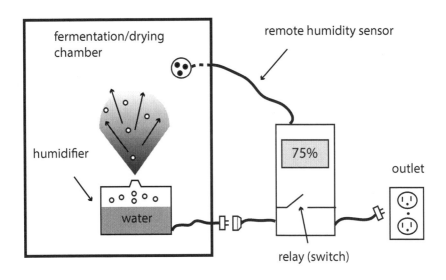

Fig. 12.11 Single stage humidistat with remote humidity sensor.

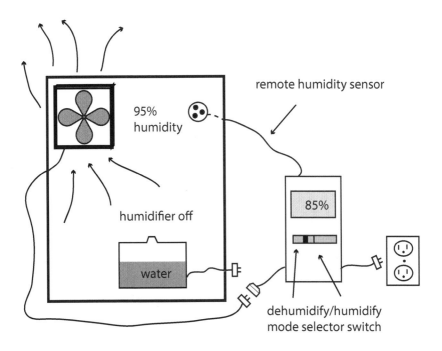

Fig. 12.12 Humidistat in "dehumidifying" mode. The fan is expelling moisture outside.

154

When the humidity sensor is placed inside of the drying chamber, the control unit may be mounted outside up to 20 feet away. It is insignificant whether a humidifier is adjustable, the most simple electricity powered unit will do as the humidistat control will accordingly switch it on and off. Note that designs that incorporate line voltage humidistats (Fig.12.10), allow for precise control of humidity only. Temperature must also be controlled and that is accomplished with a separate temperature controller (Fig. 12.2).

Hygrometer

It should be noted that an average hygrometer is rated to indicate humidity plus or minus 3% at best. In reality they are even less accurate (10%), although the more expensive calibrated units are are accurate within 1%.

Photo 12.2 Hygrometer.

Weighing Cultures and Spices

There are different sizes of teaspoons in the USA and Europe and the same recipe becomes a different recipe depending on the size of a measuring device. The only consistent method of applying ingredients is to weigh them on an accurate scale like the ones made by American Weigh Systems.

A digital scale is of immense value for weighing cultures. 5 lb of meat needs just 0.28 g (0.001 oz) of T-SPX culture. It can be roughly estimated to be a 1/8 of a teaspoon. Spices are normally added at about 1-2 g per 1 kg (2.2 lb) of meat which corresponds to about 1 flat teaspoon.

Photo 12.3 AWS Compact Digital Scale v2.0 by *American Weigh Systems.* Capacity: 100 g
Accuracy: 0.01 g (0.001 oz)

155

Separate Fermentation and Drying Chambers

Using the same chamber for fermenting and drying creates a major inconvenience when a new production must be started. Fermentation is a relatively short process and may be accomplished in 48 hours. Then the temperature and humidity is lowered and the product enters the drying stage which may continue for months occupying the drying chamber. To start a new production presents a problem which can be avoided when two or three separate chambers are involved:

- Fermentation chamber.
- Drying chamber.
- Storing chamber.

Employing one designated chamber for fermentation and another one for drying/storing allows for mixing products which were made on different days.

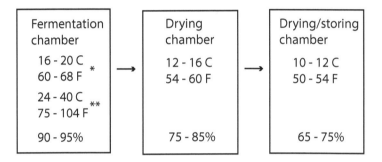

*   no starter culture used,
    if starter culture is added, slow-fermented sausage will
    require fermentation temperature of 20-24 C (68 - 76 F).
** fast culture used

Fig. 12.13 Making slow-fermented sausage in designated chambers.

Thermometers

Standard room thermometers are surprisingly accurate. The same can not be said about some inexpensive digital cable remotes. It is nice to have a cable remote thermometer with the display located outside of the chamber but make sure the cable looks strong and is jacketed. Very thin cable wires can be off the mark by a few degrees although the problem disappears when the wire is insulated. There is no need for a separate thermometer when using the line voltage thermostat as these units are very accurate.

156

Fan

To control air speed in improvised chambers such as a refrigerator is surprisingly easy. The most reliable device is a computer cooling fan as it is designed for working 24 hours a day. In addition there is a huge variety of these fans and they come in different sizes, shapes and power outputs. They can be obtained in computer stores or online.

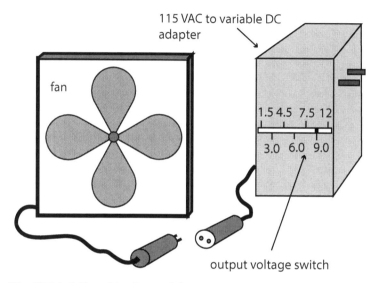

Fig. 12.14 Adjustable air speed fan.

The current draw of a typical 3" 12 VDC, 1.9 W fan is only 0.1 A. It runs from a 115 VAC adapter whose output can be set to 12, 9, 7.5 or 6 VDC. *Each voltage setting lets the fan run at a different speed.* If only a fixed DC output voltage adapter is available, a simple inexpensive and universally available device called a "potentiometer" can be attached between the fan and the adapter. The device will control the fan's speed. Keep in mind that the air fan does not remove the humid air from the chamber, it just moves it around. An opening is needed which will permit the stale air to escape. An exhaust fan can be installed, or just open the front door periodically to let the humid air out.

Final Notes

Although equipment may vary in size and nature, some criteria must not be improvised upon and this is *the temperature and the safety hurdles.* What can be flexible is the choice of physical devices that may be selected to control specific parameters. It makes little difference whether a hot plate, barbecue starter wire, fish tank heater, soldering iron or an electrical bulb will be used to raise the temperature, as long as the correct temperature is obtained.

Fermented sausages can be made in any kitchen, and a stove or baking oven can be used as a drying chamber, as long as it is big enough to accommodate hanging sausages. Depending on the insulation and the size of the unit, different heat sources may be employed, even internal light will do. The temperature can be controlled by simply switching the light bulb on and off. When making fast-fermented sausages using cultures, the optimum fermentation temperature will be higher. *That does not mean that fermentation will not take place at a lower temperature. It will, but it will progress much slower.*

The fermentation (with starter culture) should be completed in 2 days at 75° F (24° C) and 85-90% humidity. This is a high level of humidity which is present only in humid tropical climates or just after the rain. In air conditioned rooms the humidity level is only about 40% and is too low for fermentation, drying or even prolonged storing. Controlling temperature is easy and there are countless heating devices that would perform the task, but to adjust humidity one needs a humidistat control or an adjustable humidifier. Then sausages enter the drying stage which continues for about 20 days. The temperature and humidity should be gradually lowered (if possible) about 1° C and 4% humidity drop every 5 days. By doing this we will finish the drying process at about 16° C (60° F) and 70-75% humidity. Fast and medium-fermented sausages will be done now.

During the beginning of fermentation the humidity in the chamber is at high levels and is the sum of:

- The moisture in the air.
- The moisture which is created by placing a water filled pan inside of a chamber or the moisture coming from a humidifier.
- The moisture that evaporates from the sausages.

As the fermentation and drying cycles progress, less moisture will be removed from the sausages and *the relative humidity of the chamber will decrease.*

In the past when sausages were made in natural conditions, control of humidity was an ever present problem and strategically placed openings were either opened or closed. Water was manually sprayed into suction vents or wet rags were placed there. That required a lot of experience and was labor intensive. Today, the availability of temperature and humidity controllers make this task possible and easy to perform at home. Were it not for those technological breakthroughs and availability of testing equipment and starter cultures, this book would probably not be written.

158

Chapter 13

Guidelines to Sausage Recipes

It is mind boggling to see people clicking for hours and hours on a computer keyboard to find magic recipes on the Internet. Searching for the Holy Grail of a sausage. Then when they find something they like, they mess it up by applying too high smoking or cooking temperatures. The recipe of course, gets the blame. Then they look for another magic recipe again. There are some salami recipes on the Internet and all those instructions provide is this sentence: stuff the sausage and hang to dry. This is a dangerous statement and if you have made it so far reading this book you already know why.

Recipe is what the word says: "the recipe", it does not imply that one will produce an outstanding sausage. Making quality sausages has nothing to do with recipes, it is all about the meat science and the rules that govern it. All sausage making steps, especially temperature control, are like little building blocks that would erect a house. It is like the strength of the chain, which is only as strong as its weakest link. *Each step in sausage making influences the step that follows, and all those steps when perfomed correctly will, as a final result, create the quality product.*

There isn't one standardized recipe for any of the sausages. The best meat science books, written by the foremost experts in this field list different ingredients for the same sausage. Salami Milano and Salami Genoa are basically the same sausage, the difference lies mainly in meat particle size. Replacing mace with nutmeg, using white or black pepper, adding/removing a particular spice will have little final effect on a sausage. Grinding cold meat or frozen fat is more important for making a quality sausage than a pretty arrangement of expensive spices. It's all about the technology.

By adhering to the guidelines outlined in this book you have to make a great sausage. By all means look at different recipes, but be flexible and not afraid to experiment. Use ingredients that you personally like as in most cases you will make a sausage for yourself, so why not like it? When making a large amount of the product a wise precaution is to taste the meat by frying a tiny piece. After mixing meat with all ingredients there is still time for last minute changes. There is not much we can do after a sausage is stuffed. *A recipe is just a recipe and let your palate be the final judge.*

I will never forget when I made my first Polish smoked sausage that turned out very well and I proudly gave it to my friend - professional sausage maker Waldemar to try. I have included salt, pepper, garlic, and added optional marjoram. I also added nutmeg and other spices that I liked. Well my friend's judgement was as follows:

"Great sausage, but why all those perfumes?"

For him it was supposed to be the classical Polish Smoked Sausage and all it needed was salt, pepper and garlic. The moral of the story is that putting dozens of spices into the meat does not guarantee the best product. Combining meat with salt and pepper already makes a great sausage providing that you will follow the basic rules of sausage making. It's that simple. Like roasting a chicken it needs only salt, pepper, and it always comes out perfect. If you don't cure your meats properly, grind warm fat or screw up your smoking and cooking temperatures, all the spices in the world, saffron included will not save your sausage.

Dry sausages made with *pepper only* will have the wonderful mellow cheesy flavor, *which is created in time by the reaction of bacteria with meat.* Fast-fermented sausages will always exhibit this tangy and sourly flavor as flavor forming bacteria don't get sufficient time to work with meat. In this case a variety of spices, sugars and syrups can somewhat off set the acidic flavor.

Starter Cultures, Fermentation and Drying

There is not one universal temperature for fermenting, drying or even storing. There is an acceptable range of temperatures that correspond to each particular process. When starter cultures are used, the fermentation temperature can vary from the minimum to the maximum recommended by the manufacturer. Recipes in this book employ Chr. Hansen meat cultures. In order not to complicate the recipes, they are standardized on cultures which are commonly available.

Bactoferm™ T-SPX - slow-fermenting culture for *traditional fermentation profiles.* For best quality apply at temperatures not higher than 75° F (24° C) in order to prevent pH from dropping below 4.8 at any time. Add sugar at 0.5% or less. For best results use cure #2. The culture is particularly suited for the production of Southern European types of sausages, low in acidity with an aromatic flavor, such as Italian salami or French saucisson.

Bactoferm™ F-LC - fast-fermenting bio-protective culture capable of acidification as well as preventing growth of *Listeria monocytogenes.* The culture works in a wide temperature range. Low fermentation temperature (< 77° F / 25° C) results in a traditional acidification profile whereas high fermentation temperature 95-104° F (35-40° C) gives a US style product. *Use dextrose* as this culture ferments sugar slowly. Controlling *Listeria monocytogenes* is not easy as it is so widespread. It can be found in livestock, in raw materials, in humans, on processing equipment and in other locations of meat processing plants. To prevent its growth proper sanitation and proper temperature control is needed in all steps of the manufacturing process.

Fermented sausages which are made at home may be at a higher risk due to simpler conditions and lack of sophisticated test equipment. It is unlikely that sausages produced at home will meet the same rigid safety conditions as a commercial meat plant. Temperatures may be lower, equipment not properly sanitized and many other factors may increase the safety risk. For these reasons we have chosen F-LC - bioprotective culture for many recipes as it provides extra safety for the operator.

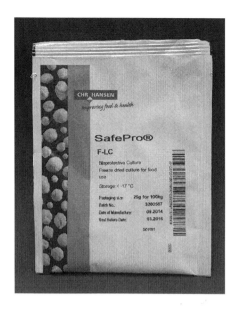

Photo 13.1 Bactoferm™ F-LC bio-protective culture.

The pH decrease of a sausage made with F-LC is faster than what is obtained with traditional culture such as T-SPX but not as fast as with F-1. By now you should realize that there is not a standard temperature that can be applied. The sausage made with T-SPX will ferment at 18°, 24° or 27° C, however, its flavor should be best at lower temperature range. Of course if you ferment at 27° C with a lot of dextrose you will get sourly taste anyhow.

LHP - fast -fermenting culture that can be applied at 80-100° F (27-38° C). The culture is recommended for the production of sausages with a sourly flavor such as American pepperoni or summer sausage.

Mold 600 - fast growing, dense, medium to very fluffy coverage. Generates a fresh camembert aroma/strong mushroom flavor and a typical scent of moss.

General Guidelines

Gdl is a great acidulant that has always been added to meat whenever a fast increase in acidity was required. Nowadays, there are widely available fast-fermenting cultures that can do the same job without creating danger of unpleasant and bitter flavors. Moreover, they are able to work at a wide range of temperatures which is of great importance in home production.

Adding different amounts of sugar has a little influence on pH drop during the first stage of fermentation providing that the temperature remains constant. The amount of acidity which the sausage acquires depends mainly on the amount of the introduced sugar.

Often people ask why dextrose and sugar are included in slow-fermented sausage recipes. The reason is the safety of the sausage and the easiest way to explain it is using a graph. A starter culture, 0.1% dextrose and 0.3% sugar are introduced to a sausage mince. It is depicted by point A on the graph. Bacteria are waking up from the freeze (lag phase) and not much happens between A and B. Depending on the temperature this can last from a few to 14 hours.

Dextrose curve - in point B lactic acid bacteria become fully active and immediately start converting dextrose into lactic acid. As the acid is produced the spoilage bacteria find the environment increasingly hostile. There is a fast pH drop which ends in point C (at the intersection of pH2 and T1) as there is no more dextrose left for lactic bacteria. The amount of developed acidity is too small to inhibit color and flavor forming bacteria *(Staphylococci)* which are growing and reacting with meat. Using more dextrose will introduce a sourly flavor and will prevent color and flavor forming bacteria from working.

At the same time lactic acid want to consume sugar, however, there is a problem; unlike dextrose which is a simple sugar, common sugar (sucrose) is a complex carbohydrate and must be first converted into dextrose (glucose) before bacteria can consume it. This conversion takes time so there is a delay. As a result lactic acid bacteria processes sugar slowly, see the rather flat sugar curve from B to E.

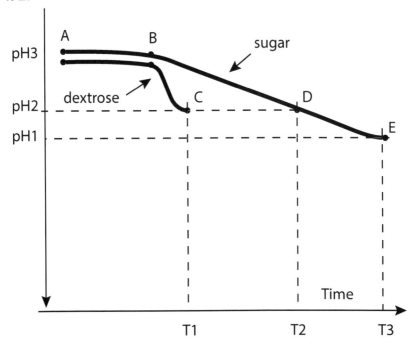

F 13.1 Fermenting with dextrose and sugar.

Dextrose processing bacteria reached pH2 (point C) in just T1 hours, however, sugar processing bacteria need T2 hours to reach the same pH drop (D). Much more time was needed to reach pH2 so more time was given to spoilage bacteria to grow and spoil the meat. Bacteria will produce lactic acid until all sugar will be exhausted in point E (pH1 and T3). Of course the total acidity will be the sum of dextrose and sugar fermentation.

Adding a little dextrose jumps up the fermentation process by allowing lactic bacteria to produce acidity faster what creates a safety hurdle sooner.

Equipment

It will be impossible to match the texture of a commercially produced fast-fermented sausage at home. In order to have the cleanest distribution of meat and fat particles the commercial producer processes frozen meat and fat. A bowl cutter produces a much cleaner cut that a grinder could ever do. A hobbyist should try to make up for this by using partially frozen meat, especially the fat in order to eliminate the problem of smearing. Mixing ground meat with our hands will also adversely contribute to texture of the sausage, however, the problem can be somewhat avoided if a very cold stainless steel mixing bowl is used. Texture problems are less visible in slow-fermented dry sausages as we have grown accustomed to irregular looks of traditionally made products.

Photo 13.2 It can be seen in the upper right corner how small fat particles can be cut in a bowl cutter.

pH of the Sausage Mix

If you have a means of measuring pH, it will be a good idea to hold off sugar calculations until pH of the meat is determined. Pork, beef, fat, skins, they all have a different pH and it is impossible to estimate pH of the sausage mass beforehand. Pork butts coming from different animals will have a different value. In some recipes such as Salami Milano wine is added which will increase acidity. In Mexican Chorizos vinegar is common and that of course will increase acidity even more. Your pH can lie anywhere between 5.7 and 6.2 and adding 1% dextrose or 1% GDL will drop it one full point to 4.7 and 5.2 respectively. Fast fermented sausages with pH of 5.2 fall within the border line of safety as its pH will increase a bit in time. If it is submitted to a few days of drying, the Aw drop will provide additional safety.

Once you know the pH of the mixed sausage mass, it is easy to calculate the dextrose that is needed. This decision will also depend on your starter culture and fermentation temperature. This reasoning applies mainly to fast-fermented sausage types as *slow-fermented sausages employ very little sugar* in order not to increase acidity. In slow fermented sausages moisture removal is the main hurdle that provides safety against bacterial spoilage and the addition of any liquids must be very carefully monitored as generally speaking it is not a good idea. Adding a little wine for this extra flavor is justified but adding water to facilitate mixing and stuffing should be avoided.

Choosing Sausage Type

Choosing the sausage type determines fermentation and drying temperatures, total production time, amount and type of sugar used, type of starter cultures and other parameters. *By now you should realize that with one recipe you can make different sausage types (slow or fast-fermented) and it is entirely up to you which way you want to go.* Twenty years ago a hobbyist had only one choice and that was a slow-fermented sausage. Today starter cultures are easily obtainable and all types of fermented sausages can be produced at home.

Let's say you have a recipe for a fresh Italian sausage and you want to make a fermented sausage out of it. All you need is to increase the percentage of salt, add sodium nitrite, starter culture and decide whether you want to wait 3 months before you can eat it or whether you want to take it with you on a hunting trip that happens in a week time.

Classical dry fermented sausages are the hardest to manufacture. They also require the most time and care. Therefore it is advised to start with semi-dry sausages first which are faster, easier and safer to produce. After they are fermented, smoked and cooked they become great snacks which can be taken everywhere. They can be left hanging in the kitchen and even though they will lose more moisture in time, they will be even microbiologically safer. Then as more experience is gained more difficult sausages can be attempted.

164

Modifying Known Sausage Recipes

There are many sausages for example Soviet, Moscow or Tambov, which belong to the dry type of sausages. The meat was cured with salt and nitrate for 5-7 days at 40° F (4° C) then cold smoked for 3-5 days below 71° F (22° C) and then dried for 25-30 days at 54-56° F (12-14° C). Of course no starter cultures were used. Those were naturally fermented sausages as the fermentation took place during the cold smoking stage. These sausages can be made faster today with starter cultures. They will also be much safer to produce at home conditions and of constant quality. By using different cultures or proper manipulation of the fermentation temperatures the same sausage recipe can produce a semi-dry or dry sausage.

To stress the point, the pepperoni recipe is presented in two forms: dry pepperoni and semi-dry pepperoni. The same sausage recipe can be used to produce a fresh, smoked or fermented sausage by changing parameters of manufacturing process. There are hundreds of sausage recipes that can be turned into fermented sausages.

For example "Kabanosy" meat stick is the smoked and cooked sausage of a semi-dry type. When the war ended and there was no refrigeration, all smoked sausages were hanging in Polish kitchens or pantries for weeks and months at the time and they only got drier and better. By adding culture and fermenting the sausage you can easily make a semi-dry or dry fermented version of the Kabanosy sausage.

You don't need a magical recipe to make a good sausage, you need to know how. Once you know *the how* you will transform any recipe into a wonderful product.

Tips and General Guidelines

- All *dry sausage* recipes contain 3% salt and the maximum amount of nitrite permissible by law. This is done in order to protect the sausage maker himself as his processing and testing equipment will not be as advanced as that of commercial processors. All semi-dry sausage recipes contain 2.5% salt. Low pH and often employed cooking process provide additional safety during manufacture of semi-dry products.

- ***Both cures (#1 and #2) contain salt and this amount is accounted for when calculating the total amount of salt in all recipes.***

- Most recipes call for grinding pork with a 3/16" (3 mm) plate. If you own only 3/8" (10 mm) use this one instead, nothing will happen to the sausage. Beef is usually ground with 1/8" (3 mm) plate.

- Dextrose (glucose) is used in semi-dry sausage recipes as fermentation times are very short and a fast pH drop is required.

- For slow-fermented sausages it is a good idea to use a combination of 1/3 dextrose and 2/3 common sugar.

- Sugar (sucrose) is used in dry sausage recipes as the fermentation time is longer and lactic acid bacteria have more time to act on. In addition a small amount of dextrose (fast fermenting sugar) is added to most *dry sausage* recipes. The reason is that dextrose being the simplest of sugars is easily metabolized by lactic acid bacteria and a small but moderately fast pH will be immediately obtained. This will provide an extra margin of safety which is very important during the first hours of the process.

- For fast fermented sausages like pepperoni, major pepperoni manufacturers overkill at adding 1.5% -2% sugar but most of Italian processors settle out between 0.4-0.8%.

- A highly accurate digital scale is needed to measure culture when making a small load of sausage.

- Sausage recipes such as Metka, Metka-Braunschweiger, Metka-Salmon Style, or Hungarian Sausage, Salami and Hungarian Salami have great academic value as they contain original instructions for making spreadable sausages as they were practiced by Polish meat plants in 1950-1990's. The sausages made according to these recipes were sold to the general public.

- Spices play an essential role in the production of any type of sausages. Spices are volatile and lose their aroma quickly. For that reason the amount of spices in slow fermented sausages may be increased as these sausages require longer processing times.

- Cold smoking is drying with smoke and it is not a continuous process. Smoke can be applied for about one hour then the sausage "rests" for one hour. The cycle is repeated again and again.

	Slow-fermented	Fast-fermented
Salt %	3.0	2.5
Sugar %	0.25 - 0.50	0.40 - 0.80
Sugar type	sucrose or dextrose + sucrose	dextrose
Gdl	None	optional
Nitrates	cure #2	cure #1
Culture *	T-SPX	F-LC, LHP
* These cultures are easily obtainable on the internet.		

Note: the majority of recipes are calculated for 5 kg (11 lb) meat because the amount of starter culture is very small. For 1 kg (2.2 lb) of meat the required amount of T-SPX culture (0.1 g) will be about 1/10 of the teaspoon and it will be difficult to measure, unless a highly accurate digital scale is available. If you have to estimate the amount is better to add a little more culture. You will not damage the sausage with more bacteria, they will simply consume sugar faster.

166

Chapter 14

Sausage Recipes
Recipe Index

CS - Cold smoked, traditional, no culture
SF - Slow-fermented, dry
FF - Fast-fermented, semi-dry

#	Name	Type	Page
1	Boerenmetworst	SF	169
2	Bydgoska	CS	170
3	Cacciatore	SF	171
4	Cervelat	FF	172
5	Chicken	FF	173
6	Chorizo	SF	175
7	Delicatessen Sausage	CS	176
8	Farmer	SF	177
9	Fuet	SF	178
10	Goteborg	SF	179
11	Gothaer	FF	180
12	Holsteiner	SF	181
13	Hungarian Dry Sausage	SF	182
14	Hungarian Smoked Sausage	CS	183
15	Kantwurst	SF	184
16	Kindziuk	CS	185
17	Landjager	SF	186
18	Lap Cheong	FF	187
19	Lebanon Bologna Traditional	CS	188
20	Lebanon Bologna with Culture	FF	189
21	Loukanka	SF	191
22	Medwurst	FF	192
23	Merguez	FF	193
24	Metka	CS	195
25	Metka Brunszwicka	CS	196
26	Metka Pomorska	CS	197

27	Metka Salmon Style	CS	198
28	Mettwurst-Braunschweiger	CS	199
29	Mortadella	SF	200
30	Moscow Sausage	FF	201
31	Nham	FF	202
32	Pepperoni	SF	205
33	Pepperoni	FF	206
34	Polish Cold Smoked Traditional	SF	207
35	Polish Smoked Sausage -Dry	SF	208
36	Polish Smoked Sausage-Semi-Dry	FF	208
37	Salami de Arles	SF	209
38	Salami Finocchiona	SF	210
39	Salami Genoa	SF	211
40	Salami - Hungarian Traditional	SF	212
41	Salami - Hungarian with Culture	SF	213
42	Salami Lombardia	SF	214
43	Salami Milano	SF	215
44	Salami Nola	SF	216
45	Salami - Polish Traditional	SF	217
46	Salami - Polish with Culture	SF	218
47	Salami Sorrento	SF	219
48	Salchichón	SF	220
49	Salmon Sausage	CS	221
50	Saucisson d'Alsace	SF	222
51	Servolatka	CS	223
52	Smoked Frankfurters	CS	224
53	Snijworst	FF	225
54	Soviet	SF	226
55	Sucuk Traditional	SF	227
56	Sucuck-Semi-Dry	FF	228
57	Summer Sausage	FF	230
58	Tambov	SF	232
59	Teewurst	CS	233
60	Tourist	SF	234
61	Thuringer	FF	235
62	Urutan	SF	236

Total 62 sausage recipes.

168

Boerenmetworst
(Dutch)

Dutch specialty dry sausage, made without garlic.

pork,   50%,   2.5 kg (5.5 lb)
lean beef, 20%,   1.0 kg (2.2 lb)
back fat,   30%,   1.5 kg (3.3 lb)

Ingredients per 5 kg (11 lb) of meat

salt, 3%, 140 g
cure #2, 12 g
dextrose (glucose), 0.3%, 15 g
pepper, 15 g
coriander, 10 g
mustard, 10 g
T-SPX culture, 0.6 g (¼ tsp)

1. Grind pork and back fat through 3/16" plate (5 mm). Grind beef with ⅛" (3 mm) plate.
2. Mix all ingredients with meat.
3. Stuff firmly into large diameter (36-40 mm) hog casings. Form 24-30" long links, then tie ends together to make a ring.
4. Ferment at 20° C (68° F) for 72 hours, 90-85% humidity.
5. Cold smoke for 12 hours (<22° C, 72° F).
6. Dry at 16-12° C (60-54° F), 85-80% humidity. In about 6-8 weeks a shrink of 30% should be achieved.
7. Store sausages at 10-15° C (50-59° F), 75% humidity.

Note: spices such as ginger and cloves are sometimes added.

Bydgoska Sausage
(Kiełbasa bydgoska surowa)

This cold smoked sausage recipe comes from the official Polish Government archives.

pork butt, 1000 g (2.2 lb)

Ingredients per 1 kg (2.2 lb) of meat

Salt, 21 g (3-1/2 tsp)
Cure # 1, 2.5 g (1/2 tsp)
Pepper, 1.5 g (1 tsp)
Marjoram, 1.0 g (1/2 tsp)
Sugar, 2.0 g (1/2 tsp)

1. **Curing.** Cut meat into 2.5-5 cm (1-2") pieces and mix with salt and Cure # 1. Pack tightly in container, cover with cloth and keep in refrigerator for 3 days.
2. Grind meat through 13 mm (3/8") plate.
3. Mix ground meat with spices until sticky.
4. Stuff into 32-36 mm hog casings forming 15 cm (6") long links. Leave links in long coils.
5. Apply a thin cold smoke for 1-1.5 days until the casings develop yellow-light brown color. Re-arrange smoke sticks or smoke carts during smoking.
6. Dry at 10-12° C (50-53° F) and 75-80% humidity until the yield is 87% in relation to the original weight of the meat. This should take about 2 weeks. Divide sausage coils into pairs.
7. Store at 12° C (53° F) or lower.

Note: 87% yield means that the finished sausage has retained 87% of its original unprocessed weight. In other words it has lost 13% of the moisture.

Cacciatore

Italian small dry sausage. Cacciatore means "hunter" in Italian and the story goes that hunters carried this sausage as a snack on long hunting trips.

lean pork, 60%, 3.0 kg (6.6 lb)
lean beef, 10%, 0.5 kg (1.1 lb)
back fat,   30%, 1.5 kg (3.3 lb)

Ingredients per 5 kg (11 lb) of meat

salt, 3%, 140 g
cure #2, 12 g
dextrose (glucose), 0.3%, 15 g
pepper, 15 g
coriander, 10 g
caraway, 10 g
red pepper, 10 g
garlic, 15 g
T-SPX culture, 0.6 g (¼ tsp)

1. Grind pork and back fat through 3/16" plate (5 mm). Grind beef with ⅛" (3 mm) plate.
2. Mix all ingredients with meat.
3. Stuff firmly into large diameter 36-40 mm hog casings or beef rounds. Make 6" long links.
4. Dip into surface mold growing solution - Bactoferm™ M-EK-4.
5. Ferment at 20° C (68° F) for 72 hours, 90-90% humidity.
6. Dry for 2 days at 18-16° C (64-60° F), 90-85% humidity.
7. Dry at 16-12° C (60-54° F), 85 -80% humidity.
8. In about 6-8 weeks a shrink of 30% should be achieved.
9. Store sausages at 10-15° C (50-59° F), 75% humidity.

Cervelat

European semi-dry sausage, an equivalent of American summer sausage. Definition covers countless recipes and sausages with the name cervelat made in many countries. You can call Thuringer, the Thuringer Cervelat or Summer Sausage the Cervelat Summer sausage and both names are correct describing the same type of sausage.

beef,	70%,	3.5 kg (7.7 lb)
pork,	30%,	1.5 kg (3.3 lb)

Ingredients per 5 kg (11 lb) of meat

salt, 2.5%, 115 g
cure #1, 12 g
dextrose, 1%, 50 g
sugar 1%, 50 g
ground black pepper, 12 g
whole black pepper, 10 g
coriander, 10 g
paprika, 10 g
whole mustard seeds, 20 g
ginger, 5 g
F-LC culture, 1.2 g (½ tsp)

1. Grind pork and beef through 3/16" plate (5 mm).
2. Mix all ingredients with meat.
3. Stuff into beef middles or fibrous casings about 60 mm diameter, form 30" links
4. Ferment at 38° C (100° F) for 24 hours, 90-85% humidity.
5. Introduce warm smoke (43° C, 110° F), 70% humidity for 12 hours. Gradually increase smoke temperature until internal meat temperature of 140° F (60° C) is obtained.
6. For a drier sausage: dry for 2 days at-22-16° C (60-70° F), 65-75% humidity or until desired weight loss has occurred.
7. Store sausages at 10-15° C (50-59° F), 75% humidity.

Chicken Fermented Sausage

Chicken thigh meat will create a better color than the breast, however, it is characterized by a high pH (6.1-6.4 for thigh and 5.6-5.8 for breast). Breast pH falls into pork pH range, unfortunately it contains little myoglobin which results in a weak color.

Chicken fat becomes semi-liquid already at room temperature and should be replaced with pork hard fat (back fat or hard fat trimmings). pH of pork fat is also high (6.2-7.0) and the sausage batter consisting of chicken meat and pork fat may have an initial value well over 6.0.

The moisture level of chicken meat is high and the Aw will be around 0.98 even after salt introduction. Chicken skin is often microbiologically dirty (contains undesirable bacteria). In addition to common pathogens that may be present in chicken meat, *Campylobacter jejuni* is typically associated with poultry meat.

The high initial pH of the sausage batter will require a longer fermentation time to drop pH below 5.3 within the prescribed time. Starter cultures which are available online are of freeze dry type and they exhibit a rather long lag phase (wake up time) before bacteria will start to produce a significant amount of lactic acid. Adding a larger amount of starter bacteria (adjusted for in this recipe) will compensate for lag time and low temperatures during fermentation. Bactoferm™ F-LC bio-protective culture might be a good choice as it inhibits *Listeria monocytogenes* and can be used at a wide range of temperatures.

Due to the high initial pH of the sausage batter it is essential to limit the time the sausage mix is left at temperatures over 15.6° C (60° F) which favors the growth of *Staphylococcus aureus*.

chicken meat,	80%,	4.0 kg (8.8 lb)
back fat or pork fat trimmings,	20%,	1.0 kg (2.2 lb)

Ingredients per 5 kg (11 lb) of meat

salt, 3%, 140 g
cure # 2, 12 g
dextrose (glucose), 1.0%, 50 g
sugar, 0.3%, 15 g
pepper, 15 g
coriander, 10 g
ground mustard, 10 g
allspice, 10 g
garlic, 25 g
F-LC culture, 2.4 g (1 tsp)

1. Grind chicken and back fat through 3/16" plate (5 mm).
2. Mix all ingredients with meat.
3. Stuff firmly into large diameter (36-40 mm) hog casings.
4. Ferment according to the table below.
5. Optional: cold smoke (< 22° C, 72° F) from time to time during fermentation.
6. Dry according to the table below.
7. Drying may continue past 18 days but the sausage will be much drier.

Recommended times and temperatures for making fermented poultry sausage ref. 29

Fermentation			
Temperature		Humidity %	Duration
° C	° F		
6	43	90	24 hrs
14	57	90	6 hrs
18	64	85	6 hrs
22	72	85	6 hrs
18	64	85	6 hrs
14	57	85	24 hrs
Drying			
14	57	75	18 days

Chorizo

In Spain and South American countries the chorizo sausage is made from coarsely chopped pork and seasoned with pepper, paprika and garlic. Spanish smoked paprika (sweet, bittersweet or hot) known as Pimentón gives it its deep red color. Mexican Chorizo is made from pork that is ground and seasoned with chile peppers, garlic and vinegar. It is moister and much hotter than the Spanish chorizo.

lean pork, ham or butt (20% fat), 5 kg (11 lb)

Ingredients per 5 kg (11 lb) of meat

salt, 3%, 140 g
cure #2, 12 g
dextrose, 0.2%, 10 g
sugar, 0.2%, 10 g
pepper, 30 g
pimentón (smoked paprika), 100 g
oregano, 10 g
garlic, 45 g
T-SPX culture, 0.6 g (¼ tsp)

1. Grind pork through ⅜" plate (8 mm).
2. Mix all ingredients with meat.
3. Stuff firmly into 32-36 mm hog casings, form 6" links.
4. Ferment at 20° C (68° F) for 72 hours, 90-85% humidity.
5. Dry at 16-12° C (60-54° F), 85-80% humidity, for 1-2 months.
6. Store sausages at 10-15° C (50-59° F), 75% humidity.

Spanish Chorizo types:

Chorizo Andaluz: pork, salt, black pepper, pimentón, cloves, garlic, white dry wine.
Chorizo Calendario: pork, beef, salt, pepper, garlic, oregano.
Chorizo Cantipalos: pork, salt, pimentón, garlic, oregano.
Chorizo Castellano: pork, salt, hot pimentón, sweet pimentón, garlic, oregano.
Chorizo Navarro: pork, salt, sweet pimentón, garlic.
Chorizo Riojano: pork, salt, hot pimentón, sweet pimentón, garlic.
Chorizo Salmantino: lean meat, salt, pimenón, garlic, oregano.

Delicatessen Sausage
(Kiełbasa delikatesowa)

This cold smoked sausage recipe comes from the official Polish Government archives.

lean pork, 400 g (0.88 lb)
beef, 400 g (0.88 lb)
back fat, 200 g (0.44) lb

Ingredients per 1 kg (2.2 lb) of meat

Salt, 28 g (5 tsp)
Cure # 2, 2.5 g (1/2 tsp)
Sugar, 4.0 g (3/4 tsp)
Pepper, 2.0 g (1 tsp)
Sweet paprika, 1.0 g (1/2 tsp)
Ginger, 1.0 g (1/2 tsp)
Nutmeg, 1.5 g (3/4 tsp)
Garlic, 1.5 g (1/2 clove)

1. **Curing.** Cut meat into 2.5-5 cm (1-2") pieces and mix with salt and Cure # 1. Pack tightly in container, cover with cloth and keep in refrigerator for 3 days.
2. Grind all meats and fat through 5 mm plate.
3. Mix ground meats with spice until mixture feels sticky.
4. Place the mixture in a container for 24 hours at 2-4° C (35-40° F) which is refrigerator temperature.
5. Stuff into 60 mm synthetic fibrous casings.
6. Place sausages in a container one on top of another and hold for 4-5 days at 2-4° C (35-40° F), 85-90% humidity. Remove and hang for 2-3 days at 8-10° C (46-50° F), 80-85% humidity.
7. Apply cold smoke for 2-3 days until brown in color.
8. Cool in air to 10-12° C (50-53° F) or lower. Hold at this temperature, 75-85% humidity for 7-10 days.

Farmer Sausage

Coarsely ground sausage with manually cut fat pieces. Besides its rustic look and different size grind the recipe differs very little from the classic Italian salamis.

pork (butt),	30%,	1.5 kg (3.3 lb)
beef (chuck),	50%,	2.5 kg (5.5 lb)
back fat or fat pork trimmings	20%,	1.0 kg (2.2 lb)

Ingredients per 5 kg (11 lb) of meat

salt, 3%, 140 g
cure # 2, 12 g
dextrose, 0.3%, 15 g
ground white pepper, 15 g
T-SPX culture, 0.6 g (¼ tsp)

1. Grind pork through ⅜" plate (12 mm). Manually dice back fat or pork fat trimmings into 1/4" (6 mm) pieces. Grind beef with 3/8" (5 mm) plate, partially freeze and regrind again through 1/8" (3 mm) plate.
2. Mix all ingredients with meat.
3. Stuff firmly into 60 mm beef middles or protein lined fibrous casings. Make 16" long links.
4. Ferment at 20° C (68° F) for 72 hours, 90-85% humidity.
5. Cold smoke below 20° C (68° C) with thin smoke for 24 hours.
6. Dry at 16-12° C (60-54° F), 85-80% humidity, for 2-3 months. The sausage is dried until around 30-35% in weight is lost.
7. Store sausages at 10-15° C (50-59° F), 75% humidity.

Fuet-Spanish Salami

Fuet is a Spanish pork sausage, dry cured, like salami. Sausage is frequently found in Cataluña, Spain. Unlike the Butifarra, another in the family of Catalan sausages, fuet is dry cured. The name fuet means "whip" in the Catalan language.

lean pork,	70%,	3.5 kg (7.7 lb)
back fat,	30%,	1.5 kg (3.3 lb)

Ingredients per 5 kg (11 lb) of meat

salt, 3%, 140 g
cure #2, 12 g
dextrose (glucose), 0.3%,15 g
pepper, 15 g
paprika, 20 g
garlic, 20 g
T-SPX culture, 0.6 g (¼ tsp)

1. Grind pork and back fat through 3/16" plate (5 mm).
2. Mix all ingredients with meat.
3. Stuff firmly into hog, beef middles or 38-50 protein lined fibrous casings.
4. Ferment at 20° C (68° F) for 72 hours, 90-85% humidity.
5. Dry at 16-12° C (60-54° F), 85-80% humidity for 1-2 months. The sausage is dried until around 30-35% in weight is lost.
6. Store sausages at 10-15° C (50-59° F), 75% humidity.

Some fuets are covered with white mold, others not. Mold-600 culture can be applied.

Goteborg

Swedish dry sausage. Smoked.

pork (butt),	40%,	2.0 kg (4.4 lb)
beef (chuck),	40%,	2.0 kg (4.4 lb)
pork cheeks or belly,	20%,	1.0 kg (2.2 lb)

Ingredients per 5 kg (11 lb) of meat

salt, 3%, 140 g
cure # 2, 12 g
dextrose (glucose), 0.2%, 10 g
sugar, 10 g
white pepper, 15 g
cardamom, 10 g
coriander, 10 g
T-SPX culture, 0.6 g (¼ tsp)

1. Grind pork and back fat through 3/16" plate (5 mm). Grind beef with ⅛" plate.
2. Mix all ingredients with meat.
3. Stuff firmly into 60 mm beef middles or protein lined fibrous casings. Make 16" long links.
4. Ferment at 20° C (68° F) for 72 hours, 90-85% humidity.
5. Cold smoke below 20° C (68° C) with thin smoke for 24 hours.
6. Dry at 16-12° C (60-54° F), 85-80% humidity, for 2-3 months. The sausage is dried until around 30-35% in weight is lost.
7. Store sausages at 10-15° C (50-59° F), 75% humidity.

Gothaer

German semi-dry sausage.

| lean pork, | 80%, | 4.0 kg (8.8 lb) |
| beef, | 20%, | 1.0 kg (2.2 lb) |

Ingredients per 5 kg (11 lb) of meat

salt, 2.5%, 115 g
cure #1, 12 g
dextrose, 1%, 50 g
black pepper, 12 g
F-LC culture, 1.25 g (½ tsp)

1. Grind pork through 3/16" plate (5 mm). Grind beef through 1/8" (3 mm) plate.
2. Mix all ingredients with meat.
3. Stuff into beef middles or fibrous casings 40-60 mm, 20" long.
4. Ferment at 24-30° C (75-86° F) for 24 hours, 90-85% humidity.
5. Apply warm smoke (43° C, 110° F), 70% humidity, for 6 hours. Gradually increase smoke temperature until meat reaches 140° F (60° C) internal temperature.
6. For a drier sausage: dry for 3 days at 22-16° C (60-70° F), 65-75% humidity or until desired weight loss has occurred.
7. Store sausages at 10-15° C (50-59° F), 75% humidity.

Holsteiner

German dry sausage.

beef (chuck),	60%,	3.0 kg (6.6 lb)
pork (butt),	40%,	2.0 kg (4.4 lb)

Ingredients per 5 kg (11 lb) of meat

salt, 3%, 140 g
cure #2, 12 g
dextrose (glucose), 0.2%, 10 g
sugar, 0.2%, 10 g
ground white pepper, 10 g
cracked white pepper, 5 g
T-SPX culture, 0.6 g (¼ tsp)

1. Grind pork through 3/16" plate (5 mm). Grind beef with 1/8" plate.
2. Mix all ingredients with meat.
3. Stuff firmly into 60 mm beef middles or protein lined fibrous casings. Make 16" long links.
4. Ferment at 20° C (68° F) for 72 hours, 90-85% humidity.
5. Apply a thin cold smoke at 20° C (68° C) for 24 hours.
6. Dry at 16-12° C (60-54° F), 85-80% humidity, for 2-3 months. The sausage is dried until around 30-35% in weight is lost.
7. Store sausages at 10-15° C (50-59° F), 75% humidity.

Hungarian Dry Sausage

Although this sausage carries Hungarian name it has been always made in Poland and might as well be considered a local product.

lean beef,	30%,	1.5 kg (3.3 lb)
pork back fat,	70%,	3.5 kg (7.7 lb)

Ingredients per 5 kg (11 lb) of meat

salt, 3%, 140 g
cure # 2, 12 g
dextrose (glucose), 0.2%, 10 g
pepper, 10 g
sweet paprika, 15 g
T-SPX culture, 0.6 g (¼ tsp)

1. Grind meat through 2 mm plate. Refreeze and grind again. Cut back fat into 15 mm (¾") pieces.
2. Mix all ingredients with ground meat and diced back fat.
3. Stuff firmly into beef middles or 3" protein lined fibrous casings.
4. Ferment at 20° C (68° F) for 72 hours, 90-85% humidity.
5. Cold smoke for 4 days (<22° C, 72° F). You can smoke during fermentation.
6. Dry at 16-12° C (60-54° F), 85-80% humidity for 2-3 months.
7. Store sausages at 10-15° C (50-59° F), 75% humidity.

Hungarian Smoked Sausage
(Kiełbasa węgierska wędzona)

This cold smoked sausage recipe comes from the official Polish Government archives.

| beef, | 300 g (0.66 lb) |
| pork back fat, | 700 g (1.54 lb) |

*Ingredients per **1 kg (2.2 lb)** of meat*

Salt, 21 g (3-1/2 tsp)
Cure # 1, 2.5 g (1/2 tsp)
Pepper, 1.5 g (3/4 tsp)
Sweet paprika, 1.5 g (3/4 tsp)

1. Curing. Cut back fat into strips, rub in 2/3 (16 g) salt into fat strips and hold for 10 days in refrigerator. Back fat does not need Cure #1. Cut meat into 2.5-5 cm (1-2") pieces and mix with 1/3 (8 g) salt and all Cure #1. Pack tightly in container, cover and keep in refrigerator for 3 days.
2. Grind beef through 2-3 mm plate. Dice back fat into 15 mm (5/8") cubes.
3. Mix ground beef with pepper until sticky. Mix back fat with paprika and then mix all together.
4. Stuff firmly into 40 mm beef rounds or hog casings and form rings. Tie both ends with twine.
5. Hang for 1-2 days at 2-4° C (35-40° F), 85-90-% humidity.
6. Apply cold smoke for 2-3 days until yellow in color.
7. Cool in air to 10-12° C (50-53° F) or lower. Keep refrigerated.

Kantwurst

Kantwurst is an original Austrian dry sausage, very unique in its characteristic square shape.

lean pork, 80%, 4.0 kg (8.8 lb)
back fat, 20%, 1.0 kg (3.3 lb)

Ingredients per 5 kg (11 lb) of meat

salt, 3%, 140 g
cure # 2, 12 g
dextrose, 0.3%, 15 g
pepper, 15 g
coriander, 10 g
caraway, 10 g
garlic, 15 g
T-SPX culture, 0.6 g (¼ tsp)

1. Grind pork and back fat through 3/16" plate (5 mm).
2. Mix all ingredients with meat.
3. Stuff loosely (80% capacity) into large diameter fibrous casings (70 mm). Place stuffed sausage between two boards with some weight on top to flatten the sausage. Then move to a fermentation room.
4. Ferment at 20° C (68° F) for 96 hours, 95-90% humidity.
5. Remove boards and wipe off any slime that might have accumulated under boards.
6. Dry at room temperature until casings are dry to the touch. Hang square shaped sausages on smokesticks.
7. Cold smoke (20° C, 68° F) for a few hours to prevent growth of mold.
8. Dry for 2 days at 20-18° C (68-64° F), 90-85% humidity. Apply smoke from time to time.
9. Dry at 16-12° C (60-54° F), 85-80% humidity. In about 8 weeks a shrink of 30% should be achieved.
10. Store sausages at 10-15° C (50-59° F), 75% humidity.

Kindziuk

This is a well known product of Lithuania, known in Poland as Kindziuk ("Skilandis" in Lithuanian).

lean pork (ham),	80%,	4.0 kg (8.8 lb)
fresh belly,	20%,	1.0 kg (2.2 lb)

Ingredients per 5 kg (11 lb) of meat

salt, 3.3%, 155 g
cure #2, 12 g
sugar, 0.1%, 5 g
pepper, 15 g
smashed garlic, 15 g
pure alcohol, 190 proof, (American *EverClear* 190 proof), 50 ml

1. Cut meat and belly into 1.5" pieces and mix with pepper and smashed garlic.
2. Fry salt briefly on a hot pan (removes moisture), stirring often. Rub salt thoroughly into the meat. Add sugar, cure #1 and alcohol.
3. Mix everything well together. Stuff firmly into pork stomach, bladder or large fibrous casing (60 mm). Avoid creating air pockets.
4. Hang for at least 10 days in a cool, dry and ventilated area. This is when curing, drying and fermenting are taking place.
5. Cold smoke (below 18° C, 64° F) for 3 weeks, applying smoke 3-4 hours daily. On the last day of smoking add juniper berries or juniper twigs into the fire.
6. Store in a dark, cool and dry place.

Originally the ingredients were stuffed into pork stomach or bladder. The stomach was sewn and the bladder was tied off with butcher twine.
Then the casing was placed between two wooden boards and pressed together. The boards were tied with twine and hung (see step 4).
Pure alcohol evaporates and removes moisture.
Original Kindziuk was smoked with alder wood.

Landjager

Landjager is a German sausage similar to Austrian Kantwurst as both sausages are flattened during fermentation, which gives them a rectangular shape.

fat pork,	70%,	3.5 kg (7.7 lb)
lean beef,	30%,	1.5 kg (3.3 lb)

Ingredients per 5 kg (11 lb) of meat

salt, 3%, 140 g
cure #2, 12 g
dextrose, 0.3%, 15 g
pepper, 15 g
cumin, 10 g
nutmeg, 10 g
T-SPX culture, 0.6 g (¼ tsp)

1. Grind pork through 3/16" plate (5 mm). Grind beef through ⅛" (3 mm) plate.
2. Mix all ingredients with meat.
3. Stuff loosely (80% capacity) into 32-36 mm hog casings. Make links 8" (20 cm) long. Place stuffed sausage between two boards with some weight on top to flatten the sausage. Then move to a fermentation room.
4. Ferment at 20° C (68° F) for 72 hours, 95-90% humidity.
5. Remove boards and wipe off any slime that might have accumulated under boards.
6. Dry at room temperature until casings are dry to the touch. Hang square shaped sausages on smokesticks.
7. Cold smoke (< 20° C, 68° F) for a few hours to prevent growth of mold.
8. Dry at 16-12° C (60-54° F), 85 -80% humidity. In about six weeks a shrink of 30% should be achieved.
9. Store sausages at 10-15° C (50-59° F), 75% humidity.

Lap Cheong

Chinese sausage is a dried, hard sausage usually made from pork meat and a high content of fat. The Chinese name for sausages is "Lap Chong" which means the "winter stuffed intestine" or "waxed intestine" because "chong" not only means "intestine" but also "sausage". This sausage is normally smoked, sweetened, and seasoned. It is used as an ingredient in many dishes in some parts of southern China, including Hong Kong and countries in Southeast Asia. It is for example, used in fried rice, noodles and other dishes. Chinese sausage formulations are unique, based on a long tradition. Ingredients such as monosodium glutamate, soy sauce and sugar are added to the sausages in very high levels. The addition of selected Chinese rice wines or even scotch or sherry are common for certain quality products.

pork butts, 70/30%, 5 kg (11 lb)
(If using lean pork or lean pork trimmings add 30% of back fat).

Ingredients per 5 kg (11 lb) of meat

salt, 2.5%, 115 g
cure #1, 12 g
dextrose (glucose), 1%, 50 g
sugar, 4%, 200 g
cinnamon, 10 g
chinese rice wine, 1/2 cup, 125 ml
monosodium glutamate, 12 g
F-LC culture, 1.2 g (½ tsp)

1. Grind pork and back fat through ⅜" plate (10 mm).
2. Mix all ingredients with meat.
3. Stuff firmly into narrow hog or sheep casings 18-26 mm and form 5-6" (15 cm) long links.
4. Ferment at 38° C (100° F) for 12 hours, 90-85% humidity.
5. Apply light smoke at 45° C (115° F), 70% humidity for 6 hours. The sausage is still fermenting (F-LC culture is able to produce lactic acid at this temperature).
6. Gradually increase smoke temperature until internal meat temperature becomes 154° F (68° C).
7. Store sausages at 10-15° C (50-59° F), 75% humidity.

The traditional Chinese way, still applied today, is a time consuming operation of cutting meat by hand into small cubes. Chinese are fond of using MSG (monosodium glutamate), but it may be removed from the recipe.

Lebanon Bologna
(traditional method)

This well known American sausage has its roots in the town of Lebanon, Pennsylvania, where it was made by German settlers. This is a semi-dry, fermented, heavily smoked, *all-beef* sausage which is not cooked. The traditional process (no starter cultures) calls for curing beef at 4-6° C (40-43° F) for 10 days.

beef, 100%,   5.0 kg (11.0 lb)

Ingredients per 5 kg (11 lb) of meat

salt, 3%, 140 g
cure #1, 12 g
dextrose, 1%, 50 g
sugar, 3 %, 150 g
black pepper, 15 g
allspice, 7,5 g
cinnamon, 10 g
cloves, (ground), 7,5 g
ginger, 10 g

1. Curing. Grind beef with a large plate (3/4", 20 mm), mix with salt, cure #1 and sugar and keep for 10 days at 4-6° C (40-43° F).
2. Grind cured beef through 1/8 - 3/16" (3-5 mm) plate.
3. Mix ground meat with all ingredients.
4. Stuff sausage mix into 40-120 mm casings. Natural beef middles, collagen or fibrous casings. The larger casings are tied and stockinetted or laced with butcher twine for support as this is a large and heavy sausage.
5. Cold smoke for 4-8 days at < 22° C, 72° F, 85% humidity.
6. For a drier sausage: dry at 16-12° C (60-54° F), 85-80% humidity.
7. Store sausages at 10-15° C (50-59° F), 75% humidity.

Final pH around 4.2-4.4, water activity 0.93-0.96, it is a moist sausage but extremely stable due to its low final pH. The sausage is often left for 3 days at 4-6° C (40-43° F) for additional ripening. The sausage was traditionally cold smoked for 7 days in winter months and 4 days in the summer.

Lebanon Bologna
(with starter culture)

beef,   5.0 kg (11.0 lb)

Ingredients per 5 kg (11 lb) of meat

salt, 2.5%, 115 g
cure #1, 12 g
dextrose 1%, 50 g
sugar, 3%, 150 g
black pepper, 15 g
allspice, 7.5 g
cinnamon, 10 g
cloves, (ground), 7.5 g
ginger, 10 g
T-SPX culture, 0.6 g (¼ tsp)

1. Grind beef through 1/8 - 3/16" (3-5 mm) plate.
2. Mix ground beef with all ingredients, including starter culture.
3. Stuff sausage mix into 40-120 mm casings. Natural beef middles, collagen or fibrous casings. The larger casings are tied and stockinetted or laced with butcher twine for support as this is a large and heavy sausage.
4. Ferment at 24° C (75° F) for 72 hours, 90-85% humidity.
5. Cold smoke for 2 days at < 22° C 72° F, 85% humidity.
6. For a drier sausage: dry at 16-12° C (60-54° F), 85-80% humidity.
7. Store sausages at 10-15° C (50-59° F), 75% humidity.

Final pH around 4.6, water activity 0.93-0.96, it is a moist sausage but extremely stable due to its low final pH. The sausage is often left for 3 days at 4-6° C (40-43° F) for additional ripening.

If no cold smoke is available, smoke with hot smoke for 6 hours. Start at 110° F (43° C), then gradually increase temperature and smoke at 120° F (49° C) for 3-4 hours.

Traditionally made Lebanon Bologna is not cooked. To comply with increasingly tougher government regulations for preventing the growth of *E. coli 0157:H7* most manufacturers subject this sausage to a heat treatment:

Lebanon Bologna - according to compliance guidelines for fermented products. *Instructions are listed for the purpose of stressing the importance of the control of some of the pathogenic bacteria, in this case E.coli 0157:H7 which creates a safety hazard in products made with beef. This is how the commercial producer will make the sausage in order to be on the safe side.*

Process to achieve a 7-log10 reduction of *Salmonella* and *E.coli 0157:H7.*

Ingredients:	boneless lean beef - 10% fat
	salt - 3.5%
	potassium nitrate - 12 ppm
	sodium nitrite - 200 ppm
Fermentation:	12 hrs at 80° F, then at 100° F until pH of 4.7 or 5.2 is reached
Heat:	110° F (44° C) for 20 hrs, OR
	115° F (47° C) for 10 hrs, OR
	120° F (49° C) for 3 hrs

Reference: Ellajosyula, K.E., S. Doores, E.W. Mills, R.A. Wilson, R.C. Anantheswaran, and S.J. Knabel. 1998. *Destruction of Escherichia coli 0157:H7 and Salmonella typhimurium in Lebanon Bologna by interaction of fermentation, pH, heating temperature, and time.* J. Food Prot. 61(2):152-7.

Loukanka

Loukanka is a very well known Bulgarian dry sausage. It is formed into a traditional flat shape and it has great keeping qualities.

lean pork, ham, butt, loin	80%,	4.0 kg (8.8 lb)
pork back fat or fat trimmings,	20%,	1.0 kg (2.2 lb)

Ingredients per 5 kg (11 lb) of meat

salt, 3%, 140 g
cure #2, 12 g
dextrose, 0.2%, 10 g
garlic, 1%, 50 g
cumin, 1%, 50 g
T-SPX culture, 0.6 g (¼ tsp)

1. Grind lean pork and fat through 3/16" plate (5 mm).
2. Mix all ingredients with meat.
3. Stuff firmly into 28-30 mm hog casings.
4. Ferment at 20° C (68° F) for 72 hours, 90-85% humidity. At the beginning of the fermentation process place weight on sausages to flatten them out.
5. Dry at 16-12° C (60-54° F), 85-80% humidity for about 1-2 months.
6. Store sausages at 10-15° C (50-59° F), 75% humidity.

Loukanka has very little tang owing to a small amount of sugar.

Medwurst

Swedish sausages are characterized by the addition of potatoes and this semi-dry Medwurst is no exception.

pork (butt, picnic),	80%,	4.0 kg (8.8 lb)
back fat or bacon,	20%,	1.0 kg (2.2 lb)

Ingredients per 5 kg (11 lb) of meat

salt, 2.5%, 115 g
cure #1, 12 g
dextrose 1%, 50 g
sugar 0.5%, 25 g
white pepper, 12 g
granulated or powdered onion, 25 g (5 Tbsp)
allspice, 10 g
boiled potatoes, 1 kg
F-LC culture, 1.25 g (½ tsp)

Potato contains about 2% carbohydrates (sugars). pH of fresh potato is 7.50.

1. Boil potatoes.
2. Grind all meats through 5 mm (3/16") plate. Re-freeze and grind again through 3mm (1/8") plate.
3. Mix everything together, add 1 cup of water.
4. Stuff into 35-40 mm hog casings, beef middles or fibrous casings.
5. Ferment at 75° F (24° C), 80-85% humidty for 72 hours.
6a. Apply cold smoke for about 1 hour every day. Cook to 140° F (60° C) internal meat temperature *OR*
6b. Smoke for 6 hours at 115° F (46° C) gradually raising temperature until sausage reaches 140° F (60° C) internal temperature.

Merguez

Merguez a spicy, short sausage from North Africa that is made with lamb or beef and flavored with spices. Spices such as paprika, cayenne or harissa, a hot chili paste, all give Merguez sausage its red color. Sold by street vendors in Paris, can also be found in London, Belgium and New York. Merguez, the French transliteration of the Arabic word mirqaz, is a spicy small sausage used in Tunisia and Algeria.

Many recipes call for Harrisa Paste which is nothing more than a combination of the spices that are already listed above in ingredients (garlic, cumin, olive oil, hot chili peppers and coriander).

Making Harrisa paste:

1. Place 4 oz of red hot chilies in a bowl and cover with hot water for two hours, then drain.
2. In a blender process ¼ cup garlic cloves, ¼ cup ground cumin, ½ cup ground coriander, ¼ cup salt, drained chillies and ½ cup olive oil. Add olive oil slowly until a thick paste is produced. For a finer consistency rub paste through a sieve.

You can make a smaller amount of paste: 1 garlic clove crushed and finely chopped, ½ Tbsp salt, 2 Tbsp olive oil, 1 tsp cayenne pepper, ½ tsp ground cumin, ¼ tsp ground coriander. Mix ingredients in a jar and shake well. Cover with a lid.

There are Merguez sausage recipes that include coriander, oregano, fennel seeds (used in Italian sausages) and even ground cinnamon. This is a spicy sausage and in addition to the spices listed in ingredients above, please feel free to add any spices that you personally like. Merguez is often made into hamburger patties or meat balls. It is served by frying in olive oil until well browned or grilled.

Merquez is listed as a fermented sausage in the *Fermented Foods of the World: A Dictionary and Guide* by Campbell-Platt and a fast-fermented semi-dry version of the sausage is presented here.

lamb, 70/30 (lean to fat),   5 kg (11 lb)

Ingredients per 5 kg (11 lb) of meat

salt, 2.5%, 115 g
cure #1, 12 g
dextrose, 1%, 50 g
black pepper, 25 g
garlic, 30 g
cayenne pepper, 25 g
paprika, 25 g
cumin, 12 g
coriander, 10 g
olive oil, 90 g (6 Tbsp)
F-LC culture, 1.2 g (½ tsp)

1. Grind lamb through 3/16" plate (5 mm).
2. Mix all ingredients with ground lamb.
3. Stuff firmly into sheep casings 18-26 mm and form 5-6" (15 cm) long links or leave in one continuous rope.
4. Ferment at 24° C (75° F) for 48 hours, 90-85% humidity.
5. Dry at 16-12° C (60-54° F), 85-80% humidity for 18 days.
6. Store sausages at 10-15° C (50-59° F), 75% humidity.

Note: after fermenting, sausage can be fully cooked and served.

Metka
(Metka)

Metka is a cold smoked sausage that is related to German Mettwurst. Metka sausages were not cooked and this why they were less popular in summer months. With the advent of refrigeration the storing problem has been eliminated. *This cold smoked spreadable sausage recipe comes from the official Polish Government archives*

pork (butt, picnic),	60%,	600 g (1.32 lb)
beef,	40%,	400 g (0.88 lb)

Ingredients per 1 kg (2.2 lb.) of meat

Salt, 21 g,	(3-1/2 tsp)
Cure 1, 2.5 g,	(1/2 tsp)
Pepper, 1.0 g,	(1/2 tsp)
Paprika, 1.0 g,	(1/2 tsp)
Sugar, 0.2%, 2.0 g	(1/2 tsp)

1. **Curing.** Cut all meat into 5-6 cm (2") cubes, mix with salt and cure #1. Keep pork and beef separate. Pack tightly in containers and cover with a clean cloth. Place in a cooler (4-6° C, 40-42° F) for 72 hours.
2. Grind all meats through 3 mm (1/8") plate. Re-freeze and grind again.
3. Mix meats until sticky. During mixing add remaining ingredients.
4. Stuff firmly into 36-40 mm beef rounds or synthetic cellulose or fibrous casings.
5. Hang for 1-2 days at 2-6° C (35-43° F) and 85-90% humidity.
6. Apply a thin cold smoke for 1-2 days until casings develop brown reddish color.
7. Cool in air to 12° C (53° F) or lower. Store in refrigerator.

Metka Brunszwicka
(Metka brunszwicka)

Origin of this metka sausage is to be found in the German town of Brunszwik. *This cold smoked spreadable sausage recipe comes from the official Polish Government archives.*

Pork (butt, picnic), 40%,	400 g (0.88 lb)
Beef, 40%,	400 g (0.88 lb)
Jowls (or belly), skinless, 20%,	200 g (0.44 lb)

Ingredients per 1 kg (2.2 lb.) of meat

Salt, 21 g,	(3-1/2 tsp)
Cure # 1, 2.5 g	(1/2 tsp)
Pepper, 2.0 g	(1 tsp)
Paprika, 1.0 g	(1/2 tsp)
Nutmeg, 0.5 g	(1/4 tsp)

1. **Curing.** Cut meat into 5-6 cm (2") cubes, mix with salt and cure #1. Keep pork and beef separate. Pack tightly in containers and cover with a clean cloth. Place in a cooler (4-6° C, 40-42° F) for 72 hours.
2. Grind all meats through 2 mm plate, refreeze and grind again *OR* grind once and then emulsify in a food processor without adding water. Add spices when grinding or emulsifying.
3. Stuff firmly into 40 mm beef middles or fibrous casings. Form 8-10" (20-25 cm) links.
4. Hang for 1-2 days at 2-6° C (35-43° F) and 85-90% humidity.
5. Apply a thin cold smoke for 1-2 days until casings develop brown color.
6. Cool in air to 12° C (53° F) or lower. Store in refrigerator.

Metka Pomorska
(Metka pomorska)

Metka Sausage has its origin in the Northern areas of Poland known as Pomerania (Pomorze). *This cold smoked spreadable sausage recipe comes from the official Polish Government archives.*

Beef, 30%,   300 g (0.66 lb)
Back fat or fat trimmings, 70%,   700 g (1.84 lb)
Around 5% (50 g, 0.11 lb) of pork fat may be replaced with beef fat.

Ingredients per 1 kg (2.2 lb.) of meat

Salt, 21 g   (3-1/2 tsp)
Cure # 1, 1.5 g   (1/3 tsp)
Pepper, 2.0 g   (1 tsp)
Paprika, 1.0 g   (1/2 tsp)
Sugar, 2.0 g   (1/2 tsp)

1. Curing. Cut meat into 2.5-5 cm (1-2") pieces and mix with salt and cure #1. Pack tightly in container, cover with cloth and keep in refrigerator for 3 days.
2. Grind all meats through 2 mm plate, refreeze and grind again *OR* grind once and then emulsify in food processor without adding water. During emulsifying the temperature of the meat should not exceed 15° C (59° F).
3. Mix meat, fat and spices together *without* adding water.
4. Stuff into 50 mm synthetic cellulose or fibrous casings. Form straight 20-25 cm (8-10") long links.
5. Hang for 1-2 days at 10° C (50° F) and 85-90% humidity.
6. Apply a thin cold smoke for 1-2 days until casings develop light brown color.
7. Cool in air to 12° C (53° F) or lower.

197

Metka Salmon Style
(Metka łososiowa)

There is no salmon inside though the name may imply it. Certain Polish meat products that call for bacon or pork loin in a recipe have the "salmon" nickname added. For instance, Smoked Pork Loin-Salmon Style. The reason is that the loin resembles the shape of a salmon. Both pork loin and salmon are very popular in Poland and are considered delicacies. *This cold smoked spreadable sausage recipe comes from the official Polish Government archives.*

Beef, 20%,	200 g	(0.44 lb)
Pork belly, skinless, 80%,	800 g	(1.76 lb)

Ingredients per 1 kg (2.2 lb.) of meat

Salt, 21 g	(3-1/2 tsp)
Cure # 1, 2.5 g	(1/2 tsp)
Pepper, 2.0 g	(1 tsp)
Nutmeg, 0.5 g	(1/4 tsp)
Paprika, 1.0 g	(1/2 tsp)

1. **Curing.** Cut meat into 5-6 cm (2") cubes, mix with salt and cure #1. Keep pork and beef separate. Pack tightly in containers and cover with a clean cloth. Place in a cooler (4-6° C, 40-42° F) for 72 hours.
2. Grind all meats through 2 mm plate, refreeze and grind again *OR* grind once and then emulsify in food processor without adding water. Add spices when grinding or emulsifying.
3. Stuff firmly into 40 mm beef middles or fibrous casings. Form 8-10" (20-25 cm) links.
4. Hang for 12 hours at 10° C (50° F) and 85-90% humidity.
5. Apply a thin cold smoke for 10-12 hours until casings develop gold brown color.
6. Cool in air to 12° C (53° F) or lower. Store in a refrigerator.

Mettwurst-Braunschweiger

German spreadable sausage.

beef,	30%,	1.5 kg	(3.30 lb)
pork butt,	30%,	1.5 kg	(3.30 lb)
pork belly,	40%,	2.0 kg	(4.40 lb)

Ingredients per 5 kg (11 lb) of meat

salt, 2.6 %, 120 g
cure #1, 12 g
dextrose, 0.2%, 10 g
pepper, 12 g
paprika, 3 g
mace, 3 g
juniper extract* 5 g, (1/2 Tbsp)
T-SPX culture, 0.6 g (¼ tsp)

1. Grind all meats through ⅛" (3 mm) plate. Re-freeze meats and grind again twice. You may grind once and then emulsify in the food processor without adding water.
2. Add all ingredients, starter culture included, during this step.
3. Stuff firmly into 40-60 mm beef middles or fibrous casings. Form 8-10" (20-25 cm) links.
4. Ferment for 48 hours at 18° C (64° F), 75% humidity.
5. Apply cold smoke for 12 hours at 18° C (64° F).
6. Store in a refrigerator.

Notes: cold smoking is drying with smoke and it is not a continuous process. Smoke is applied for about one hour, then the sausage "rests" for one hour. The cycle is repeated again and again.
* insert 20 g of crushed juniper berries into 120 ml (½ cup) vodka or cognac and leave in a closed jar for 2-3 days. Filter the liquid from berries.

Mortadella

Mortadella is made from pork only, pork and beef or pork fat and veal. If back fat is diced into ¼" (6 mm) pieces and whole pistachio nuts are added, the resulting product will have traditional look. Mortadella is not smoked.

pork (butt),	55%,	2.75	kg (6.05 lb)
beef (chuck),	25%,	1.25	kg (2.75 lb)
back fat or hard fat trimmings,	20%,	1.00	kg (2.20 lb)

Ingredients per 5 kg (11 lb) of meat

salt, 3%, 140 g
cure #2, 12 g
dextrose, 0.2%, 10 g
sugar, 15 g
ground white pepper, 15 g
garlic, 5 g
rum, 65 ml (¼ cup)
pistachio nuts, 25 g
T-SPX culture, 0.6 g (¼ tsp)

1. Cut back fat ino ¼" (6 mm) cubes and set aside.
2. Grind pork through 3/8" plate (10 mm). Refreeze and grind again through ⅛" plate (3 mm). Do the same with beef.
3. Mix all ingredients with meat and diced fat.
4. Stuff firmly into 100-120 mm (4-5") protein lined fibrous casings, 12" long.
5. Ferment at 20° C (68° F) for 72 hours, 90-85% humidity.
6. Preheat smokehouse (no smoke applied) to 120° F (49° C) and hold sausages at this temperature for 12 hours (to remove the moisture from the sausage). Gradually increase temperature until an internal temperature of 138° F (59° C) is obtained.
7. Cool sausages by hanging them at room temperature.
8. Dry at 16-12° C (60-54° F), 85-80% humidity. The sausage is dried until around 30-35% in weight is lost.

Note: You may make the sausage ready to eat by cooking (after step 5) to 158° F (70° C) internal meat temperature.
At your discretion the following spices may be added (around 2 g spice/1 kg of meat) : anise seed, cardamom, cinnamon, ground clove, coriander, nutmeg, juniper berries. Aromatic liquids such as curacao or rum are also often added.

Moscow Sausage

Russian semi-dry sausage.

beef,	75%,	3.75 kg (8.25 lb)
pork back fat,	25%,	1.25 kg (2.75 lb)

Ingredients per 5 kg (11 lb) of meat

salt, 2.5%, 115 g
cure #1, 12 g
dextrose, 1%, 50 g
black pepper, 15 g
nutmeg, 2 g
F-LC culture, 1.25 g (½ tsp)

1. Grind beef through ⅛" plate (3 mm). Grind back fat through 3/16" (5 mm) plate.
2. Mix all ingredients with meat.
3. Stuff into beef middles or fibrous casings 40-60 mm.
4. Ferment at 38° C (100° F) for 24 hours, 90-85% humidity.
5. Introduce warm smoke (43° C, 110° F), 70% humidity, for 6 hours. Gradually increase smoke temperature until internal meat temperature of 140° F (60° C) is obtained.
6. For a drier sausage : dry for 5 days at 22-16° C (60-70° F), 65-75% humidity or until desired weight loss has occurred.
7. Store sausages at 10-15° C (50-59° F), 75% humidity.

Nham

Nham is an uncooked, fermented semi-dry Thai sausage very popular in Asia. It is made from fresh lean pork, pork skins, cooked rice, fresh garlic and eye bird chillies. The sausage is wrapped in banana leaves or synthetic casings and fermented for 3-5 days (depending on the season and if no culture added) at about 30° C (86° F) and 50% humidity.

Rice serves not only as a value added filler but as a source of carbohydrates for lactic acid production during fermentation. Many Asian products employ rice as a fermentation source, for example "saki" - the rice wine. The fermentation is performed at high Thai ambient temperatures and there is a danger of growth of undesirable bacteria if no lactic acid is produced during the first stage of the process. For this reason glucose (dextrose) is added to jump start fermentation as cooked rice is metabolized very slowly. The pH of boiled rice is about 7.40. If stored at room temperatures (20-30° C, 68-86° F) the sausage has a shelf life of less than a week but its life can be extended by keeping it under refrigeration. Then it is served as a dish or eaten raw.

It is important to keep in mind that natural fermentations are difficult to replicate in other settings. For example, the meat mixture for Nham is traditionally wrapped in small banana leaf packets. The leaves contribute to the surface flora of the sausage, which no doubt changes the fermentation pattern.

Traditional Nham is made with Bird's Eye Chili Peppers, which are tiny very hot chillies that can be found in Malaysia, Brunei, Indonesia, Philippines and in Thailand. Although small in size compared to other types of chili, they are very hot at 50,000 to 100,000 on the Scoville pungency scale. Tabasco and cayenne peppers are rated slightly lower at 30,000-50,000 Scoville units.

| lean pork, | 70%, | 3.5 kg (7.7 lb) |
| pork skins, | 30%, | 1.5 kg (3.3 lb) |

Ingredients per 5 kg (11 lb) of meat

salt, 2.5%, 115 g
cure #1, 12 g
dextrose, 1.0%, 50 g
cooked rice, 3%, 150 g
Bird Eye Chillies, cayenne or Tabasco peppers, 100 g
garlic, 5%, raw/minced, 250 g
F-LC culture, 1.25 g (½ tsp)

Different ratios of lean pork to skins may be used: 80/20, 70/30, 60/40, 50/50 or 40/60.

1. Trim meat of all connective tissue and fat. Grind through a small plate (1/8-3/16", 3-5 mm). Trim pork skins of any visible fat and cook in water for about 1 1/2 hours. Cut de-fatted skin (rind) into 2-3 mm (⅛") thick and ¾" (20 mm) long strips. Cut Bird Eye Chillies 3-5 mm thick.
2. Mix meat, skins, rice and all other ingredients well together.
3. Stuff tightly into synthetic casings, about 30 mm diameter and 6-8" (15-20 cm) long.
4. Ferment at 30° C (86° F) for 46 hours, high humidity.
5. For a drier sausage: dry for 3 days at- 22-16° C (60-70° F), 65-75% humidity or until desired weight loss has occurred.
6. Store sausages at 10-15° C (50-59° F), 75% humidity.

Notes:

Cooked rice is commonly used between 2.5 and 4%.
Sausage contains a lot of garlic (5%). See page 81 on the antioxidant and antimicrobial effects of garlic
Ground pepper may be added at 0.1% (1 g/1 kg of meat)
Don't replace pork skins with fat. The texture and flavor of this sausage depends largely on pork skins.

If made traditionally (without starter culture):

- *Increase salt to 3% (140 g).*
- *Increase fermentation temperature to 30° C (86° F).*
- *Ferment for 3 days at 30° C (86° F) or for 5 days if temperature is lower (but equal to or higher than 24° C, 75° F).*
- *Refrigerate.*

Pepperoni - traditional, dry

Dry sausage, smoked, air dried, sometimes cooked. Pepperoni can be made from beef, pork or a combination such as 30% beef and 70% pork. Pepperoni is a lean sausage with fat content < 30%. Cheaper, fast-fermented (semi-dry) and cooked types end up as toppings to pizzas worldwide to give flavor. Traditionally made Italian pepperoni was not smoked.

pork, 70%,   3.5 kg (7.7 lb)
beef, 30%,   1.5 kg (3.3 lb)

Ingredients per 5 kg (11 lb) of meat

salt, 3%, 140 g
cure #2, 12 g
dextrose, 0.2%, 10 g
sugar, 0.3%, 30 g
black pepper, 0.3%, 15 g
paprika 0.6%, 30 g
anise seeds, cracked, 0.25%, 12.5 g
(or fennel seeds, 0.3%), 15 g
cayenne pepper, 0.3%, 15 g
T-SPX culture, 0.6 g (¼ tsp)

1. Grind pork and beef through 3/16" plate (5 mm).
2. Mix all ingredients with meat.
3. Stuff firmly into beef middles or 2" fibrous casings.
4. Ferment at 20° C (68° F) for 72 hours, 90-85% humidity.
5. Optional step: cold smoke for 8 hours (<22° C, 72° F).
6. Dry at 16 -12° C (60-54° F), 85-80% humidity. In about 6-8 weeks a shrink of 30% should be achieved.
7. Store sausages at 10-15° C (50-59° F), 75% humidity.

Pepperoni - fast fermented, semi-dry

| pork, 70%, | 3.5 kg (7.7 lb) |
| beef, 30%, | 1.5 kg (3.3 lb) |

Ingredients per 5 kg (11 lb) of meat

salt, 2.5%, 115 g
cure #1, 12 g
dextrose, 1.0%, 50 g
sugar, 1%, 50 g
black pepper, 0.3%, 15 g
paprika 0.6%, 30 g
anise seeds, cracked, 0.25%, 12.5 g
(or fennel seeds, 0.3%), 15 g
cayenne pepper, 0.3%, 15 g
F-LC culture, 1.25 g (½ tsp)

1. Grind pork and beef through 3/16" plate (5 mm).
2. Mix all ingredients with meat.
3. Stuff into 60 mm beef middles or fibrous casings.
4. Ferment at 38° C (100° F) for 24 hours, 90-85% humidity.
5. Optional step: introduce warm smoke (43° C, 110° F), 70% humidity, for 6 hours.
6. Gradually increase smoke temperature until internal meat temperature of 140° F (60° C) is obtained.
7. For a drier sausage: dry for 2 days at 22-16° C (60-70° F), 65-75% humidity or until desired weight loss has occurred.
8. Store sausages at 10-15° C (50-59° F), 75% humidity.

Note: original Italian pepperoni is not smoked.

Pepperoni - according to compliance guidelines for fermented products. *Instructions are listed for the purpose of stressing the importance of the control of some of the pathogenic bacteria, in this case E.coli 0157:H7 which creates a safety hazard in products made with beef. This is how the commercial producer will make the sausage in order to be on the safe side.*

Ingredients:	75% pork, 25% beef with 32% fat
	dextrose 0.63%
	2% salt
	sodium nitrite 0.25% (156 ppm)
	fast starter culture (*Pediococcal* bacteria strain),
	8.0 log10 cfu/g of batter
Fermentation:	36° C (96.8° F), 90% humidity, to pH 4.8
Drying:	13° C (55.4° F), 65% humidity for 18 days to MPR
	(*moisture to protein ratio*) of equal or less than 1:6.1
Slicing:	1.9 g/slice
Storage:	packed in air - 28 days at 21° C (69.8° F)
	packed under vacuum - 60 days at 21° C (69.8 F)

Reference: Faith, N.G., N. Parniere, T. Larson, T.D. Lorang, and J.B. Luchansky. 1997. *Viability of E. coli 0157:H7 in pepperoni during the manufacture of sticks and the subsequent storage of slices at 21, 4 and -20 C under air, vacuum and CO2.* Int. J. Food Microbiol. 37:47-54.

Pepperoni

Ingredients:	75% pork, 25% beef with 32% fat
	dextrose 0.63%
	2% salt
	sodium nitrite 0.25% (156 ppm)
	fast starter culture (*Pediococcal* bacteria strain),
	8.0 log10 cfu/g of batter
Fermentation:	36° C (96.8° F), 85-90 humidity, to pH 5.0 or less
Heat:	63° C (145° F) instantaneous, OR
	53° C (128° F) for 60 minutes
	Cold showered to internal temperature of 27° C (80° F)
	or less.
Drying:	13° C (55° F), 65% humidity, to MRP 1:6.1 (15-21 days).

Reference: Hinkens, J.C., N.G. Faith, T.D. Lorang, P. Bailey, D. Buege, C. Kaspar and J.B. Luchansky. 1996. *Validation of pepperoni processes for control of E. coli 0157:H7.* J. Food Prot. 59 (12):1260-66.

Polish Cold Smoked Sausage

(Polska kiełbasa wędzona)

The following is the original recipe and instructions for making Polish Cold Smoked Sausage as made by Polish meat plants in 1950-1990's.

lean pork, (ham, lean butt), 40%, 2.0 kg (4.4 lb)
pork trimmings (butt),   60%, 3.0 kg (6.6 lb)

Ingredients per 5 kg (11 lb) of meat

salt 2.5%, 115 g
cure #2, 12 g
sugar, 10 g
pepper, 7.5 g
marjoram, 5 g
garlic, 10 g

1. Cut meat into 5-6 cm (2") cubes, mix with salt, sugar and cure #2. Pack tightly in a container and cover with a clean cloth. Place in a cooler (4-6° C, 40-42° F) for 72-96 hours.
2. Grind meats through 1/2" (13 mm) plate.
3. Add remaining ingredients and mix well until feels sticky.
4. Stuff firmly into 32-36 hog casings. Form 12" (30-35 cm) long links but leave them in a continuous coil.
5. Hang for 1-2 days at 2-6° C (35-42° F) and 85-90% humidity.
6. Apply a thin cold smoke (below 22° C, 72° F) for 1-1.5 days until the casings develop yellow-light brown color.
7. Dry at 10-12° C (50-53° F), 75-80% humidity, until sausages lose 13% of its original weight. Divide into pairs.
8. Store at 10° C (53° F) or lower.

Polish Smoked Sausage - dry type
(made with culture)

lean pork,   40%,   2.0 kg (4.4 lb)
pork trimmings,   60%,   3.0 kg (6.6 lb)

Ingredients per 5 kg (11 lb) of meat

salt, 3%, 140 g
cure #2, 12 g
dextrose, 0.2%, 10 g
sugar, 0.2%, 10 g
pepper, 10 g
marjoram, 5 g
garlic, 10 g
T-SPX culture, 0.6 g (¼ tsp)

1. Grind meats through 3/16" (5 mm) plate.
2. Mix all ingredients with meat.
3. Stuff firmly into 32-36 hog casings. Form 12" (30-35 cm) long links but leave them in a continuous coil.
4. Ferment at 20° C (68° F) for 48 hours.
5. Smoke with a thin cold smoke (below 22° C, 72° F) for 24 hours until the casings develop yellow-light brown color. The sausage continues to ferment.
6. Dry for 30 days at 10-12° C (50-53° F), 85-75% humidity.
7. Store sausages at 10-15° C (50-59° F), 75% humidity.

Polish Smoked Sausage - semi-dry type
(made with culture)

lean pork,   40%,   2.0 kg (4.4 lb)
pork trimmings,   60%,   3.0 kg (6.6 lb)

Ingredients per 5 kg (11 lb) of meat

salt, 2.5%, 115 g
cure #1, 12 g
dextrose, 1%, 50 g
pepper, 7.5 g
marjoram, 5 g
garlic, 10 g
F-LC culture, 1.25 g (½ tsp)

1. Grind meats through 3/16" (5 mm) plate.
2. Mix all ingredients with meat.
3. Stuff firmly into 32-36 hog casings. Form 12" (30-35 cm) long links but leave them in a continuous coil.
4. Ferment at 38° C (100° F) for 24 hours, 90-85% humidity.
5. Introduce warm smoke (43° C, 110° F), 70% humidity, for 6 hours. Gradually increase smoke temperature until internal meat temperature of 140° F (60° C) is obtained. Sausage is microbiologically stable and ready to eat.
6. For a drier sausage: dry at 22-16° C (60-70° F), 65-75% humidity until desired weight loss has occurred.
7. Store sausages at 10-15° C (50-59° F), 75% humidity.

Salami de Arles

There are no spices in this recipe so the flavor of this salami depends entirely on:

- • the quality of raw materials.
- • good manufacturing practices.

Make sure that beef is well trimmed, without sinews, gristles or fat. The same applies to regular pork trimmings, some fat is acceptable but no sinews and tough trimmings.

pork trimmings (butt),	40%, 2.5 kg (5.5 lb)	
beef (chuck),	30%, 1.5 kg (3.3 lb)	
lean pork (butt, ham),	30%, 1.0 kg (2.2 lb)	

Ingredients per 5 kg (11 lb) of meat

salt, 3%, 140 g
cure #2, 12 g
dextrose, 0.2%, 10 g
sugar, 0.2%, 10 g
T-SPX culture, 0.6 g (¼ tsp)

1. Grind pork and back fat through ⅜ - ½" (10-12 mm) plate. Grind beef with ⅜" (10 mm), refreeze and grind again with ⅛" (3 mm) plate.
2. Mix all ingredients with meat.
3. Stuff firmly into 60-70 mm beef middles or protein lined fibrous casings. Make 12" long links.
4. Ferment at 20° C (68° F) for 72 hours, 90-85% humidity.
5. Dry at 16-12° C (60-54° F), 85-80% humidity for 2-3 months. The sausage is dried until around 30-35% in weight is lost.
6. Store sausages at 10-15° C (50-59° F), 75% humidity.

If mold is desired spray with M-EK-4 mold culture after stuffing.

Salami Finocchiona

There is a story that a thief stole a fresh salami at a fair near the Italian town of Prato and hid it in a field of wild fennel. When he picked it up a few days later, he discovered that the sausage developed a wonderful aroma from the fennel.

lean pork, (ham, butt, loin)   80%, 4.0 kg (8.8 lb)
pork back fat or fat trimmings,   20%, 1.0 kg (2.2 lb)

Ingredients per 5 kg (11 lb) of meat

salt, 3%, 140 g
cure #2, 12 g
dextrose, 0.2%, 10 g
sugar, 0.2%, 10 g
white pepper, 10 g
black peppercorns, 25 g
whole fennel seeds (dried), 15 g (1 Tbsp)
garlic, 10 g
red wine (Chianti), 120 ml (½ cup)
T-SPX culture, 0.6 g (¼ tsp)

1. Grind meat and fat through 3/16" plate (5 mm).
2. Mix all ingredients with ground meat.
3. Stuff firmly into beef middles or 46-60 mm protein lined fibrous casings.
4. Ferment at 20° C (68° F) for 72 hours, 90-85% humidity.
5. Dry at 16-12° C (60-54° F), 85-80% humidity for about 30 days. The sausage is dried until around 30-35% in weight is lost.
6. Store sausages at 10-15° C (50-59° F), 75% humidity.

Notes:

The following spice and herb combination can be found in some recipes:
spices: 4 parts coriander, 3 parts mace, 2 parts allspice, 1 part fennel.
herbs: 3 parts marjoram, 1 part thyme, 1 part basil.
To make 5 kg sausage about 7 g of spices and 4 g of herbs are needed.

Salami Genoa

Salami Milano and Salami Genoa are very similar and they both incorporate different proportions of raw materials. Some typical combinations: 50/30/20, 40/40/20 (this recipe) or 40/30/30. Salami Genoa is also known as Salami di Alessandra.

lean pork trimmings (butt),	40%,	2.0 kg (4.4 lb)
beef (chuck),	40%,	2.0 kg (4.4 lb)
pork back fat or fat trimmings	20%,	1.0 kg (2.2 lb)

Ingredients per 5 kg (11 lb) of meat

salt, 3%, 140 g
cure #2, 12 g
dextrose, 0.2%, 10 g
sugar, 0.3%, 15 g
white pepper, 15 g
garlic, 10 g
T-SPX culture, 0.6 g (¼ tsp)

1. Grind pork and back fat through ⅜" plate (10 mm). Grind beef with ⅛" plate.
2. Mix all ingredients with ground meat.
3. Stuff firmly into beef middles or 46-60 mm protein lined fibrous casings. Make links 16-20" long.
4. Ferment at 20° C (68° F) for 72 hours, 90-85% humidity.
5. Dry at 16-12° C (60-54° F), 85-80% humidity for 2-3 months. The sausage is dried until around 30-35% in weight is lost.
6. Store sausages at 10-15° C (50-59° F), 75% humidity.

Notes:

If mold is desired spray with M-EK-4 mold culture after stuffing.
The following spice and herb combination can be found in some recipes:

- spices: 4 parts coriander, 3 parts mace, 2 parts allspice, 1 part fennel

- herbs: 3 parts marjoram, 1 part thyme, 1 part basil.

To make 5 kg sausage about 7 g of spices and 4 g of herbs are needed.
Some recipes ask for the addition of red wine and you may add around 120 ml (½ cup).

Salami - Hungarian
(Salami węgierskie)
Traditional method

Although this salami carries a Hungarian name, it has been always made in Poland and might as well be considered a local product. *The following is the official Polish Government recipe for making traditional salami that comes from 1956 archives. It makes a great reading.*

Pork, 80%,	800 g (1.76 lb)
Pork back fat, 20%,	200 g (0.44 lb)

Ingredients per 1 kg (2.2 lb) of meat

Salt, 28 g (5 tsp)
Cure #2, 5 g (1 tsp)
Pepper, 4.0 g (2 tsp)
Paprika, 2.0 g (1 tsp)
Sugar, 2.0 g (1/2 tsp)
Garlic, 3.5 g (1 clove)

1. Cut meat into 10 cm (3-4") pieces and place in a slightly raised container with holes in the bottom to allow for draining of liquid. Leave for 24 hours at 1-2° C (33-35° F), then grind with ¾" plate and leave for additional 2-3 days. During that period turn meat around 1-2 times. Leave sheets of unsalted back fat for 2-3 days at -2° C (28° F) to - 4° C (24° F) and then cut into 3 mm (⅛") cubes.
2. Mix meat, back fat, salt, nitrite and spices together. Grind through 3 mm (⅛") plate.
3. Leave the sausage mass for 36-48 hours at 2-4° C (35-40° F).
4. Stuff firmly into 55-60 mm beef middles. Make links 16-18" long. Lace up with twine: once lengthwise and every 4-5 cm (1.5-2") across. The ends tied up with a twine, 10-12 cm (4-5") hanging loop on one end.
5. Hang for 2-4 days at 2-4° C (35-40° F), 85-90% humidity.
6. Apply a thin cold smoke 16-18° C (60-64° F) for 5-7 days, until dark red color is obtained.
7. Dry in a dark, lightly drafty area at 10-12° C (50-53° F), humidity 90%, for 2 weeks until salami develops white, dry mold on outside. If green mold appears it has to be wiped off and the sausages moved for 4-5 hours to a drier place. Then they may go back to the original room for drying.
8. Place sausages covered with white mold for 2-3 months in a dark and lightly drafty area at 12-16° C (54-60° F), 75-85% humidity, until about 63% yield is obtained.

Salami - Hungarian

The Hungarian salami is a unique sausage which is smoked and has mold. In the traditional process the use of starter cultures and sugars are not allowed. The sausage should not exhibit any acidity. The recipe below contains very little sugar, just to provide a margin of safety during the first stage of fermentation.

lean pork, 80%, 4.0 kg (8.8 lb)
back fat, 20%, 1.0 kg (2.2 lb)

Ingredients per 5 kg (11 lb) of meat

salt, 3%, 140 g
cure #2, 12 g
dextrose, 0.2%, 10 g
white pepper, 15 g
paprika, 30 g
garlic, 20 g
Tokay wine (Hungarian sweet wine), 60 ml (¼ cup)
T-SPX culture, 0.6 g (¼ tsp)

1. Grind pork and back fat through 3/16" plate (5 mm).
2. Mix all ingredients with ground meat.
3. Stuff firmly into beef middles or 3" protein lined fibrous casings.
4. Ferment at 20° C (68° F) for 72 hours, 90-85% humidity.
5. Cold smoke for 4 days (<22° C, 72° F). You can smoke during fermentation.
6. Dry at 16-12° C (60-54° F), 85-80% humidity for 2-3 months.
7. Store sausages at 10-15° C (50-59° F), 75% humidity.

Salami Lombardia

Although smoking is not mentioned in the instructions, this salami is sometimes given a very light cool smoke after fermentation.

lean pork (butt, ham),	45%,	2.25 kg (4.95 lb)
beef (chuck),	20%,	1.00 kg (2.20 lb)
regular pork trimmings	35%,	1.75 kg (3.85 lb)

Ingredients per 5 kg (11 lb) of meat

salt, 3%, 140 g
cure #2, 12 g
dextrose, 0.3%, 15 g
whole white pepper, 15 g
garlic, 10 g
T-SPX culture, 0.6 g (¼ tsp)

1. Grind pork and back fat through 3/16" plate (5 mm). Grind beef with ⅛" plate.
2. Mix all ingredients with ground meat.
3. Stuff firmly into large hog casings or 40-60 mm protein lined fibrous casings. Make 12-16 " long links.
4. Ferment at 20° C (68° F) for 72 hours, 90-85% humidity.
5. Dry at 16-12° C (60-54° F), 85-80% humidity for 1-2 months. The sausage is dried until around 30-35% in weight is lost.
6. Store sausages at 10-15° C (50-59° F), 75% humidity.

Salami Milano

Salami Milano and Salami Genoa are very similar and they both incorporate different proportions of raw materials. Some typical combinations: 50/30/20 (this recipe), 40/40/20 or 40/30/30. Salami Genoa is also known as Salami di Alessandra. Salami Milano is chopped somewhat finer than Salami Genoa.

lean pork (butt, ham),	50%, 2.5 kg (5.5 lb)
beef (chuck),	30%, 1.5 kg (3.3 lb)
pork back fat or fat trimmings	20%, 1.0 kg (2.2 lb)

Ingredients per 5 kg (11 lb) of meat

salt, 3%, 140 g
cure #2, 12 g
dextrose, 0.2%, 10 g
sugar, 0.3%, 15 g
white pepper, 15 g
garlic, 10 g
T-SPX culture, 0.6 g (¼ tsp)

1. Grind pork and back fat through 3/16" plate (5 mm). Grind beef with ⅛" plate.
2. Mix all ingredients with ground meat.
3. Stuff firmly into 80 mm protein lined fibrous casings. Make 25" long links.
4. Ferment at 20° C (68° F) for 72 hours, 90-85% humidity.
5. Dry at 16-12° C (60-54° F), 85-80% humidity for 2-3 months. The sausage is dried until around 30-35% in weight is lost.
6. Store sausages at 10-15° C (50-59° F), 75% humidity.

Notes:

If mold is desired spray with M-EK-4 mold culture after stuffing.
The following spice and herb combination can be found in some recipes:
spices: 4 parts coriander, 3 parts mace, 2 parts allspice, 1 part fennel
herbs: 3 parts marjoram, 1 part thyme, 1 part basil.
To make 5 kg sausage about 7 g of spices and 4 g of herbs are needed.
Some recipes ask for the addition of red wine. Salami is an Italian sausage so why not add 120 ml (1/2 cup) of Italian red wine like Chianti.

Salami Nola

This salami is lightly smoked and this is why it differs from other Italian salamis. It is also more coarsely ground and formed into shorter links.

lean pork (butt, ham),	50%,	2.5 kg (5.5 lb)
regular pork trimmings (butt),	50%,	2.5 kg (5.5 lb)

Ingredients per 5 kg (11 lb) of meat

salt, 3%, 140 g
cure #2, 12 g
dextrose, 0.2%, 10 g
sugar, 0.2%, 10 g
cracked black pepper, 15 g
ground red pepper, 10 g
allspice, 10 g
T-SPX culture, 0.6 g (¼ tsp)

1. Grind pork through ⅜" plate (10 mm).
2. Mix all ingredients with ground pork.
3. Stuff firmly into 60 mm beef middles or protein lined fibrous casings. Make 8" (20 cm) long links.
4. Ferment at 20° C (68° F) for 72 hours, 90-85% humidity.
5. Apply thin cold smoke (< 20° C, 68° F) for a few hours.
6. Dry at 16-12° C (60-54° F), 85-80% humidity for 1 month. The sausage is dried until around 30-35% in weight is lost.
7. Store sausages at 10-15° C (50-59° F), 75% humidity.

Salami-Polish
(Salami)
Traditional method

Although salami is of Italian origin, almost every country has its own version and Poland is no exception. *The following is the official Polish Government recipe for making this sausage that comes from 1956 archives.*

Pork,	40%,	400 g (0.88 lb)
Beef,	30%,	300 g (0.66 lb)
Pork back fat,	30%,	300 g (0.66 lb)

Ingredients per 1 kg (2.2 lb) of meat

Salt, 28 g (5 tsp)
Cure # 2, 5.0 g (1 tsp)
Pepper, 3.0 g (1 tsp)
Cardamom, 0.5 g (1/4 tsp)
Sugar, 2.0 g (1/2 tsp)

1. Cut meat into 5-6 cm (2") pieces, mix with 2/3 salt, sugar and Cure #1. Place in a slightly raised container with holes in the bottom to allow for draining of curing liquid. Leave for 5 days at 2-4° C (35-40° F). Cut back fat into strips and rub in 1/3 of the salt. Back fat does not require nitrite (Cure #1) and can be kept separately at 2-4° C (35-40° F).
2. Grind pork with 5 mm plate, grind beef with 3 mm plate and manually cut back fat into 5 mm pieces.
3. Mix meats with spices and back fat. Do not add water.
4. Stuff into 55-60 mm beef middle casings. Do not add water. Make links 16-18" long. The ends tied up with a twine, 10-12 cm (4-5") hanging loop on one end.
5. Hang for 4 days at 2-4°C (35-40°F), 85-90% humidity.
6. Hang in a dark, slightly drafty area for 6-8 weeks, 10-12° C (50-54° F), 80-85% humidity. If wet mold appears,wash it off with warm, salty water, then wipe it dry with a clean cloth. When sausages loose about 30% weight and start developing dry mold, wipe them off and send for smoking.
7. Cold smoke with thin smoke for 4-6 days until dark red color is obtained. Store below 12° C (53° F).

Yield of a finished product in relation to the original weight - 63%.

Salami - Polish
With culture

Most countries make their own version of salamis and so does Poland. The following is the popular recipe.

lean pork,	40%,	2.0 kg (4.4 lb)
lean beef,	30%,	1.5 kg (3.3 lb)
back fat,	30%,	1.5 kg (3.3 lb)

Ingredients per 5 kg (11 lb) of meat

salt, 3%, 140 g
cure #2, 12 g
dextrose, 0.3%, 15 g
pepper, 15 g
cardamom, 2.5 g
T-SPX culture, 0.6 g (¼ tsp)

1. Grind pork and back fat through 3/16" plate (5 mm). Grind beef with ⅛" (3 mm) plate.
2. Mix all ingredients with ground meat.
3. Stuff firmly into beef middles or 3" protein lined fibrous casings.
4. Ferment at 20° C (68° F) for 72 hours, 90-85% humidity.
5. Cold smoke for 12 hours (<22° C, 72° F).
6. Dry at 16-12° C (60-54° F), 85-80% humidity. In about 6-8 weeks a shrink of 30% should be achieved.
7. Store sausages at 10-15° C (50-59° F), 75% humidity.

Salami Sorrento

Italian Salami.

lean pork (butt, ham),	60%,	3.00 kg (6.60 lb)
beef (chuck),	20%,	1.00 kg (2.20 lb)
regular pork trimmings	20%,	1.00 kg (2.20 lb)

Ingredients per 5 kg (11 lb) of meat

salt, 3%, 140 g
cure #2, 12 g
dextrose, 0.3%, 15 g
ground white pepper, 15 g
whole white pepper. 15 g
garlic. 10 g
T-SPX culture, 0.6 g (¼ tsp)

1. Grind pork and back fat through 3/16" plate (5 mm). Grind beef with ⅛" plate.
2. Mix all ingredients with ground meat.
3. Stuff firmly into 40-60 mm protein lined fibrous casings. Make 12" long links.
4. Ferment at 20° C (68° F) for 72 hours, 90-85% humidity.
5. Dry at 16-12° C (60-54° F), 85-80% humidity for 1 month. The sausage is dried until around 30-35% in weight is lost.
6. Store sausages at 10-15° C (50-59° F), 75% humidity.

Salchichón

Spanish "salchichón" can be dried, dried/smoked and even cooked. Typical meat is pork, but recipes with other meats such as ox, veal, or even a horse meat can be found in Spanish books. Quite often pork liver is added. A typical traditional method of making these sausages at home was to add salt, nitrate and spices to meat and then hang the sausage for 4-5 days in the kitchen or in the open air outside. Then sausage was transferred to a dry and drafty area where it remained for 2-3 months. After that time it was ready for consumption. Most traditionl Spanish recipes don't include sugar at all which results in little acidity. Due to low temperatures fermentation is very slow and pH drop is low. Basically, the sausage was not fermented but just air-dried like American beef jerky. We do not advocate this kind of manufacture at home and what follows below is a typical Spanish salchichon recipe which is properly fermented and air dried.

lean pork,   70%,   3.5 kg (7.7 lb)
pork back fat,   30%,   1.5 kg (3.3 lb)

Ingredients per 5 kg (11 lb) of meat

salt, 3%, 140 g
cure #2, 12 g
dextrose, 0.2%, 10 g
lactose 0.8% (non fat dry milk - 80 g)
black pepper, 15 g
cinnamon, 3 g
cloves (ground), 3 g
nutmeg, 2 g
garlic, 7.5 g
T-SPX culture, 0.6 g (¼ tsp)

1. Grind pork and back fat through ⅜" plate (8 mm).
2. Mix all ingredients with ground meat.
3. Stuff firmly into beef middles or 46-60 mm protein lined fibrous casings.
4. Ferment at 20° C (68° F) for 72 hours, 90-85% humidity. Cold smoke (optional) for 8 hours.
5. Dry at 16-12° C (60-54° F), 85-80% humidity for 1-2 months. The sausage is dried until around 30-35% in weight is lost.
6. Store sausages at 10-15° C (50-59° F), 75% humidity.

Salmon Sausage
(Kiełbasa łososiowa)

There is no salmon in this recipe. In Poland certain high quality products carry the name "salmon" to imply that the product is of the high quality. *This cold smoked sausage recipe comes from the official Polish Government archives.*

lean pork,	800 g (1.76 lb)
beef,	200 g (0.44 lb)

*Ingredients for **1 kg (2.2 lb)** of meat*

Salt, 24 g (4 tsp)
Cure #1, 2.5 g (1/2 tsp)
Sugar, 1.0 g (1/2 tsp)
Pepper, 2.0 g (1 tsp)
Sweet paprika, 1.0 g (1/2 tsp)
Nutmeg, 1.0 g (1/2 tsp)
Garlic, 1.5 g (1/2 clove)

1. Curing. Cut meat into 2.5-5 cm (1-2") pieces and mix with salt and Cure # 1. Pack tightly in container, cover with cloth and keep in refrigerator for 3 days.
2. Cut pork class I into 20 mm (3/4 ") pieces. grind beef class II through 3 mm plate.
3. Mix ground meats with spices.
4. Stuff into 36 mm hog casings.
5. Hang at 2-4° C (35-40° F) 85-90% humidity for 4-6 days, then at 10-12° C (50-53° F), 75-80% humidity for 3-4 days.
6. Apply cold smoke for 3-4 days until dark red color is obtained.
7. Cool and store sausages in air at 10-12° C (50-53° F) for about 6-8 days.

Saucisson d'Alsace

French dry sausage.

lean pork, 80%,	4.0 kg (8.8 lb)
back fat, 20%,	1.0 kg (2.2 lb)

Ingredients per 5 kg (11 lb) of meat

salt, 3%, 140 g
cure #2, 12 g
dextrose, 0.2%, 10 g
lactose 1%, (non fat dry milk-100 g),
white pepper, 15 g
garlic, 5 g
nutmeg, 2.5 g
cloves, 2.5 g
cinnamon, 2.5 g
dark rum, 50 ml (5 Tbsp)
T-SPX culture, 0.6 g (¼ tsp)

1. Grind pork and back fat through 3/16" plate (5 mm).
2. Mix all ingredients with ground meat.
3. Stuff firmly into beef middles or 3" protein lined fibrous casings.
4. Ferment at 20° C (68° F) for 60 hours, 90-85% humidity.
5. Cold smoke for 12 hours (<22° C, 72° F).
6. Dry at 16-12° C (60-54° F), 85-80% humidity for 1-2 months.
7. Store sausages at 10-15° C (50-59° F), 75% humidity.

Servolatka
(Serwolatka miękka)

This cold smoked sausage recipe comes from the official Polish Government archives.

| beef, | 650 g (1.43 lb) |
| pork belly, skinless, | 350 g (0.77 lb) |

*Ingredients per **1 kg** (2.2 lb) of meat*

Salt, 21 g (3-1/2 tsp)
Cure #1, 2.5 g (1/2 tsp)
Pepper, 1.5 g (3/4 tsp)
Coriander, 0.5 g (1/4 tsp)
Paprika, 1.0 g (1/2 tsp)

1. **Curing.** Cut meat into 2.5-5 cm (1-2") pieces and mix with salt and Cure # 1. Pack tightly in container, cover with cloth and keep in refrigerator for 3 days.
2. Grind beef class I without connective tissue and pork belly through 5 mm plate. Beef class I with connective tissue and beef class IV through 2-3 mm plate. Partially freeze and grind again.
3. Mix all meats with spices until sticky.
4. Stuff firmly into 65 mm synthetic fibrous casings forming 25 cm (10") links.
5. Hang for 1-2 days at 2-4° C (35-40° F), 85-90% humidity.
6. With cold smoke for 1-2 days until brown.

Smoked Frankfurters
(Frankfurterki wędzone)

This cold smoked sausage recipe comes from the official Polish Government archives.

lean pork,	500 g (1.1 lb)
pork,	500 g (1.1 lb)

Ingredients per 1 kg (2.2 lb) of meat

Salt, 21 g (3-1/3 tsp)
Cure #1, 2.5 g (1/2 tsp)
Sugar, 2.0 g (1/3 tsp)
Pepper, 1.5 g (3/4 tsp)
Nutmeg, 0.5 g (1/4 tsp)

1. Curing. Cut meat into 2.5-5 cm (1-2") pieces and mix with salt and Cure # 1. Pack tightly in container, cover with cloth and keep in refrigerator for 3 days.
2. Grind pork through 8 mm plate.
3. Mix pork with all ingredients until sticky.
4. Stuff into 22 mm or larger sheep casings. Form 15-18 cm (6-7") links leaving them in a continuous coil.
5. Hang for 8 hours at 2-4° C (35-40° F), 85-90-% humidity or for 1 hour at room temperature.
6. Apply cold smoke for 6-8 hours until light brown.
7. Dry at 10-12° C (50-53° F) until test sausages display 84% yield.

Snijworst
(Dutch Cervelat)

Dutch semi-dry sausage.

lean beef,	20%,	1.0 kg (2.20 lb)
pork,	40%,	2.0 kg (4.40 lb)
pork belly,	30%,	1.5 kg (3.30 lb)
back fat,	10%,	0.5 kg (1.10 lb)

Ingredients per 5 kg (11 lb) of meat

salt, 2.5%, 115 g
cure #1, 12 g
dextrose, 1%, 50 g
black pepper, 12 g
coriander, 10 g
nutmeg, 5 g
mace, 5 g
F-LC culture, 1.25 g (½ tsp)

1. Grind all meats through 3/16" plate (5 mm).
2. Mix all ingredients with ground meat.
3. Stuff into beef middles or fibrous casings 90-100 mm.
4. Ferment at 24° C (75° F) for 48 hours, 90-85% humidity.
5. Dry for 1 month at 16-12° C (60-54° F), 85-75% humidity.
6. Store sausages at 10-15° C (50-59° F), 75% humidity.

Soviet Sausage

Russian dry sausage.

lean pork,	50%,	2.5 kg (5.5 lb)
pork fat,	30%,	1.5 kg (3.3 lb)
beef,	20%,	1.0 kg (2.2 lb)

Ingredients per 5 kg (11 lb) of meat

salt, 3%, 140 g
cure #2, 12 g
dextrose, 0.3%, 15 g
white pepper, 15 g
cardamom, 10 g
allspice, 7.5 g
Madeira wine or brandy, 125 ml (½ cup)
T-SPX culture, 0.6 g (¼ tsp)

1. Grind pork and back fat through 3/16" plate (5 mm). Grind beef with 1/8" (3 mm) plate.
2. Mix all ingredients with meat.
3. Stuff firmly into beef middles or 3" protein lined fibrous casings.
4. Ferment at 20° C (68° F) for 72 hours, 90-85% humidity.
5. Cold smoke for 24 hours (<22° C, 72° F).
6. Dry at 16-12° C (60-54° F), 85-80% humidity. In about 6-8 weeks a shrink of 30% should be achieved.
7. Store sausages at 10-15° C (50-59° F), 75% humidity.

Sucuk
(slow-fermented - traditional)

The Turkish Sucuk (Soudjouk) is the most popular dry fermented meat product in Turkey and other Middle Eastern Countries. As most of those countries practice Muslim it comes as no surprise that pork is not included in the recipe and the sausage is made from beef and lamb. The Turkish Food Codex (2000) states that high quality ripened sucuks should have pH values between 5.2 and 5.4.

| lean beef, | 70%, | 3.5 kg (7.7 lb) |
| lean lamb/mutton, | 30%, | 1.5 kg (3.3 lb) |

Ingredients per 5 kg (11 lb) of meat

salt, 3.0%, 140 g
cure #2, 12 g
dextrose, 0.3%, 15 g
black pepper, 0.5%, 25 g
red pepper 0.5%, 25 g
cumin, 1%, 50 g
garlic, 1%, 50 g
allspice, 0.2%, 10 g
olive oil, 0.25%, 12 g (1 Tbsp)
T-SPX culture, 0.6 g (¼ tsp)

1. Grind beef and lamb through 3/16" plate (5 mm).
2. Mix all ingredients with meat.
3. Stuff firmly into 38 mm casings.
4. Ferment at 20° C (68° F) for 72 hours, 90-85% humidity.
5. Dry at 16-12° C (60-54° F), 85-80% humidity for 1 month.
6. Store sausages at 10-15° C (50-59° F), 75% humidity.

Notes:

Cinnamon and cloves are often added.
Original sucuks are made with sheep tail fat (40% beef, 40% lamb, 20% sheep tail fat).
Sucuk is a very lean sausage.
Olive oil (up to 5%) is added as a replacement for beef fat, which has poor sensory qualities.

Sucuk
(fast-fermented - heat treated)

Following American trends, some Turkish sucuck manufacturers start to pre-cook sucucks after a very short fermentation. Primary reasons are: shorter production time, elimination of pathogens during cooking (safer product) and lower costs of production.

lean beef	60%,	3.00 kg (6.60 lb)
lean lamb/mutton,	25%,	1.25 kg (2.75 lb)
beef tallow or sheep tail fat,	15%,	0.75 kg (1.65 lb)

Ingredients per 5 kg (11 lb) of meat

salt, 2.5 %, 115 g
cure #1, 12 g
dextrose, 1.0 %, 50 g
black pepper, 0.5%, 25 g
red pepper 1.0%, 50 g
cumin, 1%, 50 g
garlic, 1%, 50 g
allspice, 0.5%, 25 g
cinnamon, 0.1%, 5 g
cloves 0.1%, 5 g
F-LC culture, 1.25 g (½ tsp)

1. Grind beef, lamb and lamb fat through 3/16" plate (5 mm).
2. Mix all ingredients with meat.
3. Stuff firmly into 38 mm collagen or fibrous casings.
4. Ferment at 24° C (75° F) for 48 hours, 90-85% humidity.
5. Cook to 63° C (145° F) internal meat temperature.
6. Shower with cold water to below 10° C (50° F).
7. Store in a refrigerator.

Sucuk (Soudjouk) - according to compliance guidelines for fermented products. *Instructions are listed for the purpose of stressing the importance of the control of some of the pathogenic bacteria, in this case E.coli 0157:H7 which creates a safety hazard in products made with beef. This is how the commercial producer will make the sausage in order to be on the safe side.*

Process to achieve at least a 5-log10 reduction of *E.coli 0157:H7*

Ingredients:	ground beef	(20% fat or less)
	salt	1.9%
	sodium nitrite	0.25% or 156 ppm
	starter culture	Bactoferm™ LCP or equivalent, 8.0 log10 cfu/g of batter
	dextrose 1.5%	
Fermenting/ Drying	3 days at 24° C (75.2° F), 90-95% humidity, then 3 days at 22° C (71.6° C), 80-85% humidity until moisture is about 40%, then	
Heating	48.8° C (120° F), 70% humidity for 1 hour, then at 54.4° C (130° F), 70% humidity until product internal temperature reaches 54.4° C (130° F).	

Reference: Calcioglu, M. N.G. Faith, D.R. Buege, and J.B. Luchansky. 2001. *Viability of E. coli 0157:H7 in Turkish style Soudjouk.* Food Microbiology, Vol 20, Issue 2, April 2003, p. 169-177.

Summer Sausage

Summer sausage is an American semi-dry fermented sausage made of pork and beef, although sausages made from beef alone are common. The sausage was made in winter time and after drying and storing it was consumed in the summer when working in the field. Summer sausage displays a long shelf life without refrigeration and is often used as a component of food for gift baskets along with different cheeses and jams. Diameter of casings varies from 40-120 mm and so does the length of the sausage.

pork, 70%, 3.5 kg (7.7 lb)
beef, 30%, 1.5 kg (3.3 lb)

Ingredients per 5 kg (11 lb) of meat

salt, 2.5%, 115 g
cure #1, 12 g
dextrose, 1%, 50 g
sugar 0.5%, 25 g
black pepper, 12 g
coriander, 10 g
whole mustard seeds, 20 g
allspice, 7.5 g
nutmeg, 3 g
garlic, 7.5 g
F-LC culture, 1.25 g (½ tsp)

1. Grind pork and beef through 3/16" plate (5 mm).
2. Mix all ingredients with ground meat.
3. Stuff into beef middles or fibrous casings about 60 mm.
4. Ferment at 30° C (86° F) for 24 hours, 90-85% humidity.
5. Introduce warm smoke (43° C, 110° F), 70% humidity, for 6 hours. Gradually increase smoke temperature until internal meat temperature of 140° F (60° C) is obtained.
6. For a drier sausage: dry for 3 days at 22-16° C (60-70° F), 65-75% humidity or until desired weight loss has occurred.
7. Store sausages at 10-15° C (50-59° F), 75-80% humidity.

Note: some sausages may contain around 10% diced cheddar cheese.

Summer Sausage - according to compliance guidelines for fermented products. *Instructions are listed for the purpose of stressing the importance of the control of some of the pathogenic bacteria, in this case E.coli 0157:H7 which creates a safety hazard in products made with beef. This is how the commercial producer will make the sausage in order to be on the safe side.*

Ingredients:	beef with 11% fat	
	salt	2.5%
	sodium nitrite	0.26% (156 ppm)
	starter culture	fast starter culture (*Pediococcal* bacteria strain), 8.0 log10 cfu/g of batter
	glucose (dextrose)	1.0% for target pH 4.6
		0.3% for target pH 5.0

Fermenting: at constant 80% humidity

         1 hour   at 29.4° C (85° F)
         1 hour   at 32.2° C (90° F)
         1 hour   at 35.0° C (95° F)
         1 hour   at 37.8° C (100° F)
         8 hours   at 40.6° C (105° F) until pH 4.6 or 5.0

summer sausage fermented to pH 4.6
         heat to internal temperature of 54.4° C (130° C) with 60% humidity - achieves a 7-log10 reduction of *E.coli 0157:H7*

summer sausage fermented to pH 5.0
         heat to internal temperature of 54.4° C (130° F) with 60%
         humidity   for 30 minutes - achieves the min. 5-log10 of *E. coli 0157:H7*

         heat to internal temperature of 54.4° C (130° F) with 60%
         humidity for 60 minutes - achieves a 7-log10 of E. coli
         0157:H7

Reference: Calcioglu, M., N.G. Faith, D.R. Buege and J.B. Luchansky. 1997. *Viability of E. coli 0157:H7 in fermented semidry low-temperature-cooked beef summer sausages.* J.Food Prot. 60 (10):1158-62.

Tambov Sausage

Russian dry sausage.

pork,	20%,	1.0 kg (2.2 lb)
pork bellies,	40%,	2.0 kg (4.4 lb)
quality beef ,	40%,	2.0 kg (4.4 lb)

Ingredients per 5 kg (11 lb) of meat

salt, 3%, 140 g
cure #2, 12 g
dextrose, 0.3%, 15 g
pepper, 15 g
nutmeg, 3 g
T-SPX culture, 0.6 g (¼ tsp)

1. Grind pork and beef through 3/16" plate (6 mm). Manually dice belly into ¼" (6 mm) cubes or grind through ⅜" (10 mm) plate.
2. Mix all ingredients with meat.
3. Stuff firmly into beef middles or 3" protein lined fibrous casings.
4. Ferment at 20° C (68° F) for 72 hours, 90-85% humidity.
5. Cold smoke for 24 hours (< 22° C, 72° F).
6. Dry at 16-12° C (60-54° F), 85-80% humidity. In about 6-8 weeks a shrink of 30% should be achieved.
7. Store sausages at 10-15° C (50-59° F), 75% humidity.

Teewurst

German spreadable sausage.

beef,	20%,	1.0 kg	(2.20 lb)
lean pork,	30%,	1.5 kg	(3.30 lb)
fat bacon,	25%,	1.25 kg	(2.75 lb)
back fat,	25%,	1.25 kg	(2.75 lb)

Ingredients per 5 kg (11 lb) of meat

salt, 2.5 %, 115 g
cure #1, 12 g
dextrose 0.3%, 15 g
white pepper, 12 g
allspice, 2,5 g
dark rum, 15 g (1 Tbsp)
T-SPX, 0.6 g (¼ tsp)

1. Grind all meats through ⅛" (3 mm) plate. Re-freeze meats and grind again twice. You may grind once and then emulsify in the food processor without adding water. Add all ingredients, starter culture included, during this step.
2. Mix all together.
3. Stuff firmly into 40 mm beef middles or fibrous casings. Form 8-10" (20-25 cm) links.
4. Ferment for 48 hours at maximum 18° C (64° F), 75% humidity.
5. Apply cold smoke for 12 hours at 18° C (64° F).
6. Store in a refrigerator.

Tourist Sausage

Russian dry sausage. Small sizes made these sausages a convenient item to carry when travelling, hence the name tourist.

pork,	20%,	1.0 kg (2.2 lb)
pork bellies,	40%,	2.0 kg (4.4 lb)
lean beef,	40%,	2.0 kg (4.4 lb)

Ingredients per 5 kg (11 lb) of meat

salt, 3%, 140 g
cure #2, 12 g
dextrose, 0.3%, 15 g
pepper, 15 g
caraway, 7.5 g
garlic, 15 g
T-SPX culture, 0.6 g (¼ tsp)

1. Grind pork and beef through 3/16" plate (6 mm). Manually dice bacon into ¼" (6 mm) cubes or grind through ⅜" (10 mm) plate.
2. Mix all ingredients with meat.
3. Stuff into hog casings 32-36 mm and form 8" (20 cm) long links.
4. Ferment at 20° C (68° F) for 72 hours, 90-85% humidity.
5. Cold smoke for 12 hours (< 22° C, 72° F).
6. Dry at 16-12° C (60-54° F), 85-80% humidity. In about 6-8 weeks a shrink of 30% should be achieved.
7. Store sausages at 10-15° C (50-59° F), 75% humidity.

Thuringer

Semi-dry partially or fully cooked, smoked beef and pork sausage.

pork,	70%,	3.5 kg (7.7 lb)
beef,	30%,	1.5 kg (3.3 lb)

Ingredients per 5 kg (11 lb) of meat

salt, 2.5%, 115 g
cure #1, 12 g
dextrose, 1%, 50 g
black pepper, 12 g
coriander, 10 g
whole mustard seeds, 20 g
allspice, 7.5 g
F-LC culture, 1.25 g (1/2 tsp)

1. Grind pork and beef fat through 3/16" plate (5 mm).
2. Mix all ingredients with meat.
3. Stuff into beef middles or fibrous casings 40-120 mm.
4. Ferment at 30° C (86° F) for 24 hours, 90-85% humidity.
5. Introduce warm smoke (43° C, 110° F), 70% humidity, for 6 hours. Gradually increase smoke temperature until internal meat temperature of 140° F (60° C) is obtained.
6. For a drier sausage: dry for 2 days at 22-16° C (60-70° F), 65-75% humidity or until desired weight loss has occurred.
7. Store sausages at 10-15° C (50-59° F), 75% humidity.

Urutan
(Balinese Fermented Sausage)

Urutan is a Balinese traditional dry fermented sausage whose technology differs from the European Sausages. No nitrite/nitrate is used in the process and the sausage owes its yellowish-brown color to turmeric (main ingredient of curry powder). Laos powder (*Galanga pinata* spice) and aromatic ginger (*Kaempferia galangal*) contribute greatly to its Eastern flavor. The climate in Bali is hot and the sausage is fermented at 25° C (77° F) at night and at 50° C (122° F) during the day. Such warm temperatures permit fast fermentation which is accomplished within 5 days. Urutan is not smoked.

lean pork,	70%,	3.5 kg (7.7 lb)
back fat,	30%,	1.5 kg (3.3 lb)

(or 100% fatty pork butt)

Ingredients per 5 kg (11 lb) of meat

salt, 3%, 140 g
cure #2, 12 g
dextrose, 0.5%, 25 g
sugar, 0.5%, 25 g
black pepper, 0.5%, 25 g
garlic, 2%, 100 g
red chili pepper (cayenne family), 1%, 50 g
ginger, 0.5%, 25 g
turmeric, 1%, 50 g
laos powder*, 1.5%, 75 g
T-SPX culture, 0.6 g (1/4 tsp)

1. Grind meat and fat through 3/16" plate (6 mm).
2. Mix all ingredients with ground meat.
3. Stuff into collagen or sheep casings 24-26 mm and form 5" (12 cm) long links.
4. Ferment at 24° C (75° F) for 72 hours, 90-85% humidity.
5. Dry for two weeks at 16-12° C (60-54° F), 85-80% humidity.
6. Store sausages at 10-15° C (50-59° F), 75% humidity.

Notes:

Nitrate has been added to the recipe to provide a safety hurdle.
Traditional recipe calls for 5% garlic (similar to Thai Nham sausage) to provide extra safety. See page 81 on the antioxidant and antimicrobial effects of garlic.
*Laos powder (*Galanga pinata*) - the aromatic, peppery, ginger-like spice is indigenous to Southeast Asia. Its pungent cardamom-like eucalyptus flavor enhances the overall flavor profiles of Thai and Indonesian cuisines. Used in pungent Thai curry pastes, meat marinades and stir-fries. Added to Indonesian spice pastes that are rubbed on duck and fish.

Chapter 15

Troubleshooting Problems

ACIDIFICATION

pH too low

- Too much sugar has been added.
- Fermentation has continued too long. This will apply mainly to fast-fermented sausages where the process is relatively short. The fermentation can be stopped with a heating process what will inactivate lactic acid bacteria and any unused sugar will offset an acidic taste of the sausage. If thermal process did not take place or was applied late, lactic acid bacteria converted all sugar into acid.

Acidification too slow

- Too low fermentation temperature.
- Insufficient sugar has been added.
- Freeze dried culture has been kept in water too long. Culture can be introduced directly into meat, however, placing it for 10-15 minutes in a small amount of water will shorten its *lag phase*. The benefit is twofold: it is easier to distribute culture in meat uniformly and the culture will react with meat faster. Similar procedure is employed for yeasts.
- Culture was introduced to sausage mince, however, the mince was kept too long in a cooler before stuffing. This has largely extended culture's lag phase.
- Wild bacteria have outgrown culture and has taken over the process. This might be due to the insufficient amount of culture added, too little salt or incorrect fermentation temperature.
- Too much salt was added. Adding more than 4% inhibits growth of lactic acid bacteria. It will also inhibit culture which is a mixture of different bacteria strains.
- Stuffed sausages have been kept in a cooler too long. This has extended culture's lag phase.
- Culture was mixed with salt, nitrite or spices and kept too long before being introduced into meat. This inactivated the culture or triggered the wrong type of fermentation. The culture should be introduced at the last moment, the meat should be stuffed and the sausages should enter the

fermentation chamber.

- Too rapid moisture loss may leave insufficient water for bacteria to conduct fermentation. This will be even more pronounced in sausages with a higher fat content as the fat contains less water than a lean meat.

Acidification too fast

- Too high temperature.
- Too much water was added during processing.
- Sausages contained a very large proportion of lean meat which resulted in higher Aw.
- The sausages were too warm when placed in fermentation chamber.
- Too much dextrose was added either by itself or in sugar combination.
- Too long fermentation time.

No acidification

- No culture added.
- Insufficient amount of sugar was added to sausage mince.
- Culture was inactivated by directed contact with salt, cure (nitrite) or mixed with chlorinated water.
- Culture was stored at too high temperature.
- Fat content of the sausage was unusually high.

MOISTURE

Insufficient moisture loss

- Too high humidity during drying.
- Excessive air speed and/or too low humidity in the beginning of the proces has created a dry rim so that moisture cannot escape from the inside to the surface.
- Excessive smoke too early in the process has cooked surface proteins thereby retarding moisture removal.
- Fat smearing prevented moisture loss.
- Fermentation temperature was too high causing fat melting inside of the casing and preventing moisture ecaping to the surface.

Too much moisture loss (drying too fast)

- Humidity too low.
- Air spped too high.

FLAVOR

Souring of product, post processing

- Insufficient heat treatment did not stop fermentation.

238

- Too much sugar added, some lactic acid bacteria survived process and triggered secondary fermentation.
- Too slow drying, fermentation continued due to a high moisture and left over unfermented sugar.
- Product was stored at too high temperature what triggered secondary fermentation.

Off-odor

- Poor quality raw materials were used. There were too many bacteria present.
- Some spoilage bacteria survived fermentation and drying process.
- Poor sanitation practices introduced undesirable bacteria during processing,
- Poor sanitation practices introduced undesirable bacteria during packing or storage.
- Too fast drying created hard surface which prevented moisture removal. Inside of the sausage remained moist and became breeding ground for bacteria. The sausage looks fine on outside, but the inside is spoiled.
- Old, stale natural casings.

COLOR

Discoloration - green or grey coloration

- Fat smearing or hard surface ring prevented moisture removal making inside of the sausage grey.
- Insufficient amount of sodium nitrite.
- Insufficient amount of curing and color forming bacteria *(Staphylococci* and *Micrococcaceaae*) naturally present in meat if starter culture was not added. Problem even worse if only potassium nitrate was used.
- Chemical acidifier was used.
- Casing treated with too much potassium sorbate.
- An excessive growth of yeast on the surface.

TEXTURE

Mushy product

- Meat not perfectly fresh.
- Using meat with too much connective tissue.
- Grinding and mixing meat at too high temperature. This usually holds true for home production, especially when a large proportion of fat is present.
- Too little salt added.

Soft sausage

- Not enough salt.
- Too much soft fat.
- Too high pH.
- Too little sugar.
- Lack of culture.
- Too high processing temperature.
- Incomplete drying.

Hard surface ring

- To low humidity.
- Too fast air speed.
- Too warm smoke.

Grey surface ring

- Too high humidity during ripening or storage.
- Wet smoke.
- Too low storage temperature.

Poor meat and fat particle definition

- Too much soft fat.
- Too high processing temperature.
- Cutting/grinding knife not sharp.
- Mixing too long.

Greasy sausage

- Too high processing temperature.
- Too high fermentation temperature.
- Too long mixing time, especially at high temperature.
- Smoke too warm.
- Storage temperature too high.
- Too much soft fat.
- Dull grinder knife.

Unwanted Mold

Too much humidity and/or not enough air speed during fermentation, drying or storage.

Cultured Mold

Uneven distribution. Starter culture old. Culture applied too late. Sausage was smoked.

Problems Related to Spreadable Sausages

Symptom	Problem	Solution
Poor spreadability	too much lean meat	add more fat or vegetable oil
	too many large hard fat particles	use softer fat
	fat particles too large	use smaller grinder plate
	Smoking temperature too high	keep below 22° C
	too rapid pH drop - too much sugar or Gdl	decrease the amount
	too fast ripening or storing	keep humidity at <80%, decrease air speed
Visible grey areas inside	too much light meat added	use meat from older animals
	too little or too much nitrite	change dosage
	bacteria count too high	use fresher meat and/ or improve manufacturing conditions
Greasy sausage, dripping fat, premature rancidity	too much soft fat	replace some soft with hard fat
	sausage mass too warm	keep below 20° C, mix materials at lower temperature
	meat and fat too warm	keep in cooler
	dull grinder knife	use sharp knife
	too warm smoke	apply cold smoke below 22° C
	high storage temperature	store at 10-15 C, 75% humidity
Split sausage	meat with a high bacteria count	use fresh meat and enforce correct safety practices
	cracked sausage	do not force casing on a stuffing tube

Loose or wrinkled casings	fat was not distributed properly and did not envelop lean meat particles what resulted in too fast drying	increase the amount of fat, add more soft fat or some vegetable oil. Soak natural casings longer in water
	too much sugar promoted growth of undesirable bacteria	add less sugar
	too high temperature	keep temperature below 24° C
Grey rim	too long ripening or storing at high humidity	adjust humidity
	too cold storage	store above 5° C
	too early application of smoke	apply smoke when the texture is red
	smoke too wet	keep smoke humidity <75%
Sourly and vinegar like taste	fermentation temperature too high	process at <24° C
	different strains of wild bacteria fermenting	use proper starter culture
Black and brown spots	salt not properly dissolved	mix properly

Appendix - Supplementary Information

All About Nitrates

Cured meats develop a particular pink-reddish color due to the reaction that takes place between meat myoglobin and nitrate/nitrite. If an insufficient amount of nitrate/nitrite is added to the meat the cured color will suffer. This may be less noticeable in sausages where the meat is ground and stuffed but if we slice a larger piece like a ham, the poorly developed color will be easily noticeable. Some sections may be gray, some may be pink and the meat will not look appetizing.

About 50 ppm (parts per million) of nitrite are needed to cure meat. Some of it will react with myoglobin and will fix the color, some of it will go into other complex bio-chemical reactions with meat that develop a characteristic cured meat flavor. If we stay within Food and Drug Administration guidelines (1 oz. cure #1 per 25 lbs. of meat – about 1 level teaspoon of cure #1 for 5 lbs of meat) we are applying 156 ppm of nitrite which is enough and safe at the same time.

Curing with Nitrates/Nitrites

We had been and are still using nitrates because:

- We like our meats to be red not only when they are fresh but after cooking or smoking too.
- Nitrates can preserve meat's natural color. The same piece of ham when roasted will have a light brown color and is known as roasted leg of pork. Add some nitrates to it, apply smoke or boil it and it becomes ham with its characteristic flavor and pink color.
- Nitrates impart to meat a characteristic cured flavor.
- Nitrates prevent the transformation of botulinum spores into toxins thus eliminating the possibility of food poisoning.

What's Better, Nitrate or Nitrite?

Both nitrates and nitrites are permitted to be used in curing meat and poultry with the exception of bacon, where nitrate use is prohibited. Sodium nitrite is commonly used in the USA (cure #1) and everywhere else in the world but many commonly available cures contain both nitrite and nitrate. There is not much difference between nitrate or nitrite, the final result is basically the same. The difference between nitrate and nitrite is as big as the difference between wheat flour and the bread that was baked from it. Curing bacteria force nitrate to release nitrite. Pure sodium nitrite is an even more powerful poison than nitrate as you need only about ⅓ of a tea-spoon to put your life in danger, where in a case of nitrate you may need 1 teaspoon or more. So all these explanations that nitrite is safer for you make absolutely no sense at all. Replacing nitrate with nitrite eliminates questions like: do I have enough nitrite to cure the meat? In other words, it is more predictable and *it is easier to control the dosage.* Another good reason for using nitrite is that *it is effective at low temperatures* 36-40° F, (2-4° C), where nitrate likes temperatures around 46° F, (8° C). By curing meats at lower temperatures we slow down the growth of bacteria and *we extend the shelf life* of a product. When nitrates were used alone, *salt penetration was usually ahead of color development.* As a result large pieces of meat were too salty when fully colored and had to be soaked in water. This problem has been eliminated when using nitrite. Nitrite works much faster and the *color is fixed well before salt can fully penetrate the meat.*

Nitrate Safety Concerns

There has been much concern over the consumption of nitrates by the general public. Studies have shown that when nitrites combine with by-products of protein (amines in the stomach), that leads to the formation of nitrosamines which are carcinogenic (cancer causing) in laboratory animals. There was also a link that when nitrates were used to cure bacon and the latter one was fried until crispy, it helped to create nitrosamines. In order to accomplish that the required temperatures had to be in the 600° F (315° C) range. Most meats are smoked and cooked well below 200° F (93° C) so they are not affected. Those findings started a lot of unnecessary panic in the 1970's about the harmful effects of nitrates on our health. Millions of dollars were spent, a lot of research was done, many researchers had spent long sleepless nights seeking fame and glory, but no evidence was found that when nitrates are used within the established limits they can pose any danger to our health.

A review of all scientific literature on nitrite by the National Research Council of the National Academy of Sciences indicates that nitrite does not directly harm us in any way. All this talk about the danger of nitrite in our meats pales in comparison with the amounts of nitrates that are found in vegetables that we consume every day. The nitrates get to them from the fertilizers which are used in agriculture. Don't blame sausages for the nitrates you consume, blame the farmer. It is more dangerous to one's health to eat vegetables on a regular basis than a sausage.

How Much Nitrite is Dangerous

According to the report prepared in 1972 for the U.S. Food and Drug Administration (FDA) by Battele-Columbus Laboratories and Department of Commerce, Springfield, VA 22151 – the fatal dose of potassium nitrate for humans is in the range of 30 to 35 grams (about two tablespoons) consumed as a single dose; the fatal dose of sodium nitrite is in the range of 22 to 23 milligrams per kilogram of body weight. A 156 lbs adult (71 kg) would have to consume 14.3 pounds (6.5 kg) of cured meat containing 200 ppm of sodium nitrite at one time. Taking into consideration that nitrite is rapidly converted to nitric oxide during the curing process, the 14.3 lbs amount will have to be doubled or even tripled. The equivalent amount of *pure* sodium nitrite consumed will be 1.3 g. *One gram (1 ppm) of pure sodium nitrite is generally accepted as a life threatening dose.* As nitrite is mixed with large amounts of salt, it would be impossible to swallow it at least from a culinary point of view.

Nitrates and the Law

Maximum in-going nitrite and nitrate limits in PPM (parts per million) for Meat and Poultry Products as required by the U.S. Food Safety and Inspection Service are:

Curing Agent	Curing Method			
	Immersion Cured	Massaged or Pumped	Comminuted	Dry Cured
Sodium Nitrite	200	200	156	625
Potassium Nitrite	200	200	156	625
Sodium Nitrate	700	700	1718	2187
Potassium Nitrate	700	700	1718	2187

For this reason, *nitrate is no longer permitted in any bacon* (pumped and/or massaged, dry cured, or immersion cured). As a matter of policy, the Agency requires a minimum of 120 ppm of ingoing nitrite in all cured "Keep Refrigerated" products, unless the establishment can demonstrate that safety is assured by some other preservation process, such as thermal processing, pH or moisture control. This 120 ppm policy for in going nitrite is based on safety data reviewed when the bacon standard was developed. Take note that *nitrosamines can only be formed when products are heated above 266° F (130° C)*. This can only happen when cured bacon is fried or cured sausage is grilled. The majority of cured and smoked meats never reach such high temperatures.

There is no regulatory minimum in-going nitrite level for cured products that have been processed to ensure their shelf stability (such as having undergone a complete thermal process, or having been subjected to adequate pH controls, and/ or moisture controls in combination with appropriate packaging). By the time meats are consumed, they contain less then 50 parts per million of nitrite. It is said that commercially prepared meats in the USA contain about 10 ppm of nitrite when bought in a supermarket. Nitrite and nitrate are not permitted in baby, junior or toddler foods.

Cure #1 (also known as Instacure #1, Prague Powder #1 or Pink Cure #1 is a mixture of 1 oz of sodium nitrite (6.25%) to 1 lb of salt. It must be used to cure all meats that will require smoking at low temperatures.

Cure #2 (also known as Instacure #2, Prague Powder #2 or Pink Cure #2). Cure #2 is a mixture of 1 oz of sodium nitrite (6.25%) along with 0.64 oz of sodium nitrate (4%) to 1 lb of salt. It must be used with any products that do not require cooking, smoking or refrigeration and is mainly used for products that will be air cured for a long time like country ham, salami, pepperoni, and other dry sausages. Both cure #1 and cure #2 contain a small amount of FDA approved red coloring agent that gives them a slight pink color thus eliminating any possible confusion with common salt and that is why they are sometimes called "pink" curing salts.

A.3 Botulism

Botulism, once known as a sausage disease, is a rare but serious food borne disease that can be fatal. The symptoms of botulism include difficulty swallowing, talking, breathing, and double vision. Without medical care, respiratory failure and death are likely. Botulism symptoms typically appear within 18 to 36 hours of eating the contaminated food, although it can be as soon as four hours and last up to eight days. Food borne botulism can be especially dangerous because many people can be poisoned at once. Sausages are the second biggest source of food contamination and food poisoning, second only to home-canned food products.

The optimal temperature range for the growth of botulinum bacteria is 78-95° F (26-35° C) and it significantly slows down at 118° F (48° C). When these bacteria feel threatened, they envelop themselves within a few hours in protective shells called "spores" which can be killed by heating them to 240° F (115° C) temperature what requires the use of a pressure canner. Boiling water temperature 212° F (100° C), will kill them as well if boiled for 5 hours. At 140° F (60° C) botulinum spores do not develop into toxins, although they are heat resistant.

FA1. Botulinum spore.

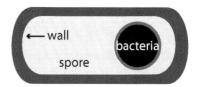

Fortunately, we are seldom exposed to *Cl. botulinum* bacteria in their "vegetative" (growing) phase when they produce toxin. Because *Cl.botulinum* hate oxygen, the air which is present in soil and water threatens them. *Cl.botulinum* bacteria immediately envelop themselves within a protective shell. They do not multiply, they just patiently remain inside waiting for more favorable conditions. Similarly to plant seeds, they can survive harmlessly in soil and water for many years. Then when the opportunity arises they emerge from their shells and become vegetative bacteria (actively growing). During this growing stage they produce toxin. It is the toxin that kills, not the bacteria.

Where Does Botulism Come From?

Cl. botulinum is found in soil and aquatic sediments all over the world. Like plant seeds, they can lie dormant for years. They are not threatening until they encounter an adequate environment for growth. The spores that germinate produce the deadly botulinum toxin. To grow they require a slightly acidic, oxygen free environment that is warm and moist. That is exactly what happens when smoking meats:

1. First of all meats contain a lot of moisture. Water is then also added to sausages to facilitate stuffing. Hams and other meats are pumped up with water.

2. Lack of oxygen – when smoking we intentionally decrease the amount of available air. This allows our sawdust or wood chips to generate lots of smoke.

3. Temperatures between 40° and 140° F - most smoking is done at this temperature range. The most dangerous range is from 78-95° F (26-35° C) and that fits into the "warm smoking" method. Bacteria thrive at this temperature range and smoking process creates ideal conditions for *Cl. botulinum* to grow.

How to Prevent Botulism

The answer lies in the use of *nitrates/nitrites*. When present, they prevent the transformation of *C. botulinum* spores into toxins. It is almost like applying a vaccine to eliminate a disease. By curing meats with nitrites we protect ourselves from possibly contracting a deadly disease. Nitrites are cheap, commonly available, and completely safe in amounts recommended by the Food and Drug Administration. So why not use them? All commercial plants do. Nitrites are needed only when smoking meats or making fermented sausages. You don't need nitrites when barbecuing or grilling as the temperatures are high enough to inhibit the development of botulinum spores into toxins.

A.4 Trichinae

There are some cold smoked pork products and sausages that will not be submitted to the cooking process and they can be at risk of being infected with trichinae. Trichinae is an illness caused by the consumption of raw or under cooked pork or wild game meat infected with *"trichinella spiralis."* Deers are herbivores; they eat leaves from trees, bushes and shrubs and they don't contract the disease. Trichinae is a parasitic nematode (round worm) that can migrate from the digestive tract and settle in the form of cysts in various muscles of the body. The disease is almost non-existent in American pork due to their strictly controlled feed, but it can still be found in meats of free roaming animals. The illness is not contagious, but the first symptoms appear within 1-2 days of eating contaminated meat. They include nausea, diarrhea, vomiting, abdominal pain, itchy skin, and may be mistaken for the flu.

Trichinae in pork is killed by raising its internal temperature to 137° F (58° C). The U.S. Code of Federal Regulations requires pork to be cooked for 1 minute at 140° F (60° C). Traditionally made fermented sausages, also called dry or slow-fermented sausages are normally never cooked and the heat treatment does not apply here. They are cured with a higher percentage of salt which kills *trichinae* too. Fortunately, *storing pork at low temperatures also kills trichinae.* For a home sausage maker the easiest to apply procedure is listed in the Table 1- Required Period of Freezing at Temperature Indicated. What follows is a complete reprint of the regulations for treatment of pork to destroy trichinae.

PART 318 - ENTRY INTO OFFICIAL ESTABLISHMENTS; REINSPECTION AND PREPARATION OF PRODUCTS

§ 318.10   Prescribed treatment of pork and products containing pork to destroy trichinae.

(a)(1) All forms of fresh pork, including fresh unsmoked sausage containing pork muscle tissue, and pork such as bacon and jowls, other than those covered by paragraph (b) of this section, are classed as products that are customarily well cooked in the home or elsewhere before being served to the consumer. Therefore, the treatment of such products for the destruction of trichinae is not required.

(2) Pork from carcasses or carcass parts that have been found free of trichinae as described under paragraph (e) or (f) of this section is not required to be treated for the destruction of trichinae.

(b) Products named in this paragraph, and products of the character hereof, containing pork muscle tissue (not including pork hearts, pork stomachs, and pork livers), or the pork muscle tissue which forms an ingredient of such products, shall be effectively heated, refrigerated, or cured to destroy any possible live trichinae, as prescribed in this section at the official establishment where such products are prepared: Bologna, frankfurter, vienna, and other cooked sausage; smoked sausage; knoblauch sausage; mortadella; all forms of summer or dried sausage, including mettwurst; flavored pork sausages such as those containing wine or similar flavoring materials; cured pork sausage; sausage containing cured and/or smoked pork; cooked loaves; roasted, baked, boiled, or cooked hams, pork shoulders, or pork shoulder picnics; Italian-style hams; Westphalia-style hams; smoked boneless pork shoulder butts; cured meat rolls; capocollo (capicola, capacola); coppa; fresh or cured boneless pork shoulder butts, hams, loins, shoulders, shoulder picnics, and similar pork cuts, in casings or other containers in which ready-to-eat delicatessen articles are customarily enclosed (excepting Scotch-style hams); breaded pork products; cured boneless pork loins; boneless back bacon; bacon used for wrapping around patties, steaks and similar products; and smoked pork cuts such as hams, shoulders, loins, and pork shoulder picnics (excepting smoked hams, and smoked pork shoulder picnics which are specially prepared for distribution in tropical climates or smoked hams delivered to the Armed Services); ground meat mixtures containing pork and beef, veal, lamb, mutton, or goat meat and other product consisting of mixtures of pork and other ingredients, which the Administrator determines at the time the labeling for the product is submitted for approval in accordance with part 317 of the regulations in this subchapter or upon subsequent reevaluation of the product, would be prepared in such a manner that the product might be eaten rare or without thorough cooking because of the appearance of the finished product or otherwise. Cured boneless pork loins shall be subjected to prescribed treatment for destruction of trichinae prior to being shipped from the establishment where cured.

(c) The treatment shall consist of heating, refrigerating, or curing, as follows:
(1) Heating. (i) All parts of the pork muscle tissue shall be heated according to one of the time and temperature combinations in the following table:

Minimum Internal Temperature		Minimum Time
° F	° C	
120	49.0	21 hours
122	50.0	9.5 hours
124	51.1	4.5 hours
126	52.2	2 hours
128	53.4	1 hour
130	54.5	30 minutes
132	55.6	15 minutes
134	56.7	6 minutes
136	57.8	3 minutes
138	58.9	2 minutes
140	60.0	1 minute
142	61.1	1 minute
144	62.2	Instant

(ii) Time and temperature shall be monitored by a calibrated recording instrument that meets the requirements of paragraph (d) of this section, except for paragraph (c)(1)(iv).

(iii) The time to raise product temperature from 60° F to 120° F shall not exceed 2 hours unless the product is cured or fermented.

(iv) Time, in combination with temperatures of 138° F to 143° F, need not be monitored if the product's minimum thickness exceeds 2 inches (5.1 cm) and refrigeration of the product does not begin within 5 minutes of attaining 138° F (58.9° C).

(v) The establishment shall use procedures which insure the proper heating of all parts of the product. It is important that each piece of sausage, each ham, and other product treated by heating in water be kept entirely submerged throughout the heating period; and that the largest pieces in a lot, the innermost links of bunched sausage or other massed articles, and pieces placed in the coolest part of a heating cabinet or compartment or vat be included in the temperature tests.

(2) Refrigerating. At any stage of preparation and after preparatory chilling to a temperature of not above 40° F or preparatory freezing, all parts of the muscle tissue of pork or product containing such tissue shall be subjected continuously to a temperature not higher than one of those specified in table 1, the duration of such refrigeration at the specified temperature being dependent on the thickness of the meat or inside dimensions of the container.

Table 1. Required Period of Freezing at Temperature Indicated			
° F	° C	Group 1 (Days)	Group 2 (Days)
5	- 15	20	30
- 10	- 23.3	10	20
- 20	- 28.9	6	12

(i) Group 1 comprises product in separate pieces not exceeding 6 inches in thickness, or arranged on separate racks with the layers not exceeding 6 inches in depth, or stored in crates or boxes not exceeding 6 inches in depth, or stored as solidly frozen blocks not exceeding 6 inches in thickness.

(ii) Group 2 comprises product in pieces, layers, or within containers, the thickness of which exceeds 6 inches but not 27 inches and product in containers including tierces, barrels, kegs, and cartons having a thickness not exceeding 27 inches.

(iii) The product undergoing such refrigeration or the containers thereof shall be so spaced while in the freezer as will insure a free circulation of air between the pieces of meat, layers, blocks, boxes, barrels, and tierces in order that the temperature of the meat throughout will be promptly reduced to not higher than 5° F, −10 °F, or −20 °F, as the case may be.

(iv) In lieu of the methods prescribed in Table 1, the treatment may consist of commercial freeze drying or controlled freezing, at the center of the meat pieces, in accordance with the times and temperatures specified in Table 2.

Table 2—Alternate Periods of Freezing at Temperatures Indicated		
Maximum Internal Temperature		Minimum Time
° F	° C	
0	- 17.8	106 hours
- 5	- 20.6	82 hours
- 10	- 23.3	63 hours
- 15	- 26.1	48 hours
- 20	- 28.9	35 hours
- 25	- 31.7	22 hours
- 30	- 34.5	8 hours
-35	- 37.2	1/2 hour

(v) During the period of refrigeration the product shall be kept separate from other products and in the custody of the Program in rooms or compartments equipped and made secure with an official Program lock or seal. The rooms or compartments containing product undergoing freezing shall be equipped with accurate thermometers placed at or above the highest level at which the product undergoing treatment is stored and away from refrigerating coils. After completion of the prescribed freezing of pork to be used in the preparation of product covered by paragraph (b) of this section the pork shall be kept under close supervision of an inspector until it is prepared in finished form as one of the products enumerated in paragraph (b) of this section or until it is transferred under Program control to another official establishment for preparation in such finished form.

(vi) Pork which has been refrigerated as specified in this subparagraph may be transferred in sealed railroad cars, sealed motortrucks, sealed trailers, or sealed closed containers to another official establishment at the same or another location, for use in the preparation of product covered by paragraph (b) of this section. Such vehicles and containers shall be sealed and transported between official establishments in accordance with §325.7 of this subchapter.

(3) Curing - (i) Sausage. The sausage may be stuffed in animal casings, hydrocellulose casings, or cloth bags. During any stage of treating the sausage for the destruction of live trichinae, except as provided in Method 5, these coverings shall not be coated with paraffin or like substance, nor shall any sausage be washed during any prescribed period of drying. In the preparation of sausage, one of the following methods may be used:

Method No. 1. The meat shall be ground or chopped into pieces not exceeding three-fourths of an inch in diameter. A dry-curing mixture containing not less than 3⅓ pounds of salt to each hundredweight of the unstuffed sausage shall be thoroughly mixed with the ground or chopped meat. After being stuffed, sausages having a diameter not exceeding 3½ inches, measured at the time of stuffing, shall be held in a drying room not less than 20 days at a temperature not lower than 45° F, except that in sausage of the variety known as pepperoni, if in casings not exceeding 1⅜ inches in diameter measured at the time of stuffing, the period of drying may be reduced to 15 days. In no case, however, shall the sausage be released from the drying room in less than 25 days from the time the curing materials are added, except that sausage of the variety known as pepperoni, if in casings not exceeding the size specified, may be released at the expiration of 20 days from the time the curing materials are added. Sausage in casings exceeding 3½ inches, but not exceeding 4 inches in diameter at the time of stuffing, shall be held in a drying room not less than 35 days at a temperature not lower than 45° F, and in no case shall the sausage be released from the drying room in less than 40 days from the time the curing materials are added to the meat.

Method No. 2. The meat shall be ground or chopped into pieces not exceeding three-fourths of an inch in diameter. A dry-curing mixture containing not less than 3⅓ pounds of salt to each hundredweight of the unstuffed sausage shall be thoroughly mixed with the ground or chopped meat. After being stuffed, sausage having a diameter not exceeding 3½ inches, measured at the time of stuffing, shall be smoked not less than 40 hours at a temperature not lower than 80° F, and finally held in a drying room not less than 10 days at a temperature not lower than 45° F. In no case, however, shall the sausage be released from the drying room in less than 18 days from the time the curing materials are added to the meat. Sausage exceeding 3½ inches, but not exceeding 4 inches in diameter at the time of stuffing, shall be held in a drying room, following smoking as above indicated, not less than 25 days at a temperature not lower than 45° F, but in no case shall the sausage be released from the drying room in less than 33 days from the time the curing materials are added to the meat.

Method No. 3. The meat shall be ground or chopped into pieces not exceeding three-fourths of an inch in diameter. A dry-curing mixture containing not less than 3⅓ pounds of salt to each hundredweight of the unstuffed sausage shall be thoroughly mixed with the ground or chopped meat. After add mixture with the salt and other curing materials and before stuffing, the ground or chopped meat shall be held at a temperature not lower than 34° F for not less than 36 hours. After being stuffed, the sausage shall be held at a temperature not lower than 34° F for an additional period of time sufficient to make a total of not less than 144 hours from the time the curing materials are added to the meat, or the sausage shall be held for the time specified in a pickle-curing medium of not less than 50° strength (salometer reading) at a temperature not lower than 44° F. Finally, sausage having a diameter not exceeding 3½ inches, measured at the time of stuffing, shall be smoked for not less than 12 hours. The temperature of the smokehouse during this period at no time shall be lower than 90° F; and for 4 consecutive hours of this period the smokehouse shall be maintained at a temperature not lower than 128° F. Sausage exceeding 3½ inches, but not exceeding 4 inches, in diameter at the time of stuffing shall be smoked, following the prescribed curing, for not less than 15 hours. The temperature of the smokehouse during the 15-hour period shall at no time be lower than 90° F, and for 7 consecutive hours of this period the smokehouse shall be maintained at a temperature not lower than 128° F. In regulating the temperature of the smokehouse for the treatment of sausage under this method, the temperature of 128° F shall be attained gradually during a period of not less than 4 hours.

Method No. 4. The meat shall be ground or chopped into pieces not exceeding one-fourth of an inch in diameter. A dry-curing mixture containing not less than 2½ pounds of salt to each hundredweight of the unstuffed sausage shall be thoroughly mixed with the ground or chopped meat. After add mixture with the salt and other curing materials and before stuffing, the ground or chopped sausage shall be held as a compact mass, not more than 6 inches in depth, at a temperature not lower than 36° F for not less than 10 days. At the termination of the holding period, the sausage shall be stuffed in casings or cloth bags not exceeding 3⅓ inches in diameter, measured at the time of stuffing. After being stuffed, the sausage shall be held in a drying room at a temperature not lower than 45° F for the remainder of a 35-day period, measured from the time the curing materials are added to the meat. At any time after stuffing, if the establishment operator deems it desirable, the product may be heated in a water bath for a period not to exceed 3 hours at a temperature not lower than 85° F, or subjected to smoking at a temperature not lower than 80° F, or the product may be both heated and smoked as specified. The time consumed in heating and smoking, however, shall be in addition to the 35-day holding period specified.

Method No. 5. The meat shall be ground or chopped into pieces not exceeding three-fourths of an inch in diameter. A dry-curing mixture containing not less than 3⅓ pounds of salt to each hundredweight of the unstuffed sausage shall be thoroughly mixed with the ground or chopped meat. After being stuffed, the sausage shall be held for not less than 65 days at a temperature not lower than 45° F. The coverings for sausage prepared according to this method may be coated at any stage of the preparation before or during the holding period with paraffin or other substance approved by the Administrator.

Method No. 6. (A) Basic requirements. The meat shall be ground or chopped into pieces not exceeding three-fourths of an inch in diameter. A dry-curing mixture containing not less than 3.33 pounds of salt to each hundredweight of the unstuffed sausage, excluding the weight of dry ingredients, shall be thoroughly mixed with the ground or chopped meat. After the curing mixture has been added, the sausage shall be held for two time periods, a holding period and a drying period. The holding period will be for a minimum of 48 hours at a room temperature not lower than 35° F. This holding period requirement may be fulfilled totally or in part before the drying period and then the remainder, if any, after the drying period or as an extension of the drying period. During the drying period, the sausage shall be held in a drying room at a temperature not lower than 50 (10.0° F (10.0° C) for a period of time determined by Tables 3A, 3B, and 4. The length of the drying period, established in (c)(3)(i)(A), may be modified as provided in paragraphs (c)(3)(i)(B) and (c)(3)(i)(C) of this section.

Table 3A - **Sausage Drying Room Times** by Method No. 6	
Diameter of casing at time of stuffing[1]	Days in drying room[2]
1 inches	14
1½ inches	15
2 inches	16
2½ inches	18
3 inches	20
3½ inches	23
4 inches	25
4½ inches	30
5 inches	35
5½ inches	43
6 inches	50

[1]The drying room times for flattened or oval sausages shall use a diameter derived by measuring the circumference and dividing by 3.14 (pi).

[2]Drying room time may be modified as set forth in Tables 3B and 4.

253

(B) Reduction in Drying Room Time. During the holding period, the sausage may be smoked or fermented. If the temperature is increased to 70 °F. (21.1 °C) or higher, while the sausage is being held after adding curing materials but before the drying period, the subsequent drying room times prescribed for this method may be reduced according to the schedule in Table 3B. No interpolation of values is permissible.

Table 3B - **Percentage Reduction in Drying Room Time** (Table 3A) Permitted by Holding Times and Temperatures Prior to Drying[1]									
Min. Time in hours	Degree F								
	70°	75°	80°	85°	90°	95°	100°	105°	110	120
	Degree C								
	21.1°	23.9°	26.7°	29.5°	32.2°	35.0°	37.9°	40.6°	43.3	48.9
24	4%	5%	8%	10%	15%	23%	37%	57%	90%	[3]100
48	9%	12%	18%	25%	35%	49%	88%	[3]100	[3]100	[3]100
72	14%	19%	28%	39%	55%	74%	[3]100	[3]100	[3]100	[3]100
96	19%	26%	38%	53%	75%	98%	[3]100	[3]100	[3]100	[3]100
120	24%	33%	48%	67%	95%	[3]100	[3]100	[3]100	[3]100	[3]100

[1]In computing the days to be deducted the number with any fraction shall be rounded to the next lower whole number and shall be deducted from the required total drying time. Example: Sausage stuffed in 3 inch; diameter casing requires 20 days in the drying room (from Drying Room Times, Table 3A). If allowed to ferment, after the addition of curing materials, at 80° F for 48 hours, the 20 day drying time may be reduced 18% (from Table 3B). Eighteen percent of 20 day equals 3.6 days. Twenty days minus 3 days equals 17 days. The total drying time required in the drying room, therefore, will be 17 days.

[2]Either room temperature or internal product temperature shall be used for sausages that will be subsequently dried to a moisture-protein ratio of 2.3:1 or less. Internal product temperature shall be used for all other sausages.

[3]Trichinae will be destroyed during fermentation or smoking at the temperature and length of time indicated. Therefore no drying room period is required for products so treated.

(C) Reduced Salt Content - Drying Room Times. Salt content of less than 3.33 pounds for each hundredweight of sausage formulation, excluding dry ingredients, (such as salts, sugars, and spices), may be permitted provided the drying time is increased according to the schedule contained in Table 4.

Trichina Treatment of Sausage by Method No. 6:

Table 4 - **Reduced Salt Content - Drying Room Times** [Required percentage increase in drying room time (table 3A) for added salt of less than 3.33 pounds per hundredweight of sausage]	
Minimum pounds of salt added to sausage[1]	Increase in drying room time[2]
3.3	1
3.2	4
3.1	7
3.0	10
2.9	13
2.8	16
2.7	19
2.6	22
2.5	25
2.4	28
2.3	31
2.2	34
2.1	37
2.0	40

[1]Calculate the salt content for column 1 as follows: Multiply the pounds of salt in the sausage formulation by 100. Then divide this number by the total weight of sausage formulation minus the weight of dry ingredients and round down to the next lowest 0.1%. Percents may be substituted for pounds.

Example: 120 lbs. pork, 3.56 lbs. salt, 2 lbs. spices, 0.5 lbs. wine, 1 lb. water and starter culture, 0.8 lbs. sugar, .012 lbs. sodium nitrite total weight is 127.872 lbs.

$(3.56 \times 100)/(127.872 - 3.56 - 2 - .8 - .012) = 356/121.5 = 2.93$

Therefore, the sausage drying time must be increased by 13 percent.

[2]In computing the days to be added to the required total drying time fractions shall be rounded to the next higher whole number and added to the required total drying time. Example: Sausage stuffed in 3 1/2 inch diameter casing requires 23 days in the drying room (from Drying Room Times). If the quantity of salt added per hundredweight of sausage is 2 pounds instead of 3.33 pounds, the drying room time must be increased by 40 percent (from Reduced Salt Content-Drying Room Times), or 9.2 days. The 9.2 is rounded up to 10 days and is added to the 23 days to equal 33 days. The total drying time required in the drying room, therefore, will be 33 days.

Method No. 7, Dry Sausages. (A) General Requirements. The establishment shall use meat particles reduced in size to no more than 1/4 inch in diameter. The establishment shall add a curing mixture containing no less than 2.7 pounds of salt per hundred pounds of meat and mix it uniformly throughout the product.

The establishment shall hold, heat, and dry the product according to paragraph (B) or (C) below.

(B) Holding, Heating, and Drying Treatment, Large Sausages. Except as permitted in (C) below, the establishment shall subject sausages in casings not exceeding 105 mm in diameter, at the time of stuffing, to all of the following minimum chamber temperatures and time periods.

Treatment Schedule for Sausages 105 Millimeters (4⅛ Inches) or Less in Diameter		
Minimum chamber temperature		Minimum time (hours)
° F	° C	
50	10	12
90	32.2	1
100	37.8	1
110	43.3	1
120	48.9	1
125	51.7	7

Following the preceding treatment, the establishment shall dry the sausages at a temperature not lower than 50° F (10° C) for not less than 7 days.

(C) Heating and Drying Treatment, Small Sausages. Alternatively, the establishment may subject sausages in casings not exceeding 55 mm in diameter, at the time of stuffing, to all of the following minimum chamber temperatures and time periods.

Treatment Schedule for Sausages 55 Millimeters (2 ⅛ Inches) or Less in Diameter		
Minimum chamber temperature		Minimum time (hours)
° F	° C	
50	10	12
100	37.8	1
125	51.7	6

Following the preceding heat treatment, the establishment shall dry the sausages at a temperature not lower than 50° F (10° C) for not less than 4 days.

(ii) Capocollo (capicola, capacola). Boneless pork butts for capocollo shall be cured in a dry-curing mixture containing not less than 4½ pounds of salt per hundredweight of meat for a period of not less than 25 days at a temperature not lower than 36° F. If the curing materials are applied to the butts by the process known as churning, a small quantity of pickle may be added. During the curing period the butts may be overhauled according to any of the usual processes of overhauling, including the addition of pickle or dry salt if desired. The butts shall not be subjected during or after curing to any treatment designed to remove salt from the meat, except that superficial washing may be allowed.

After being stuffed the product shall be smoked for a period of not less than 30 hours at a temperature not lower than 80° F and shall finally be held in a drying room not less than 20 days at a temperature not lower than 45° F.

(iii) Coppa. Boneless pork butts for coppa shall be cured in a dry-curing mixture containing not less than 4½ pounds of salt per hundredweight of meat for a period of not less than 18 days at a temperature not lower than 36° F. If the curing mixture is applied to the butts by the process known as churning, a small quantity of pickle may be added. During the curing period the butts may be overhauled according to any of the usual processes of overhauling, including the addition of pickle or dry salt if desired. The butts shall not be subjected during or after curing to any treatment designed to remove salt from the meat, except that superficial washing may be allowed. After being stuffed, the product shall be held in a drying room not less than 35 days at a temperature not lower than 45 °F.

(iv) Hams and pork shoulder picnics. In the curing of hams and pork shoulder picnics, one of the methods below shall be used. For calculating days per pound the establishment shall use the weight of the heaviest ham or picnic in the lot.

Method No. 1. The hams and pork shoulder picnics shall be cured by a dry-salt curing process not less than 40 days at a temperature no lower than 36 °F. The products shall be laid down in salt, not less than 4 pounds to each hundredweight of product, the salt being applied in a thorough manner to the lean meat of each item. When placed in cure, the products may be pumped with pickle if desired. At least once during the curing process, the products shall be overhauled (turned over for the application of additional cure) and additional salt applied, if necessary, so that the lean meat of each item is thoroughly covered. After removal from cure, the products may be soaked in water at a temperature not higher than 70 °F for not more than 15 hours, during which time the water may be changed once, but they shall not be subjected to any other treatment designed to remove salt from the meat except that superficial washing may be allowed. The products shall finally be dried or smoked at a time and temperature not less than a combination prescribed in Table 5 of Method No. 3.

Method No. 2. [Reserved]

Method No. 3. (A) Curing. (Other than bag curing): Establishments shall cure hams and shoulders by using a cure mixture containing not less than 70 percent salt by weight to cover all exposed muscle tissue and to pack the hock region. Total curing time consists of a mandatory cure contact time and an optional equalization time.

(B) Cure Contact Time. This is the cure contact period during which the establishment shall keep exposed muscle tissue coated with the cure mixture at least 28 days but for no less than 1.5 days per pound of ham or shoulder. Overhaul is optional so long as the exposed muscle tissue remains coated with curing mixture.

(C) Equalization. The establishment may provide an equalization period after the minimum cure contact period in (B) above to permit the absorbed salt to permeate the product's inner tissues. Equalization is the time after the excess cure has been removed from the product at the end of the cure contact period until the product is placed in the drying room and the drying period begins. The total curing time (equalization plus cure contact) shall be at least 40 days and in no case less than 2 days per pound of an uncured ham or shoulder.

(D) Removing Excess Cure. After the required cure contact period, the establishment may remove excess cure mixture from the product's surface mechanically or by rinsing up to 1 minute with water, but not by soaking.

(E) Bag Curing. Bag curing is a traditional ham curing technique in which the manufacturer wraps the ham and all of the cure mixture together in kraft paper then hangs them individually. The paper keeps the extra cure mixture in close contact with the product making reapplication of salt unnecessary and it protects the product from mites and insects. Establishments may employ the bag curing method as an alternative to (A) through (D) above. An establishment which elects to use the bag curing method shall apply a cure mixture containing at least 6 pounds of salt per 100 pounds of uncured product. The establishment shall rub the curing mixture into the exposed muscle tissue, pack the hock region with the curing mixture and use uncoated wrapping paper to wrap the product together with any remaining curing mixture. The bag cured product shall remain wrapped throughout the curing period and may or may not remain wrapped during the drying period. In any case, the curing period shall be at least 40 days but not less than 2 days per pound of an uncured ham or shoulder. After curing the cured product shall be exposed to a drying time and temperature prescribed in Table 5.

(F) Curing Temperature. During the curing period the establishment shall use one of the following procedures:

(1) The establishment shall control the room temperature at not less than 35° F (1.7° C) nor greater than 45° F (7.2° C) for the first 1.5 days per pound of an uncured ham or shoulder, and not less than 35° F (1.7° C) nor greater than 60° F (15.6° C) for the remainder of the curing period.

(2) The establishment shall monitor and record daily product temperature. The room temperature need not be controlled but days on which the product temperature drops below 35° F (1.7° C) shall not be counted as curing time. If the product temperature exceeds 45° F (7.2° C) within the first period of 1.5 days per pound of an uncured ham or shoulder or if it exceeds 60° F (15.6° C) for the remainder of the curing period, the establishment shall cool the product back to the 45° F (7.2° C) maximum during the first period or 55° F (12.8° C) maximum during the remainder of the period.

258

(3) The establishment shall begin curing product only between the dates of December 1 and February 13. The room temperature need not be controlled but the establishment shall monitor and record daily room temperatures and days in which the room temperature drops below 35° F (1.7° C) shall not be counted as curing time.

(G) Drying. After the curing period, establishments shall use one of three procedures for drying:

(1) The establishment shall subject the product to a controlled room temperature for a minimum time and minimum temperature combination prescribed in Table 5 or for a set of such combinations in which the total of the fractional periods (in column 4 of Table 5) exceeds 1.5.

(2) Establishments using uncontrolled room temperatures shall monitor and record the internal product temperature. The drying period shall be complete when from the days which can be counted as curing time, one of the time/temperature combinations of Table 5 is satisfied or when the total of the fractional values for the combinations exceeds 1.5.

(3) Establishments using uncontrolled room temperatures shall dry the product for a minimum of 160 days including the entire months of June, July, and August. This procedure is obviously dependent on local climatic conditions and no problem exists with respect to current producers who use this procedure. Future applicants shall demonstrate that their local monthly average temperatures and the local monthly minimum temperatures are equal to or warmer than the normal average temperatures and normal minimum temperatures compiled by the National Oceanic and Atmospheric Administration for Boone, North Carolina, station 31–0977, 1951 through 1980.

Monthly Temperatures (°F) for Boone NC, 1951–1980								
Jan.	Feb.	Mar.	Apr.	May	June	July	Aug.	Sep.
Normal average temperatures								
32.2	34.1	41.3	51.2	59.1	65.1	68.3	67.5	61.6
Normal minimum temperatures								
22.8	24.2	30.8	39.6	48.1	54.7	58.5	57.6	51.6

Table 5. Drying Times and Temperatures for Trichinae Inactivation in Hams and Shoulders *

Minimum Drying Temperature		Minimum days at dry-ing temperature	Fractional period for one day of drying
° F	° C		
130	54.4	1.5	.67
125	51.7	2	.50
120	48.9	3	.33
115	46.1	4	.25
110	43.3	5	.20
105	40.6	6	.17
100	37.8	7	.14
95	35.0	9	.11
90	32.2	11	.091
85	29.4	18	.056
80	26.7	25	.040
75	23.9	35	.029

* Interpolation of these times or temperatures is not acceptable; establishments wishing to use temperatures or times not in this Table shall first validate their efficacy as provided by 318.10(c)(4) of this section.

Method No. 4. (A) Cure: Establishments shall cure hams and shoulders by using a cure mixture containing not less than 71.5 percent salt by weight to cover all exposed muscle tissue and to pack the hock region. Establishments may substitute potassium chloride (KCl) for up to half of the required salt on an equal weight basis.

(B) Curing. Establishments shall apply the cure at a rate not less than 5.72 pounds of salt and KCl per hundred pounds of fresh meat. The cure shall be applied in either three or four approximately equal amounts (two or three overhauls) at separate times during the first 14 days of curing.

(C) Cure Contact Time. Establishments shall keep the product in contact with the cure mixture for no less than 2 days per pound of an uncured ham or shoulder but for at least 30 days. Establishments shall maintain the curing temperature at no less than 35° F (1.7° C) during the cure contact time.

(D) Equalization. After the cure contact period, establishments shall provide an added equalization period of no less than 1 day per pound of an uncured ham or shoulder but at least 14 days. Equalization is the time after the excess cure has been removed from the product, the end of the cure contact period, and before the drying period begins. Establishments may substitute additional cure contact days for an equal number of equalization days.

260

(E) Removing Excess Cure. After the required cure contact period, the establishment may remove excess cure mixture from the product's surface mechanically or by rinsing up to 1 minute with water, but not by soaking.

(F) Drying. After the curing period, establishments shall use one of the controlled temperature methods for drying listed in Method No. 3 of this subparagraph.

Method No. 5 (A) Curing. The establishment shall cure the ham to a minimum brine concentration of 6 percent by the end of the drying period. Brine concentration is calculated as 100 times the salt concentration divided by the sum of the salt and water concentrations.

Percent brine = $100 \times$ [salt] / ([salt] + [water])

The Agency will accept the brine concentration in the biceps femoris as a reasonable estimate of the minimum brine concentration in the ham.

(B) Drying and Total Process Times. The establishment shall dry the cured ham at a minimum temperature of 55° F (13° C) for at least 150 days. The total time of drying plus curing shall be at least 206 days.

(C) Ensuring an Acceptable Internal Brine Concentration.
(1) To establish compliance the establishment shall take product samples from the first 12 lots of production as follows: From each lot,

(i) One sample shall be taken from each of 5 or more hams;
(ii) Each sample shall be taken from the biceps femoris. As an alternative to the use of the biceps femoris, the Agency shall consider other method(s) of sampling the dry-cured hams to determine the minimum internal brine concentration, as long as the establishment proposes it and submits data and other information to establish its sufficiency to the Director of the Processed Products Inspection Division;
(iii) Each sample shall weigh no less than 100 grams;
(iv) The samples shall be combined as one composite sample and sealed in a water vapor proof container;
(v) The composite sample shall be submitted to a laboratory accredited under the provisions of §318.21 to be analyzed for salt and water content using methods from the "Official Methods of Analysis of the Association of Official Analytical Chemists (AOAC)," 15th Edition, 1990, Section 983.18 (page 931) and Section 971.19 (page 933) which are incorporated by reference. This incorporation by reference was approved by the Director of the Federal Register in accordance with 5 U.S.C. 552(a) and 1 CFR part 51. Copies may be obtained from the Association of Official Analytical Chemists, suite 400–BW, 2200 Wilson Boulevard, Arlington, VA 22201–3301. Copies may be inspected at the Office of the FSIS Hearing Clerk, room 3171, South Agriculture Building, Food Safety and Inspection Service, U.S. Department of Agriculture, Washington, DC 20250 or at the National Archives and Records Administration (NARA).

For information on the availability of this material at NARA, call 202–741–6030, or go to: http://www.archives.gov/federal_register/code_of_federal_regulations/ibr_locations.html. If the time between sampling and submittal of the composite sample to the accredited laboratory will exceed 8 hours, then the establishment shall freeze the composite sample immediately after the samples are combined;

(vi) Once the laboratory results for the composite sample are received, the manufacturer shall calculate the internal brine concentration by multiplying the salt concentration by 100 and then dividing that figure by the sum of the salt and water concentrations;

(vii) Compliance is established when the samples from the first 12 lots of production have a minimum internal brine concentration of 6 percent. Lots being tested to establish compliance shall be held until the internal brine concentration has been determined and found to be at least 6 percent. If the minimum internal brine concentration is less than 6 percent, the lot being tested shall be held until the establishment brings the lot into compliance by further processing.

(2) To maintain compliance, the establishment shall take samples, have the samples analyzed, and perform the brine calculations as set forth above from one lot every 13 weeks. Lots being tested to maintain compliance shall not be held. If the minimum internal brine concentration is less than 6 percent in a lot being tested to maintain compliance, the establishment shall develop and propose steps acceptable to FSIS to ensure that the process is corrected.

(3) Accredited laboratory results and the brine calculations shall be placed on file at the establishment and available to Program employees for review.

Method No. 6 (A) Curing. The establishment shall cure the ham to a minimum brine concentration of 6 percent by the end of the drying period. Brine concentration is calculated as 100 times the salt concentration divided by the sum of the salt and water concentrations.

Percent brine = $100 \times$ [salt] / ([salt] + [water])

The Agency will accept the brine concentration in the biceps femoris as a reasonable estimate of the minimum brine concentration.

(B) Drying and Total Process Times. The establishment shall dry the cured ham at a minimum temperature of 110° F (43° C) for at least 4 days. The total time of drying plus curing shall be at least 34 days.

(C) Ensuring an Acceptable Internal Brine Concentration.

(1) To establish compliance the establishment shall take product samples from the first 12 lots of production as follows: From each lot,

(i) One sample shall be taken from each of 5 or more hams;

(ii) Each sample shall be taken from the biceps femoris. As an alternative to the use of the biceps femoris, the Agency will consider other methods of sampling the dry-cured hams to determine internal brine concentration, as long as the establishment proposes it and submits data and other information to establish its sufficiency to the Director of the Processed Products Inspection Division;

(iii) Each sample shall weigh no less than 100 grams;

(iv) The samples shall be combined as one composite sample and sealed in a water vapor proof container;

(v) The composite sample shall be submitted to a laboratory accredited under the provisions of §318.21 to be analyzed for salt and water content using methods from the "Official Methods of Analysis of the Association of Official Analytical Chemists (AOAC)," 15th Edition, 1990, section 983.18 (page 931) and section 971.19 (page 933) which are incorporated by reference. This incorporation by reference was approved by the Director of the Federal Register in accordance with 5 U.S.C. 552(a) and 1 CFR part 51.

Copies may be obtained from the Association of Official Analytical Chemists, suite 400–BW, 2200 Wilson Boulevard, Arlington, VA 22201–3301. Copies may be inspected at the Office of the FSIS Hearing Clerk, room 3171, South Agriculture Building, Food Safety and Inspection Service, U.S. Department of Agriculture, Washington, DC 20250 or at the National Archives and Records Administration (NARA). For information on the availability of this material at NARA, call 202–741–6030, or go to: http://www.archives.gov/federal_register/code_of_federal_regulations/ibr_locations.html. If the time between sampling and submittal of the composite sample to the accredited laboratory will exceed 8 hours, then the establishment shall freeze the composite sample immediately after the samples are combined;

(vi) Compliance is established when the samples from the first 12 lots of production have a minimum internal brine concentration of 6 percent. Lots being tested to establish compliance shall be held until the internal brine concentration has been determined and found to be at least 6 percent. If the minimum internal brine concentration is less than 6 percent, the lot being tested shall be held until the establishment brings the lot into compliance by further processing.

(2) To maintain compliance, the establishment shall take samples, have the samples analyzed, and perform the brine calculations as set forth above from one lot every 13 weeks. Lots being tested to maintain compliance shall not be held. If the minimum internal brine concentration is less than 6 percent in a lot being tested to maintain compliance, the establishment shall develop and propose steps acceptable to FSIS to ensure that the process is corrected.

(3) Accredited laboratory results and the brine calculations shall be placed on file in the establishment and available to Program employees for review.

(v) Boneless pork loins and loin ends. In lieu of heating or refrigerating to destroy possible live trichinae in boneless loins, the loins may be cured for a period of not less than 25 days at a temperature not lower than 36° F by the use of one of the following methods:

Method No. 1. Application of a dry-salt curing mixture containing not less than 5 pounds of salt to each hundredweight of meats.

Method No. 2. Application of a pickle solution of not less than 80° strength (salometer) on the basis of not less than 60 pounds of pickle to each hundredweight of meat.

Method No. 3. Application of a pickle solution added to the dry-salt cure prescribed as Method No. 1 in this subdivision (v) provided the pickle solution is not less than 80° strength (salometer).

After removal from cure, the loins may be soaked in water for not more than 1 hour at a temperature not higher than 70° F or washed under a spray but shall not be subjected, during or after the curing process, to any other treatment designed to remove salt. Following curing the loins shall be smoked for not less than 12 hours. The minimum temperature of the smokehouse during this period at no time shall be lower than 100° F, and for 4 consecutive hours of this period the smokehouse shall be maintained at a temperature not lower than 125° F. Finally, the product shall be held in a drying room for a period of not less than 12 days at a temperature not lower than 45° F.

(4) The Administrator shall consider additional processing methods upon petition by manufacturers and shall approve any such method upon his/her determination that it can be properly monitored by an inspector and that the safety of such methods is adequately documented by data which has been developed by following an experimental protocol previously reviewed and accepted by the Department.

(d) General instructions: When necessary to comply with the requirements of this section, the smokehouses, drying rooms, and other compartments used in the treatment of pork to destroy possible live trichinae shall be suitably equipped, by the operator of the official establishment, with accurate automatic recording thermometers. Circuit supervisors are authorized to approve for use in sausage smokehouses, drying rooms, and other compartments, such automatic recording thermometers as are found to give satisfactory service and to disapprove and require discontinuance of use, for purposes of the regulations in this subchapter, any thermometers (including any automatic recording thermometers) of the establishment that are found to be inaccurate or unreliable.

(e) The requirements for using the pooled sample digestion technique to analyze pork for the presence of trichina cysts are:

(1) The establishment shall submit for the approval of the Regional Director its proposed procedure for identifying and pooling carcasses, collecting and pooling samples, testing samples (including the name and address of the laboratory), communicating test results, retesting individual carcasses, and maintaining positive identification and clear separation of pork found to be trichina-free from untested pork or trichina-positive pork.

(2) The establishment shall use the services of a laboratory approved by the Administrator for all required testing. Such approval shall be based on adequacy of facilities, reagents, and equipment, and on demonstration of continuing competency and reliability in performing the pooled sample digestion technique for trichinae.

(3) The establishment shall sample no less than 5 grams of diaphragm muscle or tongue tissue from each carcass or no less than 10 grams of other muscle tissue. Samples may be pooled but a pool shall not consist of more than 100 grams of sample. Sampling and sample preparation are subject to inspection supervision.

(4) Pork or products made from tested pork shall not be released as trichina free from the official establishment without treatment until the inspector in charge receives a laboratory report that the tested pork is free of trichina cysts.

(f) Approval of other tests for trichinosis in pork. The Administrator shall consider any additional analytical method for trichinosis upon petition by a manufacturer, and may approve that method upon the determination that it will detect at least 98 percent of swine bearing cysts present at a tissue density equal to or less than one cyst per gram of muscle from the diaphragm pillars at a 95 percent confidence level. Any such petitions shall be supported by any data and other information that the Administrator finds necessary. Notice of any approval shall be given in the Federal Register,and the approved method will be incorporated into this section.

[35 FR 15586, Oct. 3, 1970, as amended at 38 FR 31517; Nov. 15, 1973; 39 FR 40580, Nov. 19, 1974; 50 FR 5229, Feb. 7, 1985; 50 FR 48075, Nov. 21, 1985; 52 FR 12517, Apr. 17, 1987; 57 FR 27874, June 22, 1992; 57 FR 33633, July 30, 1992; 57 FR 56440, Nov. 30, 1992]

Information about the USA regulations about composition of sausages, hams, luncheon meats, loaves, jellied products and other meat specialties can be obtained from:

Code of Federal Regulations
Title 9: Animals and Animal Products
PART 319 - DEFINITIONS AND STANDARDS OF IDENTITY OR COMPOSITION

References:

1. American Meat Institute, *Sausage and Ready-To-Serve Meats,* (1953), Institute of Meat Packing, The University of Chicago.

2. Jim Bacus, *Utilization of Microorganisms in Meat Processing,* (1984), Research Studies Press.

3. R.H. Diebel, C.F. Niven, and G.D. Wilson, *Microbiology of Meat Curing, Some Microbiological and Realated Technological Aspects in the Manufacture of Fermented Sausages,* Applied Microbiology, 9, p. 156-161.

4. Chr. Hansen, *Bactoferm™ Meat Manual vol. 1, (2003).*

5. Geoffrey Campbell-Platt, *Fermented Foods of the World,* (1987), Butterworths.

6. Dalla Santa, O.R., Coelho, F.A., Freitas, J.R.S., Dalla Santa, H.S., Terra, N.N., *Caracteristicas de Salamis Fermentados Producidos sin Adición de Cultivo Iniciador,* Cienc. Tecnol. Aliment. 5 (3) 231-236 (2006).

7. Feiner Gerhard, *Meat Products Handbook,* (2006), Woodhead Publishing Ltd.,

8. Richard A. Holley, *Prevention of Surface Growth on Italian Dry Sausage by Natamycin And Potassium Sorbate,* Applied And Environmental Microbiology, Feb 1981, p.422-429.

9. Johnson Michael, G., James Acton, C., *Laboratory Method for Fermentation of Meat and Poultry Sausages in Fibrous Casings,* Applied Microbiology, June 1975, p. 855-856.

10. Donald M. Kinsman, *Principal Characteristics of Sausages of the World Listed by Country of Origin,* (1983) American Press.

11. Komarik, Tressler, Long, *Food Products Formulary,* Volume 1, (1974), The AVI Publishing Company.

12. Lucke F.K. (1985), *Fermented sausages,* in: Wood BJB (ed) Microbiology of fermented foods, Elsevier Applied Science. pp 41-83.

13. A. Marco, J.L. Navarro. M. Flores, *The Sensory Quality of Dry Fermented Sausages as Affected by Fermentation Stage and Curing Agents,* Eur Food Res Technol, (2008), 226:449-458.

14. Y.H.Hui, Wai-Kit Nip, Robert W. Rogers, Owen A. Young, *Meat Science and Applications,* (2001), Marcel Dekker, Inc.,

15. Marianski S. Marianski A. Marianski R., *Meat Smoking and Smokehouse Design,* Bookmagic, 2009.

16. Marianski S. Marianski A. Gebarowski M. *Polish Sausages, Authentic Recipes And Instructions,* Bookmagic 2009.

17. William R. Mende, *The Alchemist's Book of Salami and Other Fermented Sausages,* (2005).

18. J. Metaxopoulos, C. Genigeorgis, M.J. Fanelli, C. Franti, E. Cosma, *Production of Italian Dry Salami: Effect of Starter Culture and Chemical Acidulation on Staphylococcal Growth in Salami Under Commercial Manufacturing Conditions,* Applied and Environmental Microbiology,

(Nov 1981), p. 863-871.

19. John Nordal, Erik Slinde, *Characteristics of Some Lactic Acid Bacteria Used as Starter Cultures in Dry Sauage Production,* Applied and Environmental Microbiology, (Sept. 1989), p. 472-476.

20. Nyoman Semadi Antara, Nengah Sujaya, Atsushi Yokota, Kozo Asano, Fusao Tomita, *Effects of Indigenous Starter Cultures on the Microbial and Physicochemical Characteristics of Uratan, a Balinese Fermented Sausage,* Journal of Bioscience and Bioengineering, Vol 98, No 2, 92-98 (2004).

21. Pearson A.M., *Processed Meats,* (1984), AVI Publishing Company.,

22. Pederson Carl S., *Microbiology of Food Fermentations,* (1979), The AVI Publishing Company.,

23. Polskie Wydawnictwo Fachowe, *Kiełbasy Surowe,* (2004).

24. Kh.I. Sallam, M. Ishioroshi, and K. Samejima, *Antioxidant and Antimicrobial Effects of Garlic in Chicken Sausage,* Lebenson Wiss Technol., (2004); 37 (8): 849-855.

25. James L. Smith, Samuel A. Palumbo, *Microbiology of Lebanon Bologna,* Applied Microbiology, (Oct 1973), p/489-496

26. James L. Smith, Charles N. Huhtanen, John C. Kissinger, Samuel A. Palumbo, *Survival of Salmonellae During Pepperoni Manufacture,* Applied Microbiology, (Nov 1975), p. 759-763.

27. James L. Smith, Samuel A. Palumbo, *Injury to Staphylococcus aureus During Sausage Fermentation,* Applied and Environmental Microbiology, (Dec 1978), p.857-860.

28. Seran Temelli, Sahsene Anar, M.K. Cem Sen, Devrim Beyaz, *Heat Treated Turkish Style Sucuck: Evaluation of Microbial Contamination in Processing Steps,* Uludag University, J Fac Vet Med 24 (2005), 1-2-3-4, p. 81-88.

29. Toldra Fidel, *Dry-Cured Products,* (2002), Food and Nutrition Press, Inc.,

30. Toldra Fidel., *Handbook of Fermented Meat and Poultry,* (2007), Blackwell Publishing.,

31. Luc De Vyst, Frederic Leroy, *Bacteriocins from Lactic Acid Bacteria: Production, Purification, and Food Aplications,* Journal of Molecular Microbiology and Biotechnology, (2007);13:194-199.

32. Wiriyacharee Pairote, *Using Mixed Starter Cultures for Thai Nham,* Applications of Biotechnology in Traditional Fermented Foods (1992).

33. Woodburn Margy, *Starter Cultures in Traditional Fermented Meats,* Applications of Biotechnology in Traditional Fermented Foods (1992).

Useful Links

Sausage Making Equipment and Supplies

The Sausage Maker Inc. www.sausagemaker.com
Allied Kenco Sales www.alliedkenco.com
Sausage-Stuffer www.sausage-stuffer.com
LEM Products, Inc. www.lemproducts.com

Miscellaneous Equipment:

Decagon Devices Inc., Paw kit, water activity meter
www.decagon.com/pawkit
Hanna Instruments USA, Meat pH tester
www.hannainst.com/usa
Micro Essential Laboratory Inc., Meat pH testing strips
www.microessentiallab.com
Jehmco, Water tank submersible heaters, line voltage temperature controllers
www.jehmco.com
Green Air Products Inc., Temperature and humidity controllers
www.greenair.com
Franklin Time and Weather, Air speed meters, humidity sensors, thermometers etc., www.time-weather.com
The Ranco ETC Store, Ranco temperature controllers
www.rancoetc.com
American Weigh Scales, Inc., Highly accurate digital scales
www.awscales.com
Grainger, Industrial supplies
www.grainger.com

Spices:

Laos powder - The Food Locker http://www.foodlocker.com
Spanish pimentón - Ta Tienda http://www.latienda.com

Index

Other Books by Stanley and Adam Marianski

Home Production of Quality Meats and Sausages bridges the gap that exists between highly technical textbooks and the requirements of the typical hobbyist. The book covers topics such as curing and making brines, smoking meats and sausages, making special sausages such as head cheeses, blood and liver sausages, hams, bacon, butts, loins, safety and more...

ISBN: 978-0-9824267-3-9

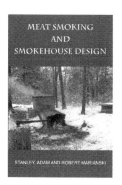

Meat Smoking And Smokehouse Design explains differences between grilling, barbecuing and smoking. There are extensive discussions of curing as well as the particulars about smoking sausages, meat, fish, poultry and wild game.

ISBN: 978-0-9824267-0-8

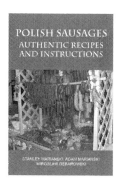

Polish Sausages Authentic Recipes And Instructions contains government recipes that were used by Polish meat plants between 1950-1990. These recipes come from government manuals that were never published before, which are now revealed in great detail.

ISBN: 978-0-9824267-2-2

Home Canning Meat, Poultry, Fish and Vegetables explains in simple language the science of canning low-acid foods such as meat, poultry, fish ans vegetables and reveals the procedures that are used by the canning industry. The material is based on the U.S. government requirements as specified in the Code of Federal Regulations and the relevant links are listed. After studying the book, a newcomer to the art of canning will be able to safely process foods at home in both glass and metal containers.

ISBN: 978-0-9836973-7-4

Home Production of Vodkas, Infusions & Liqueurs is a guide for making quality alcohol beverages at home. The book adopts factory methods of making spirits but without the need for any specialized equipment. A different type of alcohol beverage can be produced from the same fruit and the authors explain in simple terms all necessary rules.

ISBN: 978-0-9836973-4-3

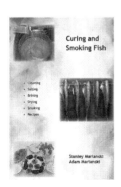

Curing and Smoking Fish provides all the information needed to understand the entire process of preparing and smoking fish, shellfish such as clams, mussels, oysters and shrimp. The subject of making brines is covered in detail and simplified by advocating the use of brine tables and testers. A collection of recipes for smoking fish, making fish spreads and preparing sauces for serving fish is included.

ISBN: 978-0-9836973-9-8

274

Sauerkraut, Kimchi, Pickles & Relishes teaches you how to lead a healthier and longer life. Most commercially produced foods are heated and that step eliminates many of the beneficial bacteria, vitamins and nutrients. However, most of the healthiest vegetables can be fermented without thermal processing. The book explains in simple terms the fermentation process, making brine, pickling and canning.

ISBN: 978-0-9836973-2-9

Making Healthy Sausages reinvents traditional sausage making by introducing a completely new way of thinking. The reader will learn how to make a product that is nutritional and healthy, yet delicious to eat. The collection of 80 recipes provides a valuable reference on the structure of reduced fat products.

ISBN: 978-0-9836973-0-5

The Amazing Mullet offers information that has been gathered through time and experience. Successful methods of catching, smoking and cooking fish are covered in great depth and numerous filleting, cleaning, cooking and smoking practices are reviewed thoroughly. In addition to mullet recipes, detailed information on making fish cakes, ceviche, spreads and sauces are also included.

ISBN: 978-0-9824267-8-4

Learn more at: **www.bookmagic.com**

Made in the USA
Lexington, KY
07 November 2018